Nancy Evans

First-rate First Lady

A Biography & Oral History

by John C. Hughes

THE WASHINGTON STATE
HERITAGE CENTER

LEGACY PROJECT

Washington
Secretary of State
SAM REED

To THE LOVE OF MY LIFE, DAN,

who made it all possible,

and to our sons, Dan, Mark and Bruce,

their wives, Celia, Deb and Christy,

and especially our remarkable grandchildren,

Eloise, Emily, Isabelle, Ben, Jackson, Grace, McKay, Andrew and John,

whose generation will help to build an even stronger world.

—NANCY EVANS

The First Lady in 1965. *Evans family album*

Biography

"She takes the winter and she makes it summer

And summer could take a few lessons from her;

Picture a tomboy in lace:

That's Nancy with the laughin' face!"

—Phil Silvers & Jimmy Van Heusen

Bright, pretty and lots of fun, Nancy Bell, a grade-school music teacher, had no shortage of suitors. In fact, two fellas proposed to her on the same Seattle park bench in the space of a week. One was a handsome engineer named Dan Evans. That was a half century ago, and although Nancy told Dan she wanted three days to think about it—"The worst three days of my life," he says—there's never been a day when she regretted saying yes.

Well, there was the muggy day in August of 1966 when she was eight months pregnant with their third son. Barefoot and wearing a maternity smock, she was scampering around the yard of the Governor's Mansion, trying to corral their enormous Irish wolfhound, Peggy, who was in heat. Her spouse and his State Patrol aide, Bill Lathrop, happened to be driving by. They waved gaily and kept right on going, not realizing their services were urgently desired. When the governor strolled into the mansion a half hour later, she was livid. "You saw me chasing that damn dog. Why didn't you stop?!" Dan stammered that he was oblivious. Nancy tried to keep scowling. Then they erupted in laughter. What a sight: The First Lady, great with child, in hot pursuit of the First Pooch. Good thing a news photographer hadn't happened by. They tell the story with relish because it is a classic slice of the sometimes goofy lives they led for the 12 years they were governor and first lady. They strived to be a normal couple—hiking, biking and skiing with their three live-wire sons, playing Pickleball and Bridge with friends between bouts with legislators and visits from presidents and premieres. Nancy also welcomed hundreds of townspeople who told her they had lived in Olympia all their lives and never been to the Governor's Mansion. During their first six months in the mansion they had 10,000 visitors. Asked how she mustered the courage to entertain all those people, Nancy says, "Ignorance is bliss!" (For the record, they did discover later on that five-year-old Dan Jr. had signed his name in the guest book a dozen times in big letters.)

They'd been married for only five years before pulling off one of 1964's biggest political upsets. In a Democratic tsunami, Lyndon B. Johnson trounced Barry Goldwater, the hero of the Republican right. But in Washington State, a former Eagle Scout bucked the tide to defeat two-term Democrat Al Rosellini. Nancy Bell Evans, 31, the daughter of a spunky suffragist and the pride of Spokane, became the youngest First Lady in state history. Her husband, Daniel J. Evans, was 39—the youngest governor ever.

Dan Evans served an unprecedented three consecutive terms and Nancy became one

Nancy, Dan, and the boys with Peggy, their Irish Wolfhound, at the Governor's Mansion in the early 1970s. *Evans family album* of the state's best-loved first ladies. Along the way, she saved the Governor's Mansion from being replaced by some characterless rambler, championed its renovation and redecoration and created a Mansion Foundation with a corps of dedicated volunteers. She was "a vivacious hostess, a serious leader and one hell of a mother, all at the same time—plus a remarkable wife," her husband says, adding that it's all still true. After 50 years together, they're still best friends, and Nancy is also the person Dan most trusts to give him a reality check.

"She really is the ying to dad's yang," says their son Bruce. "The degree to which they go back and forth on stuff is remarkable—not because they fundamentally disagree but because they just like to debate things. More than a lot of married couples, they still communicate in a very open way, which is a testimony to their marriage and why it has lasted so long."

Not-so-secret weapon

A few months after Dan was elected governor, the Legislature went into overtime and Nancy had to go it alone on an important trade mission to Tokyo. She'd never been away from her children for three weeks, but she dutifully packed her bags. The trip was a crash course in international diplomacy. Japan was a very male-oriented society, Dan notes, but Nancy was a hit with everyone she encountered and made lasting friends. "It was an enormous boost to her confidence."

The first lady was the governor's not-so-secret weapon, according to campaign workers and members of his staff. "Nancy is very smart, even-keeled and politically very savvy," says Jay Fredericksen, who was Evans' press secretary in the 1970s. "As a bonus, she has this great sense of humor." She met kings and queens, "but never let anything go to her head. In 1973, we were all back East for the Republican Governors' Conference, which Nelson and Happy Rockefeller were hosting. It was my first trip to New York City, and we were staying in an upscale hotel, so I was sort of awe-struck. I remember Nancy talking about having dinner at Rocky's town house. She said, 'My God, there's a Picasso in the bathroom!' "

Back in Olympia, Nancy had bats in her attic, although by then her campaign to make the drafty old mansion a livable place of pride for the state and its occupants was finally making real headway. Today, the mansion is the cornerstone of her legacy as first lady. When Gov. Mike Lowry and his wife Mary welcomed visitors in the 1990s, he always quipped that they were "really enjoying public housing."

Nancy Evans also sparked new interest in history and the arts in Olympia and was a founding trustee of Planned Parenthood of Thurston County. Although abortion is "not something we would ever choose," she says she has "always felt it's a woman's right, prerogative, to make that decision." She supported the 1970 statewide referendum to make abortion "legal and safe" in the early months of pregnancy. She also backed the Equal Rights Amendment and has been a longtime activist for the mentally ill and developmentally disabled. She and Dan welcomed Vietnamese refugees to Washington in the 1970s after the governor of California said there was no room at the Golden State Inn. One young immigrant couple was so grateful for their support that they named a son Evans.

Nancy's "retirement" years are devoted to an ambitious array of public service, philanthropic and cultural causes. She is vice chairman of the board of KCTS, the Seattle affiliate of the Public Broadcasting System, and active with the Northwest Parkinson's Foundation. Dan's brother and Nancy's two sisters-in-law, as well as their friend, former governor Booth Gardner, have suffered from the disease. A cancer survivor, as is her husband and their granddaughter, Eloise, she helped found the Friends of Cancer Lifeline in the late 1980s and was its first chairwoman. "She takes her responsibilities to her family, her friends and her community to the nth degree," says Barbara Frederick, Cancer Lifeline's retired executive director. "Her 'community' has reached to every corner of our state. And every single thing she's involved with she does with all her energy. Her attention to detail is just remarkable."

At Whitman College, her alma mater, she has been an overseer, trustee, fundraiser and talent scout since the early 1970s. In 2009, Whitman presented her its Scribner Award for Distinguished Service.

Involved with the Seattle Symphony since the 1960s, Nancy played a major role in generating support for the world-class Benaroya Hall, and headed the search committee for a new conductor in 2009. Her husband marvels at her moxie, and willingness to take on jobs like that. Dan and a throng of others will tell you that if you pass muster with Nancy, you're bound to be all right. She is financially savvy and a good judge of character. She makes friends and forges alliances everywhere she goes. "She's just terrific at making connections and introducing people," says former Whitman president Tom Cronin.

A natural-born campaigner

After deciding against a bid for a fourth term, Dan became president of The Evergreen State College during a critical period in its existence and went on to serve in the U.S. Senate. He is a bipartisan political icon in Washington State, and when he emphasizes that he couldn't have done it without his wife he's not just being gallant. Evans started his 1964 campaign for governor "with all the warmth and charisma of an iced halibut," according to historian Gordon Newell. He got a lot better, but Dan's handlers still sometimes called him "Old Gluefoot" because he dawdled and was bad at gripping and grinning. Nancy was a natural-born campaigner.

Dan often took his cues from Nancy—sometimes literally. He gave good speeches, but tended to talk too long. "They worked up this code, where Nancy would cough and Dan would realize he had to wrap it up," says Bill Jacobs, Dan's chief of staff when he was governor and later in the Senate. "One time he was just getting going and she coughs. He couldn't understand why because he thought he was doing pretty well. But he wrapped it up. Afterwards, she said, 'Why did you quit, Dan? That was really good.' And he said, '*Well, you coughed.*' She laughed and said, 'Well, I really had to cough!' While that's sort of a frivolous thing, it's an example of how they related to one another and the trust that they had."

Wendy Pugnetti, who worked closely with the first lady when she was assistant press secretary in 1973, says, "Nancy is warm, gracious and smart. In today's political world, she would be a shoo-in for elected office. I admired her greatly because she juggled all those roles so well and remained just Nancy."

Former U.S. Senator Slade Gorton, one of Dan's housemates in Olympia when they were young legislators, says he concluded early on that "Nancy Evans is a very strong woman. The influence she had over her husband was both significant and positive. She certainly deserves credit for saving and restoring the mansion, for which she is best known, but her political instincts and achievements go way beyond that."

Lawmakers visiting the mansion were frequently lobbied by the first lady on her favorite causes. Nancy referred to the recalcitrant ones as "some of our 17th Century legislators." Watching his wife in action, the governor would sometimes roll his eyes. And when the guests had gone, she says he might scold, "Did you have to buttonhole that one?"

While possessed of a deft touch, Nancy Evans was also her mother's daughter. Lilith (pronounced "Lie-lith") Bell, who lived to be 94, marched for suffrage as a young woman and had a "protester's streak." Mrs. Bell once told reporters that her feistiness dated to her childhood in Kansas. "I was a preacher's kid, and I resented the feeling other people had that I should be some kind of a model child."

What's in a name?

Shakespeare's immortal Juliet declared that a rose "by any other name would smell as sweet." But it's a good thing Nancy's father was joking when he suggested she should be named Vernal Equinoxia since she was born on the first day of spring in 1933. "We're going to call her 'Vernie' for short," he told the children. "Oh, Dad, you can't do that!" they said.

Her mother wanted to name her Elizabeth Ann, but the obstetrician said "she looks like a Nancy." It's a straightforward name with a dash of playfulness. She has wonderful blue eyes, a warm smile and a contagious laugh. She is simultaneously down to earth and sophisticated, and she always reminds herself that no matter where she is or who she's with, she's still just Nancy Bell from Spokane.

"It's easy to get absorbed in whatever life you're doing without remembering how you got there," Nancy says, recalling the social whirl in Washington, D.C., when Dan was a U.S. senator. "You go to a lot of embassies and on and on. So you can quickly forget who you are and where you come from....I tried very hard not to." Nor did she ever want her boys afforded special treatment just because their dad was governor. As a former teacher and diligent mom, she closely followed their schoolwork. One day, Dan Jr. brought home a report marked with an "A." Nancy was dubious. "I said, 'Why did you get an A?' And he said, 'Well, that's what they gave me.' Well, I know it was because he was Dan Evans' son, and he didn't deserve an A."

She was a surprise

Nancy's father, William L. Bell, a Stanford-educated mining engineer, was often without work during the Depression. But her parents persevered, and they loved the sound of children's laughter. Nancy was the youngest of four and a surprise. "My father was 54 when I was born," Nancy says, adding with a chuckle, "He was a very proud man, my mother said, and she was furious."

In truth, her parents and siblings—Barbara, 12 years older; Bill Jr., 9 years older, and Mary, seven years older—were all delighted with her. "I was a spoiled brat. I was doted on, and I *loved* it. I don't deny it," Nancy says, laughing at the memory. Some summers, when her father was working in Montana, Nancy would visit him. "Mother would put me on the train at night. We knew all the porters, everybody who worked on the trains....I'd be by myself, at age 6, and they'd put me in a sleeper. In the morning, they'd get me up and make sure I got dressed and everything. And my father would be there to greet me at Butte....They had a house up in the mountains, and I had a little Shetland pony that I rode all the time."

There are sad memories, too. Her brother contracted trench mouth, likely from a public drinking fountain, and in those days, before antibiotics it ate away at his lower lip. The popular teenager endured several skin grafts. Without medical insurance their parents were hard-pressed. "It was a hard time anyway in mining—a hard time everywhere in America," Nancy says, noting that there were "many mouths to feed" at the Bell house. But her parents loved having young people around. One of Bill Jr.'s friends from college moved in when he was attending law school at Gonzaga. "I never knew how many people were going to be at the dinner table because my brother and sisters would often bring people over, and my mother would say, 'Stay for dinner.' She could take nothing and make it something." Father, meantime, never lost his droll sense of humor, while Mother was "always encouraging" and the enforcer. "My parents brought me up to believe that you could do anything you want to do if you work hard," Nancy says. "There was no sense that I couldn't do things." Like many who grew up in that era, she's thrifty. "To this day I turn off the lights and scold my husband and my children for not doing so."

Then came World War II. Her brother was wounded in the Battle of the Bulge, the Nazis' go-for-broke offensive in the winter of 1944-45. "In the den, my father had on the wall a big map of Europe," Nancy recalls, "and we would try to follow Bill through his letters. You couldn't say exactly where you were because of wartime censorship. Then we learned my brother was coming through Spokane on the train on the way to Madigan Army Hospital near Tacoma. So we all went down to the train station, and I still remember this gaunt young man standing in the doorway of the train on crutches. And I thought, 'Oh my gosh, is that my brother?!' I couldn't believe it was, because he was so thin. He was so haggard looking."

Bill Bell Jr., who inherited his father's sense of humor, always said he was grateful to the Army because he was no longer self-conscious about the trench mouth scars on his lip. "People assumed it was part of the injuries he had received in the war," Nancy says, adding that "he always was a slobbery kisser." That line gives you a good idea of the Bells' upbeat outlook on life.

Nancy was "a very typical teenager," with a lot of chums, many of whom she has stayed in touch with over the years. She had been taking piano lessons since grade school from a gifted German immigrant and played for the choir and other musical productions. She was a cheerleader and rarely without a boyfriend. Many of her brother's friends were also veterans, and Nancy was impressed by their "more sophisticated" humor. "I just ate it up," she says.

Whitman calls

With graduation from Lewis & Clark High School looming in 1950, Nancy applied to several colleges. She had her heart set on Whitman, where her brother and sisters had gone. But Whitman was expensive, and Nancy was entering college on the heels of the Depression and the war. "There was financial difficulty at our house during my teens, but Mother kept saying, 'Well, don't let this detour you. There is always a way to get what you want to get.' It was always that way with Mother," Nancy recalls. "She said, 'Work hard, study hard. Maybe you can get a scholarship.' And that's what happened." Nancy competed in a classical music recital to win a music scholarship and was off to Walla Walla. "Even with a scholarship, I'm sure my mother was thinking, 'Oh, how are we going to do this?'" Nancy worked in the post office at the Student Union Building and served as an assistant to professors to help pay her tuition and expenses.

She loved Whitman's close-knitness and the whole feel of the town. Whitman has always been regarded as a very good college, but Nancy says it's now nationally recognized as a great school that draws extraordinary students. "I couldn't get into Whitman now," she says. "It's a wonderful school, and they really believe that the teachers are there to teach and not just do research. The faculty now, as then, spends a lot of time with the students. A lot of mentoring goes on besides the classroom stuff." Her affection for her alma mater and gratitude for the scholarships that allowed her—and thousands of others since—to get a first-rate liberal arts education are boundless. Her years of service as an overseer and trustee represent her commitment to keeping the doors open to bright young people. Dan Evans Jr. graduated with the Class of 1983.

Whitman grads, in other words, are loyal, which a certain University of Washington Engineering School graduate came to appreciate. When Nancy and Dan drove into Walla Walla in 1964 for her 10-year class reunion, the race for governor was in full swing. Everywhere they looked there were Dan Evans yard signs and bumper stickers. The only things they knew about him were that he had the good sense to marry a Whitmanite and that he was a Republican—in that order. Nancy says that support helped fuel Dan's upset victory.

Nancy grew up in a household where everyone talked politics. After FDR closed the gold mines during the war, her father fumed about "Roose-a-velt." (In Seattle, Dan Evans' dad, Les, was doing likewise.) However, Mr. Bell wasn't much for meetings. He liked to play devil's advocate in dinner-table debates. Mother was a Republican poll-watcher every election day, and Nancy's siblings—being much older—were active in the party. Bill Jr. managed some campaigns and Barbara Bell was a precinct committee-woman. "Everybody would enter into the discussions, so it was very much a part of our family life."

Nancy was a free-thinker, intellectually feisty like her mother, but not much of a political animal and no public speaker. When she was elected president of her sorority, Delta Gamma, her senior year, she was obliged to give the annual report for the spring alumnae banquet at the grand Marcus Whitman Hotel. "I didn't think I would get through it. I remember just gulping—ah, it was dreadful—and swallowing and not being able to go on with the words. ...I remember somebody afterwards leaning over and saying, 'Gosh that was tough, wasn't it?' And I said, 'Yes, that was very tough!' It was very memorable to me because I was so bad. I could get up and play the piano…but to speak was a real challenge. I never have been a very good public speaker, but I'm better at it now than I was."

One of the fellas she dated during her college years was Bill Cowles, heir to Spokane's two leading newspapers, *The Spokesman-Review* and *Chronicle*, and considerable real estate in the Inland Empire. "We were just friends; nothing ever serious," Nancy says, but he was a good-looking guy and a great catch for any girl. "He came to the door to pick me up, and, looking down his glasses, my father said, 'What are your prospects, young man?' I was just, 'Oh, God, Daddy!' He knew full well who Bill Cowles was, but he would do that to any man who came to the house to pick up any of his daughters."

Camas or Seattle?

Graduating from Whitman in 1954 with what amounted to a dual major in music and education, Nancy received several job offers. The two most enticing were at Camas, where she could head up the music education department, and in the Shoreline School District north of Seattle, where she would be a grade-school music teacher. The Camas job paid a lot more, but it was a rural mill town. Seattle had more attractions, including concerts and thousands of college-educated people her own age. On indoctrination day for new teachers, Nancy and a pal from Whitman met two freshly minted teachers from the University of Puget Sound. The four girls rented a house in the University District from "a wonderful little old lady." Over their front door they hung a sign that combined the names of their sororities: "Chi Chi Delta Tri."

Paramount Park Elementary School was brand new in 1954. In addition to a music teacher, they needed someone to set up a library. Miss Bell, who loved books, promptly volunteered and winged it for the first year. She returned home to Spokane for the summer break and took graduate courses at Eastern Washington State College in Cheney to fulfill her teaching credential requirements and learn more about librarianship and storytelling for grade-schoolers. "Another new school came along later, so I was teaching music at two schools and being the librarian as well. They gave me a budget and I got to order all these books." The storytelling was fun, but she really enjoyed teaching music to every class—kindergarten through sixth grade.

"One day the principal asked me to give a little talk at one of the PTA meetings. And I thought, 'Oh my God, what am I going to talk about?'" She collected an armload of tambourines, cymbals, triangles and wood blocks—the stuff she routinely handed out to kindergartners to get them enthused about making music. "I passed those out at the PTA meeting because I'd been hearing parents say, 'Well, I can't sing, so I'm sure that Johnny can't sing at all.' That was my lesson for the night. I said, 'Don't *ever* say to your children, 'I can't do this, therefore you probably can't either,' because you don't know that for a fact. Give them a chance.'" That's the Nancy Evans Theory of Elementary Education in a nutshell.

An intriguing young man

Her social life was also blossoming. "When I arrived in Seattle, I met a lot of new people and really had a wonderful time. I met a lot of great guys." One was a 32-year-old civil engineer named Dan Evans. A former naval officer, he was interested in politics and had been named the "Outstanding Freshman Legislator" of 1957.

That summer, one of Nancy's ski pals was crewing on a sailboat with Dan. She still remembers his exact words: "Nancy, I've got a young man I think you should meet." Dan joined the group for a weekend jaunt to Stevens Pass in January of 1958. He was quiet, attentive and "very good looking," Nancy says. "He kept coming along on our ski trips. Then one time I fell. All the other guys, they'd just go on, but Dan stopped. And then he asked me out."

Dan's version: "She only learned to ski because she was trying to keep up with all the guys she was dating or went skiing with. They were all pretty good skiers who wanted to go right to the top of the mountain" but "she stayed down below." Immediately smitten, Dan decided he would stick with her. Good decision. When she veered under a clump of trees "I had to get in there and pull her out. So we skied together. Then we all got together at lunch." At day's end they stopped for burgers at a diner. "It was just a place with eight or nine stools all along the bar…and I made darn sure that I sat next to her."

Nancy's first impression? "He was very quiet and shy.…He hadn't dated much. The thing I remember most, other than that he was a very nice person and a very handsome man, was his intrigue. Each time I went out with him I learned something new. I saw a man of depth. He grew on me.…He was not one of these people who just came on the first time and you learned it all. I found that very intriguing.…I loved everything I learned.…He already had done a lot of interesting things: He was an engineer, interested in politics, athletic, very competitive…served in the Navy. There were all these things that he'd done. He had a wooden sailboat that we ended up spending a lot of time sanding and waxing and varnishing.…I learned to love sailing. We would often go over to his house and sometimes have dinner."

The sailor was making headway, but the competition was fierce. One night when he arrived at Nancy's apartment to pick her up, Dan had to make a phone call. There was a datebook by the phone, so he used some naval intelligence. "It had a little rubber stamp chained to it, with the name 'Bob.' It was one of her boyfriends.…She was really very popular. So I opened it to see what was there and here's 'Bob,' 'Bob' and 'Bob.' And then there's other dates that she had (made as well). So I carefully marked down all of the free nights I could find and made sure that I asked her out on those free nights. I *really* wanted to see her more frequently. And I figured, well, if she says 'no' because she's busy and it was a free day I'll know I'm in trouble."

That spring, Nancy learned just how persistent he was. On the opening day of boating season, Dan was at the wheel of his sailboat, stopwatch in hand, ready to race. "We were about 45 seconds from the start and she decided that was the time to jump into my lap and put her arm around me. I just pushed her away....And I said, 'Nancy, we're only 30 seconds away from the start!' She was just really upset, but she found out how competitive I was."

In October, they took a weekend trip to Victoria with Nancy's sister Barbara and brother-in-law, Bill Ludders. They stayed at the Empress—the guys in one room, of course, and the girls in another—and had a wonderful time. "And then we came home to Seattle—back to my apartment. Dan said, 'Well, let's go for a walk.' And I thought, 'Well, OK, Sunday night.' So we walked up to the playfield...and we sat on the bench, and he proposed! On Saturday night of week preceding, I had been proposed to on that same bench."

She had said no immediately to the earlier proposal, even though it was "very sweet." Then when Dan proposed, "all I could think of was the week before. I was so stunned because I really had not expected it. I just couldn't say yes right then. I said, "Well, I've just got to think about it. Give me three days."

Dan was crestfallen. Nancy was confused. He slunk home. She called her mother in Spokane. "I said, 'Dan proposed and I don't know what to do!' And Mother started laughing. She'd never even met Dan, of course. I said, 'Mother, *don't laugh*. It's serious.' And she said, 'Well, of course it is. I'm laughing because how can I tell you what to do?' So she was no help. I just had to assimilate the whole idea. Then Dan came over Wednesday night and I said, 'Yes.' I knew, you know. It was just 'bingo!'"

Dan says, "I was so excited I just couldn't handle it: 'I've got to tell somebody. I've got to tell somebody!'" He still had a key to his parents' house, which was only a few blocks from Nancy's apartment. Even though it was close to midnight, he charged up the stairs, knocked on his parents' bedroom door and woke them up. Startled, they sat bolt upright in bed and said almost in unison, "What's going on?" Little wonder. That sort of exuberance—nocturnal or otherwise—was way out of character for their son.

Dan's mother "just broke into tears, she was so happy." His father just beamed. Nancy quips that Irma Evans "was just delighted that her oldest son was dating. It didn't matter what the girl was like." In truth, Dan's parents adored her and the feeling was mutual.

They were engaged on October 28th, 1958. Her parents came over from Spokane to meet Dan for the first time. Nancy was cooking dinner. Mother and daughter immediately repaired to the kitchen, leaving Daddy to work over Dan. "So there I am sitting with this kind of big, very impressive-looking man, and he says, 'Well, young man, my other sons-in-law always came to me and asked for my daughter's hand in marriage.' I'm, 'Ga, ga, ga.' I thought he was completely serious. And I really had a tough time even responding. It wasn't until later that I found out he was just putting me on."

Dan passed another test: He sat attentively through Nancy's nemesis—the grade school Christmas program, a command performance of her charges' musical skills to the tune of "O Little Town of Bethlehem" and "Frosty the Snowman."

"I'd arrange it so that we would have something on the stage of the lunchroom/auditorium/gym—*a production*. Somehow we got all the kids, plus all the parents, in that room." The future governor took note of the future first lady's organizational skills and grace under pressure. The show came off without a hitch. "I was quite pleased with myself afterwards, and Dan was *very* impressed. Each class had its own number and we had soloists. It was a lot of work."

They were married on June 6, 1959, at the Congregational Church in Spokane. The day's loveliest photo features Nancy, gorgeous in white lace, adjusting her proud 81-year-old father's boutonnière.

Dan took his bride on a honeymoon trip to Carmel and San Francisco in the first new car he'd ever owned—a "big-finned, gold Plymouth"—and took movies all along the way with his trusty Bolex.

Passionately moderate

Early on, Nancy had met most of the Dan Evans rat pack of bright young Republicans—notably Joel Pritchard, Chuck Moriarty, Jimmy Andersen, Slade Gorton, Don Moos and Tom Copeland. Dan was a classic progressive Republican in the Teddy Roosevelt mold. An Eagle Scout, he was a vigorous outdoorsman who loved to hike and sail. Early on, he was concerned about the environment and social justice issues. When he became governor, someone aptly described his agenda as "passionately moderate." The best

Nancy with her proud father. *Evans family album*

thing about Dan, Nancy says, is that he always "tried to bring people to-gether." His most famous quote is "I would rather cross the aisle than cross the people." Nancy was his political soul-mate—more liberal, perhaps, in some ways, but with solid instincts about social justice issues and fiscal re-sponsibility. Best of all, the earnest engineer dubbed "Straight Arrow" now had a wife who turned out to be a natural-born campaigner.

"Remember," Nancy says, "I grew up listening about politics....My par-ents loved to talk politics. In fact, later when she came to live with us, my mother would say, 'Now Dan, I think you ought to think about this.' And he'd say, 'Yes, yes Gom.' That's our nickname for my mother because that was what her first grandchild called her. So politics came very easily to me. When I went down to Olympia the first time I was younger than they were. So they all sort of took me under their wing."

When they were getting serious, did Dan ever say, "Well, someday I'm going to be governor; we'll have three kids, and we'll live in a mansion and have teas and receptions"? Nancy guffaws: "Obviously not! I probably would have said 'no.'...There was no talk about anything like that. I didn't know what I was getting into. At that time, the Legislature was two or three months every two years. I had no idea he would ever run for governor, and I don't think he did either."

Trip of a lifetime

Nancy quit teaching after their marriage. That September, Dan came home from the engineering office with a surprise announcement: "Well, I quit my job. Why don't we plan a trip?" Flabbergasted, Nancy said, "Well, jeep-ers, don't you have to get a job first?" Dan said they could afford it and they'd never regret it. "We had some money because we had both been out of school for long enough, and Nancy was very frugal," Dan recalls, "even though she didn't earn much as a teacher. And I had saved some money. So why not?"

They wrote letters to tourist bureaus all over Europe and ordered a car to pick up over there. On December 30th, they flew to Los Angeles, saw the Huskies shellac Wisconsin in the 1960 Rose Bowl game, then flew non-stop to Copenhagen on SAS. They proceeded to have the time of their lives, skiing for a month before wandering at will—Germany, Spain, Portugal and Paris—Europe for two on $10 a day, literally, except for lift tickets and gasoline. Not only will they always have Paris, Nancy was pregnant with Dan Jr. by the time they were homeward bound on a new ocean liner. "I can tell you where and when, but I'm not going to," she says with a wink and a laugh. "Our son knows."

Dan entered into a happy engineering partnership with Vic Gray. Daniel Jackson Evans Jr. was born on November 25, 1960. They moved from a one-bedroom apartment at Madison Park to their first house near Laurelhurst, atop a hill east of the UW campus.

Daniel Jackson Evans Sr., representing the 43rd District, was chosen House Republican floor leader in 1961. The braintrust of Evans, Pritchard, Gorton et al, had bigger things in mind. In 1963, they put together a coalition with dissident Democrats to oust Speaker John L. O'Brien, a quintessential Irish Catholic pol who since 1955 had wielded the gavel for a record four terms. They replaced him with a conservative Democrat, William S. "Big Daddy" Day, a Spokane chiropractor who was "absolutely" willing to give the Republicans some committee chairmanships. O'Brien was out-foxed, out-maneuvered and "out-flummoxed," as Jim Dolliver, the GOP consigliere, put it. "He didn't realize what was happening until the knife was going in....He came storming down the center aisle," but it was too late. The young R's had staged a coup. The enduring image of a decisive moment in the history of the Washington Legislature is O'Brien standing in the aisle glaring down at young Dan Evans, sitting stony-faced in the front row.

With his clean-cut image, Dan Evans was getting noticed around the state. In the spring of '63, after the Legislature adjourned, State Rep. Herb Hadley of Longview decided Dan ought to be governor and helped launch a "Draft Dan Evans Committee." Hadley had won election to the House in one of 1962's biggest upsets and was thinking big during a coffee hour

Speaker John L. O'Brien glares at Dan Evans as the coup unfolds. *Seattle Argus*

with some of his Cowlitz County pals. Hadley was a real estate man and the descendant of one of Longview's first families—"a classic go-getter in the Jaycees mold," says ex-senator Sid Snyder of Long Beach, one of the Legislature's foremost historians.

That May, Dan was at work in his engineering office when an AP reporter called. "She says, 'What's this about a Draft Dan Evans Committee?' I just laughed and I said, 'Draft Dan Evans for what?' And she said, 'Well, governor, of course.' And I said, 'I don't know anything about it.' And I didn't. They didn't check with me; they just decided to do it.... Herb was an enthusiast. He wanted me to run, so those guys just thought, 'Well, we'll goose this thing along.' That got me to thinking about it enough that I got Slade, Joel Pritchard, Jim Dolliver, all of those guys, together and we met at my house."

Nancy was rolling her eyes. "He'd come home saying, 'Well, they're talking about this.' And I'd say, 'Oh God!' Initially I was very skeptical of the whole prospect. I just didn't think he had a chance. I had good reason to think that way and I was pregnant with number two, Mark. That was my focus."

Bucking the tide

It was shaping up to be a Democratic year, with Lyndon Johnson looking unassailable. John F. Kennedy had been murdered in Dallas, and
Americans were likely disinclined to have three presidents in the space
of 14 months. Johnson was also running against a Republican Party that
was busy choosing up sides—Goldwater conservatives vs. Rockefeller pro-
gressives. In Washington State, Democrat Al Rosellini was seeking a third
term as governor. Conventional wisdom was that LBJ would have long
coattails. Dan Evans barely registered a blip on the pollsters' radar. Nancy
Evans told her husband something she would always say over the years
whenever they were at a crossroads: "Look—you do what you think you
ought to do, and I'll be there."

The other potential Republican candidates for governor included former
congressman Tom Pelly, Congresswoman Catherine May, Seattle Mayor
Gordon Clinton, well-known Seattle businessman Joe Gandy and Richard
G. Christensen. Only 33, Christensen was a hard-charging Lutheran minister fresh from a narrow loss to U.S. Senator Warren G. Magnuson. The
Republican Central Committee took a poll that June, Dan recalls, "and
I was sixth out of six. I was dead last with, I think, four or five percent.
And the only good news in the poll was that when they asked, 'Are these
names familiar to you,' or some question like that, I was one percent less
on who knew me than who would vote for me. And we said, 'Well, there's
something in there!'"

Dan and Nancy's dear friend, State Rep. Joel Pritchard—a future congressman and lieutenant governor—was the strategy guy. He told Dan,
"What you've got to do is invite 200 of your best friends to a 7 a.m. breakfast, ask them for money and see what happens." Dan said, "Well, geez,
Joel, 7 o'clock—how about 7:30?" "Nope," said Pritchard. "Make it tough
because you want to see who your friends really are." Some 140 Evans
fans showed up with checkbooks. "We ended up with a second breakfast
because I kept getting calls from people saying, 'Hey, Why didn't you invite

me?' We asked them to pledge or raise $50 apiece." In short order, the fledgling campaign had a $12,000 war chest. Even Nancy was impressed—still dubious, but impressed nevertheless. Besides, Dan had made two things clear from the get-go: "I will not run a deficit. I don't want to owe anybody. And I won't contribute any of my own money to the campaign, mostly because I don't have any, and I don't believe in it anyhow."

Mark Lawrence Evans was born on September 20, 1963. Nancy was now the busy mother of two. Dan was an engineer by day, politician by night and weekend, although he always carefully blocked out family time. By January of 1964, despite its enthusiasm, the Evans campaign was flat broke and "just gasping." Then two members of the Weyerhaeuser family contributed a total of $5,000, "which was huge," Dan recalls. A second poll showed him up to 11 percent. Christensen's lead had shrunk but it was still commanding. "Gandy was below us but pretty close. I was disappointed because we had worked hard for six months. But Joel Pritchard said, 'No, no, no, don't worry. This kind of thing builds. It's going to come faster and faster as time goes on. We've got a lot better campaign organization than anybody else and a lot more volunteers.' "

Nancy with Danny and Mark in 1964. *Evans family album*

No deals

By the spring of '64, the Evans campaign was gaining steam and the Gandy people wanted to cut a deal. "They tried to say, 'Well, Joel, he'll only run for one term. Why don't you have Dan run for lieutenant governor and then we'll turn it over to you?'" Pritchard said, "Nothin' doin'."

The state GOP Convention was at the University of Puget Sound in Tacoma. Cannily, Evans and Pritchard arranged with Don Moos, the permanent chairman of the convention, to have their demonstration last so they could gauge how all the other candidates had done. Gandy, the mover and shaker behind Seattle's Century 21 World's Fair, had a brass band. Christensen had "women on the warpath" in Indian costumes.

"There was this huge Christensen contingent," Nancy recalls. "And that's the part I hate about conventions—all that hoopla. I just don't like it. I can still remember standing outside the foyer of the center. Somebody on the stage was announcing, 'And now here we have Joe Gandy and Mrs. Gandy!' Laurene Gandy was just a lovely lady, and I can still see her, just putting her chin up saying to herself, 'OK, I'm going to do this!' And here was this lovely lady walking down amid the hoopla, hoopla, hoopla. Then they announced Dan, and it wasn't quite as much hoopla." But Dan told her there was a key difference: "The *delegates* were the ones that erupted into the aisles for us. Joel Pritchard had all the smarts." He'd ordered signs with "Evans" spelled out vertically so that when the delegates bobbed them up and down everyone could read what they said and they wouldn't get in anyone's way. "They had all these signs hidden down under the seats. When they started (waving them and hollering) it was so amazing! Nancy and I stood up there on the stage waving at friends as they went by. And I almost wept when I saw my father, who was the epitome of the old reticent engineer. He had a twinkle in his eye and there he was down on the floor with *two* signs—not one." Nancy says, "This quiet, dignified person was waving as wildly as he could. Dan had never seen his father doing anything like that." They both savored the moment.

Nancy's mother was watching the boys. Sadly, William Bell had died in 1962 at the age of 83. (His friends all called him by his middle name, Lawrence; the grandkids called him "Bompa.") But he knew Dan was going places and he was enormously proud of his son-in-law. Had he lived, Nancy says he would have been right next to Dan's dad—two old Republican engineers, whooping it up.

On the road

"We did hundreds of hours of coffee hours," Dan says, "and having Nancy along was a *huge* asset to me." With a second child on the way they had invited her widowed mother to come over from Spokane and stay with them. Lilith Bell had said, "Well, OK, I will for just a couple of months." She lived with them for the next 20 years and enriched their lives enormously. With "Gom" as much more than a babysitter, Nancy could hit the campaign trail with enthusiasm, confident that the boys were in good hands.

"We stormed out of (the convention) just really on a high," Dan says. In the next poll, Christensen was down to 42 percent and Evans was up to 29, leaving Gandy in the dust. Gandy's handlers made one last stab at cutting a deal before throwing in the towel. That made it a two-man race for the Republican nomination. Evans, ever the engineer, had been tracking his progress on a graph that he still has. Joel Pritchard kept saying, "Just watch—We're going to accelerate!" They calculated they were going to catch and pass Christensen around August 15th.

No one knows for sure when it happened. In fact, with Pritchard a notable exception, Dan recalls everyone saying, "This is going to be a tight race. It's going to be right up to the end."

On Primary Election Day, Dan Evans crushed Christensen by 100,000 votes. Christensen, like Joe Gandy before him when the jig was up, conceded gracefully, pinning on a bright red Evans campaign button and declaring, "My task now is to join with this man and make him the next governor of this state…" The Rosellini camp, meantime, had tried to woo crossover votes in the primary with ads that said "Thinking Republicans CANNOT: 'Go with Goldwater,' 'Crusade with Christensen'…or 'Endure with Evans.'"

Over the next eight weeks, Joel Pritchard was the James Carville of the 1964 governor's race. They emphasized Evans' Eagle Scout image and characterized Rosellini as an old pol who'd had his turn. In Washington it was as if Dan Evans was the new frontier, with a platform dubbed a "Blueprint for Progress." "Let's get our state moving again," the Evans brochures and ads declared, promising "a new legislative program designed to end the drift and stagnation of the Rosellini administration."

The emerging Evans wing of the party—which would come to be called "Mainstream Republicans"—was taking care to not hitch its bandwagon to Goldwater's. To borrow a phrase from George W. Bush, the Arizona senator was "a divider, not a uniter." Goldwater had once wished out loud that he could just lob a nuclear missile "into the men's room of the Kremlin." The right-wing John Birch Society loved that line, and it was already suspicious of Dan Evans. With good reason. (In a famous speech to the Republican State Central Committee in the fall of 1965, Evans took stock of the GOP debacle he had managed to survive, declaring: "It is now time to discard hyphenated Republicanism. The Republican Party did not achieve greatness nor will it regain greatness by being the party of radicalism or of the lunatic fringe. Extremists of neither the Right nor the Left contribute to the strength of America or her political institutions. Both feed on fear, frustration, hate and hopelessness.…The John Birch Society and its frightened satellites…meet none of the tests and follow none of the traditions of the Republican Party.")

Always positive

Dan was the underdog but increasingly upbeat as the final two months evaporated in a blur of speeches, coffee hours and commercials. At mid-October the press reported that he was being outspent by more than 4 to 1. His expenditures since the primary were estimated at $100,000, while ad agency observers calculated that Rosellini had spent $450,000.

"He was always positive," Nancy says. "He was always very good at understanding what the numbers meant at that moment in time. So he wasn't often surprised about things." Pretty soon, "I had a feeling 'this may happen.' Then I think I began thinking, 'But what if it does? What will I do then? What's going to happen to us?'

"The one thing about that campaign that I loved was not just the people we met out in the communities; it was the people here in Seattle, our friends, and others who became really good, life-long friends. You could just feel they were working for Dan because they *really* wanted to be there. It was sort of like the Obama campaign: They really wanted to be a part of it. I'm not comparing Dan to Obama in any way, but this was really a mission that they were on—and they were having fun. And *we* had fun. It was so personal. We really were with the campaign workers a lot—and you just enjoy being together....I have really good memories about that campaign."

Emmett Watson, the *Seattle P-I's* popular columnist, called Evans "a first-rate legislator...with a sincere abhorrence of political lunacy." Ross Cunningham of *The Seattle Times* said Dan represented "a combination of pragmatism and idealism," and *The Raymond Herald & Advertiser*, the leading paper in a solidly Democratic county, opined that "If anyone can restore harmony and respect between the executive and legislative branches of state government it is Evans."

Dan never wanted to be with a lot of people on election night—at least not before the ballots were all counted. "He wants to sit and watch that television and keep track of the numbers," Nancy says. "So conversation is not in there. And that has no exception. So my memory of Election Night 1964 is that we had a room at the Olympic Hotel with his family and my family, all the brothers and sisters and that sort of thing...And of course things were a little slower in counting the results in those days. But then when we knew he had won we went to the campaign office downtown."

Dan Evans had been elected Washington's 16th governor with 140,000 votes to spare. He was 39. Nancy was 31. They'd been married five years.

The campaign headquarters was going bonkers. "I remember that Dan was talking with KING-TV up on the stage...And then the reporter had his microphone right in front of my mouth. But I couldn't hear his questions because it was so noisy. And I know I stood there looking like 'Duh.' I think I was actually in a bit of a daze. I just sort of went, '*What did you say?*'...I felt so stupid standing up there. Then I was overwhelmed—in a good way."

Did she learn anything new about her husband by watching him on the campaign trail?—see him evolve? "Absolutely....I really saw him grow with his understanding of issues in a broader sense. Being around the state so much more and talking to so many more people, getting different sides to every issue. I think he had a wonderful understanding of the major issues for our state, and he learned how to articulate them in front of people.... Environmentalism came very easily to Dan because of his old Boy Scout days," Nancy says. "Ever since he was a kid at Camp Parsons he had been hiking in the Olympics. To this day he takes a hike every summer in the Olympics or the Cascades....But it was never defined in those days as the 'environment' and 'ecology,' and all those words that we are so accustomed to today. But when that whole movement came along, he was at the forefront because he felt so strongly about it."

She barely made it

Inauguration Day, January 13, 1965, dawned with Dan in Olympia, where the smoke was just clearing from a late-night battle over redistricting. Nancy was in Seattle, hustling the kids through their Cheerios and schlepping stuff into the station wagon. For a while the night before, the Republicans were threatening to swear in Dan at midnight to thwart any fast moves by the Democrats. Neither of them got much sleep. "I had to dismantle the crib that Mark slept in and put it in the trunk, and get everybody up and dressed and fed and ready to drive to Olympia to see Dan sworn in at noon."

Up and down the block, their neighbors had gathered to say goodbye. "It was wonderful....So we say goodbye, and I'm putting my inaugural gown on top of everything, over the crib in the back. The boys are in the back seat." She glanced in the rear-view mirror as they headed up the hill and saw people waving their arms, yelling, jumping up and down. "The trunk door was open and everything is falling out, including my dress," which, fortunately, was in a plastic bag. Tire tracks on a ball gown would have been quite a fashion statement.

She stuffed everything back in and high-tailed it to Olympia, arriving about an hour before the ceremony. The Rosellinis had finished moving out just before she arrived. "I had arranged for some high school kids to be there at the mansion to help carry in suitcases and to do the crib." But they couldn't figure out how it went together, so Dan's father, another engineer, came to the rescue. "Then I had to get the kids something to eat! At least I was dressed. I had just worn whatever I was going to wear for the ceremony. But the kids, we had to get them dressed. Mark was just 16 months old, and we had to get him down for his nap, and then be over there at noon. Ah, it was amazing! But we made it."

In his inaugural address, the new governor declared, "We cannot be blind to the growing requirements of health and welfare. Nor can we be indifferent to the dangers of stifling competitive spirit. We cannot solve the problems of the present with the outworn dogmas of the past. We must be bold in charting our course, resolute in our determination, compassionate in our assessment of human needs, firm in our policies, just in our laws and efficient in our administration....This administration is not frightened by the word 'liberal,' nor is it ashamed of the word 'conservative.' It does not believe that the words 'fiscal responsibility' are old fashioned, nor will it ever fear to spend money if money needs to be spent."

As usual, Nancy had read the speech in advance and felt it was both eloquent and timely, given the turbulent currents sweeping America. "I don't remember if I offered any suggestions. I sometimes did. But I was very proud of him and loved sitting in the audience and watching him deliver that speech, even though it was after a very long day."

In addition to multiple receptions, there had been a celebratory banquet before the Inaugural Ball. The governor and first lady came back to their new home to change into formal clothes. Mark was sound asleep, but 4-year-old Danny, still excited from the hubbub of the day, greeted them in his pajamas and bathrobe—together with a crew from KING-TV. Not realizing what she was getting into, Nancy had agreed weeks before to give KING's Chuck Herring an exclusive Inauguration Day interview. When the time came, however, she was feeling more like Lucy Arnaz than Jackie Kennedy. "I don't know why we ever even allowed it," Dan recalls, shaking his head at the memory of how hectic things were.

"So we're sitting in the living room being interviewed," Nancy says—she in her ball gown, Dan in his white tie and tails, with Danny between them, squirming with excitement at the prospect of being on TV. "Dan always remembers it so well because Chuck Herring said, 'And, Mrs. Evans, you are the youngest First Lady at 32.' And I say, *'I'm 31.'* Dan always thought that was very funny." Then Herring said, "Can I have a tour?" And Nancy goes, "Sure Chuck, come with me!" Danny gleefully scampered ahead. "I'm trying to take his hand and be a mother. I can look back at it and smile, but at the time I was just thinking, 'Couldn't you just stand here and be a nice, quiet little boy for a few moments?' But, no, he was very excited in this new big house, with a new big playroom."

Dan says she pulled it off with aplomb. "She explained everything beautifully. 'Here is this silver service from the battlecruiser *Olympia*,' and all that sort of thing. After it was all over I said, 'Nancy, how did you know all of that stuff?' And she said, 'Well, I just listened when I'd come to receptions'" when he was in the Legislature. "When I look back on all that I think of what a miracle it really was. We had been married for about four years; we lived in a small little house in Laurelhurst. If we had more than six people for dinner you had to turn the table 90 degrees and move it out into the living room. And suddenly you're into a huge mansion with *all* of the formality and all of the people." Nancy clearly was up to the challenge. "She didn't miss a step."

The first couple did more hand-shaking than dancing at the Inaugural

Ball. They were in a receiving line for more than three hours. Nancy's feet—and right hand—were aching. "There were so many people; we had so many friends, so many supporters. This was so exciting to them. I felt sorry for us, but worse for all those people who were getting pushed and shoved."

They returned to the mansion to find it packed with revelers. "So we finally went to bed at 4 in the morning—just exhausted because it had been a *long* day." Dan Evans left at 7 for his first day as governor. A bleary-eyed Nancy—who will tell you emphatically that she is not a morning person—was also up early to feed the boys, take an inventory of her new home and get ready for a new round of obligatory teas.

'Pretty, practical..."

In the beginning, the press invariably portrayed her as the little woman—a *resourceful* little woman, but the little woman nonetheless. She has "served as the flower in her husband's buttonhole at a score of important social functions," the AP noted. *The Olympian's* post-election headline on Nov. 11, 1964, was of the same genre: "State's New First Lady Pretty, Practical." But it did have the added advantage of being true. "The first is obvious," the story said. "The second was revealed when Nancy Evans said she hadn't made plans for moving to Olympia. 'We were so busy campaigning, and it seemed unnecessary to make plans we might never use,' she explained." But "Mrs. Daniel J. Evans has plenty of other attributes that helped her husband become the state's youngest governor…She has poise, a warm personality and an interest in politics."

With undertones of a write-up on a 4-H horse-judging competition, the story added that "she also had good feet and an excellent digestion. The feet, encased in needle-heeled shoes, traveled the long campaign trail beside those of her husband and she ate everything she was served. 'Well, sometimes I passed up the bread and potatoes at dinner,' she admitted, 'but I ate cookies and nuts at all those coffee hours. And I gained 15 pounds." She said she enjoyed campaigning because it took her to "every nook and cranny of this state," and although she "at first dreaded it," she quickly found it was fun, and everyone she met "was so friendly." The story concluded prophetically: "At 31, Nancy Evans may be the state's youngest first lady, but there will be few challenges she can't handle." As late as 1972 writers were still reducing her to a stereotype—the "pretty, pert wife who is the kind of mother very quick to wipe chocolate off the mouths of her three boys after an ice cream cone."

Settling in

Dan, Nancy, Danny, Mark and "Gom," together with enough animals to stock an ark, quickly discovered that their new 19-room home was old, with clanking radiators, a leaky roof and a mishmash of furniture, most of it pedestrian. The cold water faucets would often yield hot water, and vice versa. One bonus, Nancy quips, was that sometimes when you used the toilet you could "warm your bottom." On the other hand, if you plugged in a fan you could nearly electrocute Boots the cat.

Ethel Rosellini warned her that being the de facto CEO of the mansion wouldn't be all tea and roses. "Ethel told me about the night they were entertaining the crown prince of Norway or some such dignitary at a very big formal dinner party. It was being catered from Seattle, and when they plugged in the 50-cup coffee pots in the tiny kitchen the fuses blew and the lights went out." Oh, and another thing: There was one bathroom on the first floor. Nancy vividly recalls the day a busload of Seattle retirees pulled up in the driveway. "They all had to go to the bathroom—all 35 or 40 of them. I told them, 'There's one back there. That's it.'" Incredulous, they began to wander, looking for bathrooms. "These were elderly people. They had an urgent need. I understood that then and even better now. And there was not a thing we could do."

One day, a 7-year-old from the neighborhood came over to play with Dan Jr. The boy's dad happened to be a carpet layer. The kid took note of the threadbare treads on the grand staircase. "Gee, Mrs. Evans, you need to get my father over here. Your carpets are really old!" To which Nancy replied, "You're absolutely right. I'd like to do that."

Every November, friends would come over to help address the thousands of Christmas cards the first family sent out. They'd set up tables in the ballroom and huddle around portable heaters. But the place was still so cold that they wore overcoats as they addressed envelopes with numb fingers.

Still, Dan says Nancy did "a spectacular job of making the wretchedly decrepit mansion look pretty good" for everyone from Cub Scouts to dignitaries—including Pearl Bailey, J.P. Patches and Victor Borge. Especially during holidays she worked her magic to make it a home that radiated warmth. The mansion was "filled with grandparents, sisters, brothers, cousins and what seemed like squadrons of young children," Dan says. They'd be tricycling down the halls; skidding across the polished ballroom floor in stocking feet; playing hide-and-seek and lining up shortest to tallest so dad could take the obligatory movies before the presents were opened. Then Nancy, the former music teacher, would play the piano to accompany Christmas carols.

"As I think back on those years," says Dan Jr., "what strikes me the most and maybe the greatest compliment I can pay to Mom is how 'normal' life was from my perspective. With three children of my own now, it is easier to relate my experiences to those of my parents. ....It's truly amazing now to look back and recall how simple my life felt for how abnormal it could have been. My mom and dad both had a hand in that, but it was really my mother who made the mansion a home where three boys could and did feel right at home. We had birthday parties...had friends over to play, turned the Ballroom into an indoor basketball court, and the grand staircase was a great place to slide down the steps on sleds. I flew more than one model plane in flames from the second floor deck and played for hours in the woods behind the mansion."

Dad won a second term in 1968, after a turn on the national stage as keynoter for the Republican National Convention. *Time* magazine put the young governor on its cover, and Dan was in the running for a spot on the ticket

Evans family album

with Nixon before—ever the contrarian—he endorsed Nelson Rockefeller. Many of his advisers were disappointed. Nancy was proud of him.

Their family had grown to three sons—Danny, 8, Mark, 5, and Bruce, 2. In addition to Peggy and Boots, there was a big tabby named Scamper, and kittens of course, plus bunnies, gerbils, grandmother's guppies and, at one time, a couple of turkeys who didn't last long, nor did one of the hapless gerbils, who got loose and provided a snack for the cats.

Nancy says the only people who ask her whether Bruce was born *in* the mansion are men. Women chortle at that naiveté, although if St. Peter Hospital had been located then where it is now—way across town—instead of just around the corner and up the hill, Bruce might have been history's second mansion baby. He arrived in a hurry.

The first—and to date only—mansion baby was Margaret Hay, born upstairs on Nov. 30, 1910. She was the sixth child of Gov. Marion Hay and his wife Lizzie. The Hays were the first first family to live in the new house. How it came to be built is a story that features another formidable first lady.

A rush job

The 14,000-square-foot, red brick Georgian Revival house, though handsome, was constructed in a hurry at the wooded crest of Capitol Point in 1908 for the relatively munificent sum of $35,000. There'd been a severe national recession the year before, but the Northwest fared better than the rest of the country. This was the land of opportunity. Washington had been a state for only 19 years.

By the spring of 1908, Olympia was sprouting new buildings. The ballyhooed Alaska-Yukon-Pacific Exposition—Seattle's first world's fair—was set to open the next year. The whole state would be in the spotlight, and the governor would need a classy place to entertain visiting dignitaries, industrialists and investors. The cornerstone laying for "the mansion on the hill" drew a big crowd. Many local businesses had proclaimed a half-day holiday.

When work began on the grand new Capitol Campus in 1912, it was expected that the governor's "temporary" mansion would be torn down. The master plan envisioned the site being occupied by a twin to the neoclassical Insurance Building. But in the wake of never-ending debates over budget balancing and the priorities of government—some things never change—the mansion survived, which is not to say thrived.

Gov. Ernest Lister, a Democrat elected in 1912 in a photo-finish reminiscent of the Gregoire-Rossi election 92 years later, was so fed up with the state of the accommodations and the lack of privacy that he threatened to move out in 1913, actually did it in 1915 and lived intermittently in a downtown hotel again in 1917. Lister said the plumbing was bad, the wiring worse and the heating system a joke. The paltry budget the Legislature provided for maintenance and operations only ensured further decay, he added.

Lister had been in a running battle with the Republicans practically from Day One of his administration, hurling "denunciations right and left" as he delivered veto messages. When a contentious pork-barrel appropriations bill finally passed the House, the speaker dispatched the chief clerk and a senior member of the Roads Committee to deliver it to the governor. They ended up at the mansion just before midnight on March 7, 1913. "After repeated thunderous knocking on the front door, the two were confronted by Mrs. Lister, a determined lady with quick reflexes. When she opened the door," the clerk tossed the bill inside, "but like a skilled soccer player, the first lady drop-kicked it back across the porch" and the messengers fled into the night. The governor was livid, according to Gordon Newell, the capital city's leading historian. In his veto message the next day, Lister declared: "I want to say this right now—that if any gang of ruffians, hoodlums or window-tommies can go to the residence of the governor because it is a public building, any time of the day or night to compel him to be seen, I am ready to leave that residence and move to a private house where I can at least during the nights have a few hours of privacy that every public citizen is entitled to."

Adding insult to injury, the state auditor wanted to dock the governor $1,500 for overspending the Mansion Fund. In what became one of Nancy Evans' favorite quotes, Gov. Lister pronounced the mansion "a monument to the high cost of low bids." And some other things hadn't changed much, either. Dan Evans says he never ceased to be amazed at Nancy's skill in managing the mansion "with the inadequate pittance the Legislature would appropriate for maintenance and operations."

"Out of place"

The Governor's Mansion had been targeted for removal as early as 1928, when some legislators argued that it was out of place on the new Capitol campus and the perfect site for a legislative office building, in keeping with one comprehensive plan.

A few blocks south, there's another mansion of note that plays a role in this story. Built in 1923 by pioneer Olympia banker and financier Clarence J. Lord, the beautiful stucco and tile house is the work of Olympia architect Joseph Wohleb. He created one of the city's grandest homes in the Spanish Colonial style then popular in California. In 1939, C.J. Lord's widow and daughter donated the mansion to the state. Legislation was passed accepting the mansion generally, but not necessarily, for a museum, and there was even speculation that it might be used as a governors' residence. The following year, the Olympia chapter of the Daughters of the Pioneers staged a rally that drew members from around the state. They demanded that the Legislature designate the Lord Mansion as the State Capitol Museum, and the lawmakers and governor threw in the towel. (Today, the Lord Mansion is the State Capital Museum and Outreach Center, part of the Washington State Historical Society.)

But there's another twist: In the early 1960s, it was suggested that the

The Governor's Mansion, circa 1955. *Washington State Archives*

State Capitol Museum swap mansions with the state, giving the governor and his family a newer but better built mansion that boasted both historical and architectural significance. The notion was that by converting the Governor's Mansion into a museum, its proximity to the Capitol would attract thousands more visitors and finance a thorough renovation—a win-win. But nothing came of that.

A timely visitor

During the Rosellini administration, a bill was introduced to finance the long-planned legislative office building. That idea also went nowhere. The earthquake of 1965 raised structural concerns, and in 1966, a citizens' advisory committee recommended construction of a new mansion. A bond issue approved the previous year even included some funding. But Gov. Evans said he believed remodeling would be a "much sounder" plan and suggested that history-conscious citizens, organizations and businesses might donate funds or materials.

Nancy Evans was in full agreement, but she had her hands full doing the grocery shopping, preparing menus, arranging flowers, helping set tables, trying to find and, better yet, keep decent cooks for low wages. Her only other full-time helper was a housekeeper. Later, she had a part-time secretarial assistant. "I was *extremely* busy, what with the three children and all the things I had to oversee," Nancy recalls. "We had breakfast meetings, lunch meetings, dinner meetings, banquets, receptions and teas. I was just scurrying about, trying to keep up and thinking, 'What do I do *tomorrow*?!'"

That same year, 1966, Art McDonald, a popular KOMO-TV reporter, came to the door and asked to see the first lady. "In those days, you could come right to the front door of the Governor's Mansion," Nancy says. "I knew Art and he knew me, and we were chatting. Then he said, 'Well, I just wanted you to know that a member of the Capitol Committee (Lands Commissioner Bert Cole) has suggested that the mansion be torn down to make way for an office building, because that was the original plan for the Capitol campus.' Art said the idea was that 'a new modern, much more efficient mansion would be built somewhere else.' The Capitol Committee included the governor, the lieutenant governor and the commissioner of public lands. Without a moment's hesitation, I told Art, 'Absolutely not. We are a young state, and this is part of our history, and we need to retain it.'

"Art thanked me, excused himself and went right back over to the Capitol, where Dan was having a press conference. He said, 'Governor, I've just spoken to Mrs. Evans about the suggestion that the mansion be torn down. And she told me, 'Absolutely not. It's worth preserving.' What do you think?' And Dan said, 'That's what I think, too.' He's well trained!"

Dan, however, remembers waffling before getting his marching orders renewed. "Bert Cole was all in big favor of building a new mansion out on the point," he recalls, but Lieutenant Governor John Cherberg "wasn't sure quite what to do and neither was I. So it was kind of inconclusive that afternoon. After the (committee) meeting, we had a press conference and the press asked me my view. I said, 'Well, I don't know. Maybe a new mansion is OK.' I was kind of not willing to say too much about it because I didn't really know what the heck we ought to do. And I got home that night and the paper said, 'First Lady says, 'Save the mansion.' I asked Nancy, 'What the heck was all this about?' And she said, 'Well, I talked to a member of the press. They asked me and I told them.'…So I told her, 'Well, I guess that's our policy.' And then she was very good in saying why it needed to be saved, you know—'It may not be old now but it will never be old if we (tear it down).'"

The governor emerged the next day fully girded for battle. Moreover, the cost of securing a site, constructing and furnishing a new mansion was estimated at upwards of a shocking $2 million. With Nancy taking the lead, the couple supported a "Save the Mansion" campaign launched by the Daughters of the Pioneers—good ladies to have on your side. They attracted a strong core of supporters.

Stop-gaps

After Dan won a second term, Nancy oversaw some repairs and renovations. But they were stop-gaps, literally and figuratively: The place was still cold in winter and stuffy in summer. Wind-whipped rain invariably led to leaks. One Christmas Day, as family and friends gathered to open presents, the governor was up on the rooftop trying to figure out why water was pouring into the ballroom. Further, the floorboards sagged; there was dry-rot in the porch and the wiring was a fright. The kitchen was too small for a family of six, let alone a place that entertained en masse.

"The mansion," Nancy told Sally Gene Mahoney of *The Seattle Times* on Inauguration Day 1969, "is an unhappy subject with me." The first lady lamented that when she called the caterer to make arrangements for a large pre-function, the woman "asked me if the kitchen had been fixed. When I told her it hadn't, she said, 'Oh no—your kitchen is the worst one I've ever worked in!'"

Privacy—or the lack of it—which sore-vexed Gov. Lister, was still a problem. The mansion was both a semi-public venue and a private residence, although the private part was sometimes lost on tourists in the era before a fence was installed, together with a State Patrol guardhouse at the foot of the winding driveway. Wearing shorts, Nancy turned the corner one summer's day to encounter a couple who thought they were in a museum. "When's the tour?" they inquired. She couldn't even leave the door open on a muggy day.

Still, the governor, first lady and grandma coped with it all and added touches that made the mansion a home. Dan, who had fond memories of what it was like to be an adventuresome little boy, loved woodworking. And he was, after all, a former civil engineer, so he built a tree house with his sons. "It was a beautiful tree house," Nancy says wistfully, "and it also turned out to be a very expensive tree house. There was an old maple tree outside the mansion that had an enormous trunk with a lovely fork about 10 feet up—just a logical place to put a tree house. Dan and the boys were out there every weekend for weeks building this thing. It had a trapdoor and a ladder. Mark, who was about 4 at the time, fell through the open trapdoor and cracked his head. And of course these things always happen on the weekend when the doctors aren't available. So we dashed, as usual, to the emergency room. Mark actually had some ensuing difficulties…and we had to go to Children's Hospital a few times. Happily, the difficulties went away with time. The boys spent a lot of time in that tree house. There were no small children in the mansion for several years after we left, and eventually the tree house was removed, but I was sorry to see it go."

As for the other emergency room trips, Mark broke his leg while skiing when he was 6, while Bruce suffered serious lacerations when he ran through a glass door when he was 3. He was playing circus with his brothers while visiting his Uncle Bill. A few months earlier, busy little Bruce locked himself in the bathroom a few minutes before guests were set to arrive for a large dinner party at the mansion. Nancy says "Dan was out on the balcony checking windows to see if we could get in from there and I was frantically telling Bruce though the door, 'Turn the little button the other way like a good boy.' Just as the first guests rang the bell, he turned it and let himself out."

"My appreciation for my mother grows by the day as I drag my own kids through their childhood," says Bruce Evans. "They're 9, 6 and 4, the same number and similar spacing to my brothers and me. And to think she was doing all that while being thrust into the role of first lady at a young age. It's really remarkable to me."

"Are you coming back?

Having the mansion right across the street from his office meant that the governor could spend more time with his family, but he was still gone a lot. Nancy wrote an article about what it was like to be first lady and First Mommy. She said Dan always tried to have breakfast with his family. Almost every morning when he was about to leave for work, Mark would ask, "Are you going to the Capitol, Daddy?" When Dan said "Yes," he always knew the next question would be "Are you coming back, Daddy?" Nancy wrote that "it sounds a little fatalistic but I'm sure it must seem to Mark that his Daddy does not come back for many days, as often he does not return until long after the boys are in bed and sometimes, of course, he actually does not return for several days. And then I think, 'What a shame he can't spend more time with his father,' only to be caught short as I am preparing to go somewhere and Mark asks, 'Are you coming home, Mommy?' Don't tell me I'm gone that much, too!"

Mark Evans, who became the middle child with baby Bruce's arrival, had a knack for asking tough questions. Dan Jr., being oldest, dutifully took notes and pasted stuff in his scrapbook. When he was 10, he wrote an article for *Jack and Jill* magazine about what it was like to be the son of a governor. He said his folks assigned him and his brothers "certain jobs that have to be done regularly," noting that he had earned a five-speed bike by cleaning the garage and tetherball court and raising the flag. He liked Little League, Cub Scouts and playing with his brothers. Bruce, easy-going, funny and friendly, added spice to all their lives, Danny said. For instance, when the Apollo astronauts were poised to land on the Moon in the summer of 1969, his kid brother, then 3, was helping tend the family garden in the mansion's back yard. Bruce suddenly extracted a carrot, counted down—"Five-four-three-two-one-zero-blast off!"— then tossed it as high as he could.

In 1971, however, when Spiro Agnew visited the mansion, Bruce was uncharacteristically petulant. He refused to dress up and come downstairs with his brothers to meet the vice president of the United States. Nancy insisted, and the 4-year-old finally appeared in short pants and knee socks. With Mom bending over his shoulder, he shook hands with Agnew with downcast eyes, tears streaming down his face. Motorized Nikons whirred and newspapers all over the country published the photo. They say kids can sense things about people. Maybe Bruce knew the honored guest was a nattering nabob of hypocrisy. Agnew resigned in disgrace three years after their encounter, pleading no contest to a charge of income tax evasion. Bruce is now clerk for the U.S. Senate Appropriations Committee in Washington, D.C., and still gets teased about the photo.

As for teasing, Nancy recalls the time she was a substitute carrier on Mark's *Olympian* paper route and missed some porches. Mark, who was around 11, had a bad cold, or some such ailment, and mom sprang into action. Some customers had the effrontery to complain they'd been skipped or had soggy papers.

It seemed as if every day was a new adventure. One of Nancy's all-time favorite mansion moments came courtesy of a Cub Scout pack that arrived on Valentine's Day: "They walked in, presented me with a corsage, politely stood in line for their cookie, looked around, and, as they were leaving, each boy shook my hand like a gentleman and politely thanked me for a lovely time. But one little boy caught my heart when he pulled me down to him and said, 'The house is pretty, but I like your red dress better.' That was the nicest Valentine present I could have had."

"Gom" a Godsend

The nicest present the whole family ever had was grandma. Widowed when Nancy's father died in 1962, Mrs. Bell was persuaded to move into the mansion in 1965 to help Nancy settle in to her new role. But Gom quickly made friends in the community and enjoyed joining in the entertaining at the mansion, including having tea with Pat Nixon and Betty Ford. She became an expert on its history and could recite the provenance of its furnishings. She delighted in giving tours. Her presence was a Godsend for her daughter and the whole family. The boys adored her, and so did her son-in-law, who carefully listened to her advice, solicited or otherwise.

"Gom was the third pillar and a huge part of our childhood," says Bruce Evans. With grandma's help, "there was no feeling of absence on the part of either parent, and that's pretty remarkable given the responsibilities they had." His grandmother definitely "wasn't to be trifled with," Bruce says. "The only occasion when I had my mouth washed out with soap, around age 10, was when I said something I shouldn't have in her presence, and I'm pretty sure I never used that word around her again. . . . Her word was the word of God." After he ran through the plate glass window at his uncle's house, his grandmother urged him to stop crying and try to stay calm, "and I tried very hard because Gom wanted me to."

Dan and Nancy were rarely surprised by Lilith Bell's chutzpah. In the early 1970s, she often attended legislative sessions and hearings. Like many senior citizens, she needed a hearing aid, but found there were problems with the process and the product. "I learned what a sad need there was for standards," she told reporters. "My beauty operator had to have a license, but hearing aid salesmen did not. I began taking on legislators at cocktail parties at the mansion. When I went to the hearings, a lobbyist stopped me and said, 'Young lady, you're going to get arrested if you don't stop all that lobbying.'" Fat chance, Mrs. Bell said, but if it ever happened, she would "lobby against that, too. I believe in free speech!'"

"Dan didn't realize it at the time when he became governor," Nancy says, "but he quickly found out that there were several hundred commissions. There was the Mattress & Bedding Commission and there was a Hearing Aid Commission, so Dan said, 'Ah, I'll put Gom on that commission.' I thought he was really brave to put her on there. (But) I would run into people who were on the commission, and they said, 'Your mother is just a breath of fresh air. She comes in and tells it exactly like it is. And she tells the manufacturers what for.'"

The governor gleefully signed into law his mother-in-law's bill to regulate hearing aid sales. "She really was a dynamo on the commission because she was all for the consumer," he recalls. "She knew all the foibles and the problems and the difficulties and the costs. And so, boy, she really turned that commission upside down because she was fighting to get the cost down and the quality up. . . . She saw a need and acted. I thought it was just great. . . . 'Gom' was a wonderful help to us all and a steadying influence on the boys. She was always there. And a lot of times she was always there when we weren't. I don't know how we could have managed without her."

"Mother was a *huge* help and it really is what made it possible for me to not go crazy," Nancy says, "and she was also very sensible. Any sensibility I have I learned from her. She was very practical, and when I wasn't around she tried to keep things orderly, as much as she could, with the kids. So she was a lifesaver." The touching thing, Nancy says proudly, is that when "Gom" got older, her three grandsons always took care of her.

Mrs. Bell's four children and a hundred friends and admirers gave her a surprise 80th birthday party at the mansion in 1972. She was going strong, eager as ever to try new things. "I cut off my long hair and went up in a blimp," she boasted.

That same year, her daughter acted on a plan they'd been mulling—a foundation to help preserve the Governor's Mansion "and stimulate interest" in the donation of antiques, artwork, table settings and historically relevant artifacts. One of the first lady's key goals was to establish and maintain some consistency in the style of the mansion's furnishings. Over the years, the Georgian Revival mansion had acquired a hodge-podge of drapes and furniture, much of it purchased out of pocket by former first ladies since the Legislature was perennially tight-fisted toward the mansion. In fact, when the Hays became the first tenants in 1908, Nancy says "the ladies of Olympia actually scurried around borrowing dishes and furniture" to help them set up housekeeping. Once unpacked, Governor Hay decided they would tap into the funds allocated by the Legislature for maintenance, operations and entertaining and issue a call for bids for enough furniture to furnish the place. He decreed that the bidding would be restricted to Washington state stores. The winner, with a bid of $15,000, was Frederick & Nelson, the pioneer Seattle department store. On the whole, given the tight budget, Lizzie Hay exhibited good taste. The stately grandfather clock on the staircase landing and the massive mahogany table, buffet and 18 chairs in the State Dining Room are among the survivors. However, "each family that moved in did things as money was allowed, and oftentimes not much money," Nancy says. "Every room was sort of different, except for the original furniture that was sort of late Victorian. There was no continuity to the décor."

Founding a foundation

In 1972, architects were still sniffing that the mansion was "not architecturally wonderful and not historically ancient." Gov. Evans shot back that it was "a lot more ancient than a new one would be." Nancy redoubled her efforts to save it. "But I knew that even if we won, the state was not going to buy the furnishings appropriate for a place like this. That's when I came up with the idea of forming a foundation that would do it." She invited influential, history-minded citizens from around the state to join the cause. Forty-seven women and five men met with her at the mansion on May 30, 1972. The first lady already had two important players on board. Jean Jongeward, one of Seattle's most sought-after interior designers, agreed to donate her services, while, in a real coup, Laurene Gandy accepted Nancy's invitation to head the foundation. Mrs. Gandy was a much-admired civic activist, together with her late husband, who spearheaded Seattle's Century 21 world's fair. Its success made the Gandys the toast of the town. In 1964, you'll recall, Joe Gandy was an early GOP candidate for governor before withdrawing and lending his support to Dan Evans.

"I was so delighted when Laurene said yes," Nancy recalls, "because she was a wonderful, widely respected person and had great interest and knowledge of antiques. And my timing was impeccable because she had just lost her husband. The mansion was a new and interesting project for her to take on. I'm sure, however, that she had no idea of the amount of effort it was going to take, but she chaired the foundation for its first five formative years and did a wonderful job."

The foundation, anxious to avoid social minefields, quickly established a three-person Acceptance Committee. That simultaneously took the onus off Nancy Evans and protected the integrity of Jean

Jongeward's master plan, which called for the acquisition of furnishings circa 1780-1830 to complement the design of the house. "Everywhere I went," Nancy recalls, "somebody would say, 'Well, I have Aunt Sophie's tablecloth that would be just perfect.'" From Enumclaw to Ephrata, there were countless Aunt Sophies with a vase, a chest of drawers or an allegedly priceless rug.

"Laurene Gandy and I traveled around the state with what I called our dog and pony show, talking to people about the foundation," Nancy says. "We asked Marie Edwards, who had been the buyer for the Old World Shop at Frederick & Nelson, to help us. The shop sold antique furniture, lamps and dishes, and Marie was extremely knowledgeable. She chaired the Acceptance Committee, so it was very easy for me and anyone else involved with the foundation to be able to politely say, 'I'm sorry. We have this committee that accepts things. I will refer this to them.' It was a very good decision to sort of depoliticize acquisitions and draw on the judgment of experts."

Jongeward and Edwards, with bargain-hunting savvy to match their exquisite taste, made the rounds of East Coast antique shops. They were pleasantly surprised when they found some choice American antiques. "They thought it was going to be primarily British or English pieces, and maybe a few French pieces," Nancy says. "So that was very exciting."

The foundation had received some donations, but it was far from well-heeled, especially in the early going, and often relied on timing and the kindness of enlightened strangers. "For the fireplace mantel, Jean and Marie had bought two little pieces with crystal drops. They arrived with one of the crystals missing, so we called a big antique store in New York." While mulling that request, the appraiser asked, " 'By the way, are you a poor foundation?' We said, 'Very, very poor.' And they said, 'Well, a woman has just come in who's a customer of ours from Connecticut, and she has this demilune (crescent moon-shaped) server that she would like to donate. But she wants it to go to a poor foundation.' We qualified! It's the lovely mahogany and bird's-eye maple inlaid server that sits just off the entry hall."

The piece, circa 1800, is attributed to John Seymour, considered the greatest post-Revolutionary War furniture designer and craftsman in Boston.

Working with the experts and mobilizing the committees was "a wonderful learning experience for me," Nancy says. "I learned so much."

Four more years

"The main reason I didn't want to leave here is that I didn't want to pack," Nancy quipped to reporters after Dan won his bare-knuckle 1972 rematch with Al Rosellini. At mid-October, the resurgent Democrat had a 13-point lead in the polls. Then, in one turning point in the race, he referred to his successor as "Danny Boy" during a debate. The faux pas struck many as both patronizing of the younger man and disrespectful to the governor's office. Nancy was in the audience that Saturday morning at North Seattle Community College and says she knew immediately that Rosellini had made "a big mistake."

The Mansion Foundation, meantime, was proving to be a big success. Fundraisers were taking place all over the state by all manner of groups and organizations, Republican and Democratic women's groups, Rotary and Zonta clubs, guilds and sororities. The Boeing Company and other firms would make donations in the years to come.

Nancy asked Dan to make a guest appearance for the foundation's second-annual meeting in 1973. He had good news: The Legislature had at last appropriated $600,000 for remodeling and structural renovation of the mansion. It was going to have a new lease on life.

Renovation work got under way in the spring of 1974, after the Evans family took up temporary residence in a Colonial Revival home known as the Egbert-Ingham House. Built in 1914, it was at Columbia and 14th on the site now occupied by the Visitors' Center at the north entrance to the Capitol Campus.

Unfortunately, to paraphrase the first lady's father, the contractors discovered *Surprises Equinoxia*—expensive ones. "When they opened it up, they found out the mansion's beams were not footed properly," Nancy says. "The gravity of the house was pressing down, keeping them in place. They also found a number of pint whiskey bottles, so it's easy to understand why the house was having problems."

Much of the interior had to be virtually gutted. The final tab was nearly $2 million, but the outcome left few dissenters. The tired old mansion was transformed into a house that had all the modern conveniences—whether for banquets or family breakfasts—without compromising its integrity as a public treasure. There was new wiring, new plumbing, a modern heating and air-conditioning system and a commercial-sized kitchen. Another sorely-needed public bathroom was added on the main floor, together with a private dining room and a family living room that Nancy loves. "It is a peaceful, quiet, lovely room" brightened by soft natural light from a big Palladian window that she suggested to the architects. She first admired the design in grand old homes and palaces she and Dan visited when they bummed around Europe as newlyweds. There's a smaller version in the house they built in Seattle when they finally retired from politics.

To complete the project, two new guest rooms were added on the second floor. In all, some 4,000 square feet of living space was added on the south side of the original structure, bringing the total to 18,000 square feet.

Meantime, the Mansion Foundation had been raising funds and tracking down furnishings and artwork for the public rooms. Through pluck and luck, Nancy and the other volunteers turned out to be persuasive fundraisers and world-class scroungers. "They had teas, lunches and dinners, train rides and picnics—all sorts of events all over the state," Nancy says. "And amazing pieces kept turning up....When we moved back in September of 1974, it was truly exciting. The transformation was remarkable."

That October was dubbed "Mansion Month," with fundraisers in 35 communities. More than $45,000 was raised. Through purchases and donations, the foundation had secured furnishings then valued at a total of $350,000. Today, the mansion collection easily tops $1 million, and the work goes on. Some of the greatest furniture-makers in American history, including Duncan Phyfe, Joseph Barry and Samuel McIntire, are featured. A magnificent portrait of George Washington by Rembrandt Peale, the American master of neoclassical portraiture, is a recent acquisition. "It's one of the finest in the country," Nancy notes, explaining that the foundation owns all of the furnishings in the mansion's original public rooms, as well as artwork and antiques in other public and private areas.

"What had once been a shabby home was now a really beautiful and even more historic building—a wonderful place where the governors and their families can enjoy life and entertain with a great feeling of satisfaction, proud to invite people from around the state and around the world," the former first lady says.

"What if?"

In 1976, Dan Evans likely had a good chance to become the state's first four-term governor, but he decided 12 years was long enough. Nancy was relieved. She too was ready for something new. Meantime, Gerald Ford, who had succeeded the disgraced Nixon, was looking for a running mate. With his squeaky-clean image and progressive record, Evans was on his short list. The Evans family was vacationing at a remote Montana cabin when the Secret Service arrived for a chat. That upped the ante, and Nancy's emotions were mixed: Pride, some anxiety and a dash of excitement, although she never allowed herself to get hung up on things beyond her control.

A few weeks later, Dan was asked to be a Ford delegate-hunter at the Kansas City Convention, where the president was facing a stiff challenge from Ronald Reagan. Dan's competitive juices kicked in, and the Evans brain trust—including legendary political operative C. Montgomery "Gummie" Johnson, Chief of Staff Bill Jacobs and Joel Pritchard, now a congressman—was doing its best to boost their guy onto the ticket. Ford's son Jack was also making it clear that Dan was dad's favorite.

Shelby Scates, the *Seattle P-I's* political reporter, called Jacobs to see if he could confirm a rumor that Secret Service phone links had been installed in the governor's suite, which would have been clear evidence that Dan was among the finalists. Jacobs said that was news to him. He cupped the phone and asked the governor and Bill Lathrop, his security man, if they knew anything. Both said nope, and Scates hung up disappointed. Dan was now intrigued. He dispatched Lathrop to check out the story. When the State Patrolman returned empty handed, Jacobs said, "I've got an idea. I'll be back!" He went to a pay phone, called the Holiday Inn where they were staying and in his best Dragnet imitation pretended to be a member of Ford's Secret Service detail. He asked the assistant manager to confirm that the phone links had been installed. "Yes, sir," the man said. "They're there." Then Jacobs said, "You're the one I was talking to when I was there?" "Yes sir." "Well, would you go over with me just where they're located?" "Well, sir, you told me that no matter who called on the phone, even you, not to discuss this." "Very good!" said Jacobs "But they *are* in place?" "Yes, sir, they are." Now, that's what we call great staff work.

In the end, Ford picked Kansas Senator Bob Dole. Dan told Nancy, "I know I'd be a better candidate than he is." It wasn't sour grapes. They were both wary of Dole's sarcastic tongue. The GOP ticket went on to lose narrowly to Jimmy Carter and Walter Mondale. "That was the one time," Jacobs says, "when I felt that the VP choice made a difference—that Mondale ran a good campaign, Dole a bad one."

Would Dan have taken the spot if it had been offered? "Sure," says Nancy. "The vice-presidency…would have been a wonderful experience. Absolutely." And what about the presidency? If Nixon had picked Dan instead of Spiro Agnew in 1968, her husband could have ended up in the Oval Office. He certainly wouldn't have been involved in Watergate, and he might have won in his own right in 1976. Did she ever think about that— "What if"? Well, "not much." And if she had become first lady, would she always try to remember she was really Nancy Bell from Spokane? "No other choice," says Nancy. "That's who I am. But it's a danger. It's easy to get absorbed in whatever life you're doing without remembering how you got there—why you are there.

"When Dan was in the Senate and we moved to D.C....there were a lot of social things going on *all* the time. It's very formal there. Women dress up *all* the time. I had to buy new clothes....And there's a lot of deference paid to elected officials back there, to senators particularly. You go to a lot of embassies and on and on and on and on. So you can quickly forget who you are and where you come from....My oldest sister—my *wise* older sister Barbara—came back to visit one time and she could see all of this going on. She said, 'Don't let yourself get so involved and forget who you are and why you're here.' And I said, 'Well, I hope I don't.' She said, 'Well, I can see that it would be easy for you to get that way.' So I tried very hard not to....It's just so insidious that you're not even aware that it's happening to you. You just expect, 'Of course I can do that. I can do whatever I want because my husband is a U.S. Senator.' So I was often surprised at some of the senators' wives who were there for a long time—some are still there—and what services they expected to have provided for *them* in the Capitol, for instance. And *they* were not the senators."

Packing up

In January of 1977, when it came time to leave the Governor's Mansion, Nancy and Dan sorted through their scrapbooks, packed with the flotsam of the past 12 years—name tags from trade missions, menus, birthday cards, telegrams and notes from famous people, including Nixon, who with typical duplicity assured Dan, "Your friendship means a great deal." And from not-so-famous people thanking Dan for his stewardship of the state. "Whenever I am tempted to dismiss all politicians as crooks," a Seattle woman wrote, "you restore my faith in the system." Page after page of snapshots of the family skiing, hiking, swimming; a series of Polaroids of Dan shaving off his much-debated beard in silly stages—Fu Manchu, Pecos Bill, Hitler. So many memories. And just when the place was fixed up, it was time to leave.

"It's like having a baby," Nancy says. "You nurture a child and you raise it, and then you send it out into the world with no idea of what they're going to do. So when we left the Governor's Mansion we had deeply mixed emotions. It had been our home for 12 happy years—Dan, the three boys, my mother and all those pets."

People kept asking her, "Won't you be glad to get back to Seattle?" "And I said, 'Well, we're really happy where we are. We've really enjoyed Olympia. People think Olympia is terribly remote and provincial…But there's an ease of life here that I don't think you find in a larger city. There are things happening here and it's going to be very hard to leave Olympia." Nancy Evans' work in promoting cultural events during her years as first lady played a key role in making the capital a livelier city.

Often unmentioned is the fact Dan Evans prided himself on having a close-knit administration and he expected all of the key players—aides and departmental directors—to live in Olympia. "They became part of the community," says Jacobs, "and Nancy took an active role in the directors' wives club, which got together regularly at the mansion and did things under her leadership."

Since so many things bloom under Nancy's touch, friends and admirers gave her a unique going-away present: a new hybrid rhododendron, named in her honor. The rhodie, after all, is Washington's state flower. The Nancy Evans Rhododendron has orange-red buds that open to gorgeous amber yellow flowers in early May. It was created by Dr. Ned Brockenbrough, a Seattle surgeon who in the 1960s got hooked on the art and science of cross-breeding rhodies.

Dr. Ned Brockenbrough and the First Lady prepare to plant the "Nancy Evans Rhododendron." *Evans family album*

What next?

Dan was entertaining job offers, but most would have forced them to leave the Northwest. "My general response," the governor said in the summer of 1976, "has been 'Call me when you move your headquarters to Seattle.'" He added that a college or university presidency would be very appealing.

When Dixy Lee Ray moved into the mansion, Dan and Nancy treated the kids and Grandma to a vacation in Europe. When they returned it was to Olympia. Dan became the second president of The Evergreen State College, a job where he would need all of his political and diplomatic skills to ensure the survival of the controversial liberal arts school. Governor Ray and conservative lawmakers viewed Evergreen as an enclave of lefty professors and hippie kids with shaggy dogs.

The family moved into the president's home on Budd Inlet. It was nothing like a mansion, which was a relief in many ways, and it featured a spectacular view.

Nancy had a strong liberal arts background and real-world experience as an overseer at Whitman. She was in the trenches with her husband, lobbying to improve Evergreen's image and protect its funding. Dan Jr. was in high school, Mark in junior high and Bruce a fifth grader, so she was a busy mom, still active in cultural and philanthropic affairs—and disturbed by reports that Dixy Lee Ray's beloved poodle, Jacques, was peeing all over the mansion.

Dan burnished his image with the students and faculty when he took up famed mountain climber Willi Unsoeld's challenge to rappel down the clock tower on campus. They were happy years for Dan and Nancy, and they shored up Evergreen's reputation.

Soon, the oldest Evans boys had driver's licenses, which meant Nancy wasn't logging as many miles as taxi driver. She gave them the room to make mistakes, but kept an eye on everything. Mark says his parents "were admirably restrained," but had different styles. "Mom was the disciplinarian in some ways but never in a heavy handed fashion," he says, offering this cautionary true tale: "When I was in High School, some friends and I borrowed my parents' Volvo station wagon to go to a basketball game. On the way home, the normal road we would have turned onto was blocked off due to flooding. One of my friends suggested it would be great to drive through the water and throw up a huge spray. Being the responsible middle child, I of course demurred—for 20 seconds. I hit the gas, and boy did we ever throw a huge spray from either side of the car. Then a big spray came over the hood and the car stopped." After a moment of stunned silence, one of his friends opened a door. Water surged in, and the friend belatedly said, "Don't open the doors!" Mark rolled down a window, jumped out and landed in waist deep water. The boys finally managed to push the car back onto dry pavement.

"When I got home later that evening after wringing out the car at a friend's house, I heard my father's voice asking me to come into their room. They were both in bed. Dad looked like he had been doing the crossword with the TV on in the background, while Mom had fallen asleep. Dad lectured me briefly on staying out too late, then asked me to turn off the TV. I had been standing in the shadows because my pants were wet. Now I had to cross the room and hope he wouldn't notice. I strode over to the TV, turned it off and started to leave the room, thinking to myself, 'Thank goodness, he didn't notice anything.' But as I was leaving the room, Mom, whose eyes had never opened—or so I thought—said, 'Why are your pants wet?' That story to me captures my Mom. Even when you don't think she's looking, she's got her eyes out for her boys."

Scoop's successor

In 1983, U.S. Senator Henry M. "Scoop" Jackson died unexpectedly of a heart attack. Dan Jr. was about to graduate from Whitman, while his brothers were headed East—Mark to Williams College and Bruce to Yale. In fact, Dan and Nancy had just dropped off Bruce at SeaTac. It was a gorgeous late August afternoon. "The Evergreen president's house had a deck out in back overlooking the bay and Mt. Rainier. We were having a drink, sitting out there just talking," Nancy recalls. "And I remember I said, 'You know, now that the boys are gone...are we still going to like each other?' And Dan said, 'Well, of course.' And I said, 'I don't know, it just seems strange. What are we going to do?' It was this deep discussion....Finally I said, 'Well, I've got to go fix dinner.' And Dan says, *'Why?'* And I laughed and said, 'Well, I don't know!' So I think I sat back down and we had another drink. We went to bed and at about 11 or midnight, Dan's brother Roger called. He said, 'Have you heard the news?' Scoop Jackson had died. We had not heard the news, and the next morning, right after these two boys had gone off to school and we had talked about 'What do we do now?' the phone started ringing. The timing of everything was incredible."

Over the years, Dan had weighed running for the Senate. "We thought Maggie and Scoop were going to be there forever so why think about it?" Nancy recalls. Besides, "he just liked being governor" and being president of the college had turned out to be interesting as well. "He just didn't think that was something he wanted to do."

Over the next several days, they mulled. Dan talked with Senator Slade Gorton, his old comrade. Gorton encouraged him to seek the appointment. Secretary of State Ralph Munro, a trusted friend and former aide, prodded him to call Governor John Spellman, who would get to fill the vacancy. Dan decided "the polite thing to do" would be to talk it over with Spellman, but he was a conflicted candidate. Just before he left for the meeting with the governor, Nancy recalls, "he was walking down the hall shaking his head."

"I said, 'I'm going to tell the governor 'No.' I just don't want to do this,'" Dan recalls. "And she said, 'Look, you do what you want to do, and I'll be there. It'll be great. Whatever you do is fine.'"

On the ride from Cooper Point to the Governor's Mansion, he changed his mind. All over the radio was the news of a Korean airliner being shot down when it strayed into prohibited Soviet Union airspace. All 269 people aboard perished. It was perhaps the most dangerous moment since the

Cuban Missile Crisis. "Good God," Dan said to himself, "how can you *not* want to really get involved in resolving (things like that)? With this many problems and the challenges that we're facing you can't just back away from that." He and the governor had breakfast in the new private dining room the Spellmans were enjoying, thanks to Nancy. "I told the governor, 'You do whatever you want and I'll be very happy. But, if you think that I'm the right appointment, I'd be proud to serve.'" Spellman said he was proud to appoint Daniel J. Evans to the United States Senate.

"It was a *very* hard time," Nancy says. "One of the hardest times in our lives…because then he had to run for election in two months" if he wanted to serve out the last five years of Jackson's Senate term.

Nancy and the boys attended the swearing in, then Nancy returned alone. "Dan had to fly back there every week to learn how to be a senator. Fly home on the weekends, organize and put together a campaign, raise money.… campaign out here and then go back and do his work back there."

Pressed into service was their trusted friend Bill Jacobs, who was in D.C. on a special assignment with the U.S. Department of Labor.

Dan defeated Seattle Congressman Mike Lowry, who went on to become governor and a partner with Evans in a coalition to protect forests and wildlife. While some might conclude they're the strangest of political bedfellows—the voluble liberal Democrat and the cerebral Republican engineer— their friendship is another example of Evans' bridge-building style. It's Nancy's style, too, and she says of Lowry, "He's a love—he really is."

A frustrating job

Slade Gorton, Dan's old comrade from their days in the state Legislature, loved the Senate, but Evans was frustrated from the beginning. Dan's staff was "wonderful," Nancy says, thanks in large part to Jacobs' skill as a recruiter and organizer. But seniority—or the lack of same—permeated practically everything in the Senate.

Things were better when Nancy finally found them a tiny but charming old house not far from the Hill. Dan also landed a spot on the Foreign Relations Committee, so they met dozens of visiting dignitaries, and took a number of trips together. Jordan is the most memorable. Before King Hussein arrived for a luncheon, Nancy demonstrated her diplomatic skills and big sister wisdom. Dan's assistant, a young woman named Chris Dawson, was told she had to remain with the women while the men discussed serious issues. "She was a bright, independent, single lady and furious," Nancy recalls. "She almost turned red right there….I could see that Chris was about ready to say something, so I went over, and I think I whispered, 'Just come quietly with me.' We went to this tiny room off the entry and sat there with these Jordanian ladies. They were very nice, but we had nothing in common because all they wanted to talk about was their trips to London and Paris, and shopping. Chris was sitting there seething. And I was sitting there trying to look interested."

Dan was impressed by the way Nancy defused the situation: "Boy, she caught it so early that I don't think anybody else even ever knew….Nancy just nipped that one right in the bud. We had a more official meeting afterwards, which Chris was part of. So it all worked out….And then of course during the lunch I could hardly get a word in edgewise with the king because he was talking with Nancy the whole time."

With her deft touch and lively sense of humor, Jacobs says Nancy played a key role in keeping Dan's Senate staff revved up. They put in some long hours, but the boss's wife was a familiar face, whether for work or play. "One of the things that brought us together," the chief of staff says, "was that we played together, too, and Nancy played with us." When there was a pizza party at someone's apartment, she'd just as soon be there as at some swanky reception on the Hill.

By 1987, however, Dan had had enough of the other Washington. They were coming home. "I've lived through five years of bickering and protracted paralysis. Five years is enough," he said. "I just can't face another six years of frustrating gridlock."

Senator Strom Thurmond, the living fossil from South Carolina, once asked Nancy, "Well, Mrs. Evans, does Dan prefer being a governor or does he prefer being a senator?" Nancy replied that Dan preferred being a governor "because of the ability to set the agenda and organize things a bit more the way you would like to have them." Thurmond patted her on the behind and said, "Yeah, but the Senate is where the *power* is!" True enough, if you'd been around since the Eisenhower administration.

Jacobs offers this perspective: "I think it's important for people to understand that Dan and Nancy valued that experience in Washington, D.C., and they both worked hard at it. All governors who wind up in the U.S. Senate are frustrated at first because they don't have the executive power they did. But the main reason he decided to not stay in the Senate is that if he ran for re-election and got elected, in essence that would be where he was spending the rest of his life."

Exactly, says Nancy. Dan did hate the inertia in the Senate, "but it wasn't just that." They were both getting older. They enjoyed the museums, monuments and battlefields, met many fascinating people, but it never felt like home. They yearned for the trees, the mountains, Puget Sound on a spring day with wind in the sails.

But first they spent a stimulating semester at Harvard, where Dan was a visiting fellow in the Kennedy Institute of Government. Nancy audited classes to her heart's content, including one devoted to Beethoven, another on art history and yet another on Southern female authors. "Dan would go off to his classes, and I would put on my boots, my wool coat, my scarf, my gloves and my hat. I'd pick up my books and off I would trudge—a college student all over again. It was fun!"

"Retired"?

Settling in back home, they built a dream house not far from the park bench where Dan proposed. You would be hard pressed to find two busier, ostensibly retired people. She became a trustee at Whitman, he a regent at the UW. She found herself knee deep all over again in the Seattle Symphony

Board, plus KCTS and the Friends of Cancer Lifeline. She was surprised and deeply honored when the Nancy Bell Evans Center on Nonprofits & Philanthropy was established in 2004 as an adjunct to the Daniel J. Evans School of Public Affairs at the UW. One of the lessons of her Depression-era childhood was that "even if you didn't have much money, you could still donate your time and in any case you had an obligation to care." The Northwest Parkinson's Foundation at Evergreen Hospital at Kirkland is also close to their hearts because family members and friends have fought the incurable neurological disease.

As for cancer, it's one thing to battle it yourself, Nancy says, and quite another to see a precious grandchild desperately ill. Eloise Evans—the daughter of Dan Jr. and his wife Celia—began her harrowing bout with rhabdomyosarcoma two months before her fourth birthday. It is a cautionary tale with a happy ending. Eloise is 14 now and a competitive swimmer, her grandmother notes with pride, thanks to Seattle's Children's Hospital and a world-class oncologist named Doug Hawkins. At first, doctors thought it might be an ear infection, then tonsillitis. Nancy's daughter-in-law instinctively knew it was something more serious, so she scooped up her child and took her to the ER at Children's. "They found a mass the size of a tennis ball under her brain," Nancy recalls, still shaking her head at the close call. It was inoperable. Thirteen rounds of chemo and six weeks of radiation saved Eloise's life. Grandma and Grandpa were there every inch of the way, together with a platoon of Dan and Celia's friends, who cooked and delivered meals and offered unwavering support. Eloise's two siblings frequently lived with Dan and Nancy while their parents took turns sleeping in her hospital room. Sometimes Eloise asked her grandpa to spend the night with her at the hospital—"a rare honor" and privilege, Nancy says.

"The tumor was so fast growing. If it had slid for even a few weeks, who knows what would have happened?" Nancy says, "So I give full credit to Celia for not waiting. The thing I so often tell young mothers is, 'Listen to your children. Don't necessarily listen to the doctors because you know your child better than anybody. Follow through on your instincts.'"

The Foundation

Nancy has, of course, kept up with the Governor's Mansion Foundation. Even though the foundation had been carefully established as the legal guardian of the mansion's public rooms and furnishings, Nancy says she once worried that problems might crop up in the years to come—personality clashes between the board and first families or dust-ups with the Legislature over appropriations for maintenance. She wondered whether her successors would chafe at the restrictions and want to change things to suit their own individual styles. Over the years, in fact, she says she has made pro forma apologies to most of her successors, including Mike Gregoire, the state's first "first gentleman," for tying their hands. "When we set up the foundation, we stipulated that the governor's wife cannot do any of the decorating in the public rooms, so that the master plan would be kept intact. But they've all been very kind and said, 'We were all very happy not to have that responsibility.' It's been quite wonderful, the way they've all gotten along together."

That succeeding first families, the foundation and the state have happily coexisted as caretakers of a public trust is testimony to Nancy Evans' deft ability to bring people together to achieve good things—and have fun doing it. Like a proud parent, she is endlessly delighted with the work of the foundation. "They've continued to do a marvelous job."

Shelley Carr, the president of the foundation, says Nancy "is one very gracious, genuine, amazing woman. She has the ability to make one feel so at ease—like a loving aunt. I remember calling her a few months ago with a last-minute request for photos for a book on the families who had lived in the Governor's Mansion. She was packing to leave town for a few months, but she interrupted what she was doing, went to Dan's office, selected a number of delightful photos and made sure they were promptly mailed to me. That's going way beyond the call.

"Not only do we have Nancy to thank for saving the Governor's Mansion from demolition, the idea of setting up a foundation for the maintenance of the public rooms was ingenious. Here she was a young mother with a zillion things to attend to, and she researches how best to set up the foundation for the preservation of this oldest building on the capital campus. We are so lucky she was our First Lady. And, she's still a great supporter," Carr says.

Dan Evans Jr. says the work his mother did to preserve "such an important icon for all Washingtonians was a remarkable feat....She worked tirelessly to rebuild and redecorate, and the result is stunning. I am sure there are many visitors to the mansion today who just assume that it always looked so beautiful."

Best friends

Bill Jacobs, who met Nancy during Dan's first campaign for governor, says he realized early on that although she was only 31, she was a remarkable blend of charm and intelligence. They became good friends, especially when they ended up a long way from home in D.C. When Dan was busy with a hearing or other Senate duties, they'd go to dinner or the movies, and "sometimes I would escort her to an important function. I was always flattered to do that. I would say to Dan, 'Well we've spent most of the weekend together,' and he would go 'Really?' (almost yawning) as if to say, 'I'm not worried.' Which, kidding aside, is another insight into the trust these people had, one with the other.

"I can't imagine how difficult it must be for an elected official not to have the support and camaraderie and the wisdom of their spouse. But Dan was especially blessed. Jim Dolliver used to say that Dan's best friend—besides being his wife—was Nancy. They had great rapport and great understanding, but they would argue a lot, too. So it wasn't all harmony. That's just the way they related sometimes. They could tell one another the truth about how they felt," the former chief of staff adds.

"I also remember Jim saying early on that a governor has three responsibilities: You're the chief executive of the state; you're the First Family and you're the leader of your party. Nancy played a significant role in all three of those responsibilities. She traveled with him; they talked together; she gave advice—good advice," political and otherwise.

Jacobs adds that Nancy also deserves credit for helping Dan energize the progressive wing of the Republican Party in Washington State. "They kept it a moderate party," he says. "It's no wonder the conservatives were angry with them because (they were so effective). Having said that, they're both much more loyal Republicans than the Republican Party gives them credit for....As a team, I have never seen anything in political life like the two of them."

He says it has occurred to him lately that Nancy Evans and Hillary Clinton have several things in common, notably that they are both exceptionally smart and never hesitated to offer advice to their spouses. (Dan Evans, one could argue, was a way better listener than Bill Clinton.) Jacobs believes that "Nancy could have had her own political career, had she chosen to, because she had the ability and the popularity."

Most of all, Evans' former chief of staff adds, "They both took that role of being 'first citizen' very seriously. They knew people were looking to them—that people judged them...And they led exemplary lives as role models. Both of them are comfortable in their own skin. They know who they are—always have—and that says a lot about what kind of people they are."

Counting blessings

In a 1974 interview, the Associated Press asked Nancy to assess her "public image." After a long pause, she replied, "I'm not sure I have one. I'm probably seen as a shadow of my husband, I'm sorry to say. I don't like to be. I looked at a press release the other day that said, 'Nancy Evans, wife of Gov. Dan Evans,' and thought, 'Gee, why did they have to say 'wife of Gov. Dan Evans'? all the while knowing why they have to."

That doesn't happen much any more.

The Evans boys are happily married, have good jobs and three children apiece, which adds up to nine grandchildren to dote on—although most of them are farther away than they'd like. Dan keeps working on his autobiography, but Nancy and their friends think it's taking way too long. He admits that every time he uncovers an interesting old news story or editorial about the Evans era, he gets so fascinated that he forgets he's supposed to be writing. As an author, he really is "Old Gluefoot."

They count their blessings. They're enjoying good health and lots of stimulating activities. They're still very much in love. To observe their 50th anniversary, they recreated their trip to Carmel—without the big-finned Plymouth, but with a corkscrew, to be sure.

Looking back at an eventful life, Nancy says she dearly loved her father, but it was mother who knew best when she said, "You can do whatever you want to do; you just have to be ready to do it, and say yes."

Oral History

Research by John Hughes, Lori Larson, Dick Allen,
Bob Johnson, Miriam Bausch and Gerry Alexander
Interviews by John Hughes, April 27- 29 and July 14, 2009
Transcription by Lori Larson

John C. Hughes: The Legacy Project is with Nancy Evans, who was Washington's first lady from 1965-1977. Twelve years. Longer than any other first lady.

Nancy Evans: Well, Evelyn Langlie was also first lady for 12 years, but her husband's terms were non-consecutive. (1941-1945; 1949-1957)

Hughes: So you're tied for first lady tenure. I'd forgotten that Arthur Langlie served three terms. He was defeated for re-election by U.S. Senator Mon Wallgren, but made a comeback to beat Wallgren in 1948. Then he beat Congressman Hugh Mitchell in 1952. Langlie was 40 when he was first elected—the youngest governor in state history until a guy named Dan Evans came along in 1964.

Evans: That's right.

Hughes: Let's see if I can pass the Math WASL here: You were 31 years and 10 months old when Dan took office?

Evans: We went (into office) in January of 1965 and my birthday is in March, so, yes, that's right.

Hughes: And Dan was 39. He's 7 years and 5 months older than you. *A lot older.*

Evans: Yes. (laughs)

Hughes: Adele Ferguson, *The Bremerton Sun's* legendary capitol

Baby Nancy with a teddy bear. *Evans family album*

correspondent, told me there are three things you should never ask a woman: her weight, her age and her salary. But I'm duty bound to ask you when you were born.

Evans: In Spokane on March 21, 1933. It was the first day of spring. And my father came home to make the announcement to my three siblings. They were seven, nine, and 10 years older—Mary, Bill Bell Jr. and Barbara. They were anxiously waiting to know if it was a boy or a girl. He told them that it was a girl, and my brother was *very* disappointed. Then my father said, "And we're going to name her Vernal Equinoxia Bell." And they all said, "Oh, Dad, you can't do that!" Well, of course, he was joking. He had a wonderful sense of humor. "We're going to call her 'Vernie' for short," he said.

Hughes: In the *Time* magazine article in 1968 when Dan was on the cover as the keynoter at the Republican National Convention, it says that your dad wanted to name you that, but your mom "dissuaded" him. But it was just a joke?

Evans: Oh yes, totally.

Hughes: You're Nancy Ann Bell, right?

Evans: Ah, yes. When I was born, my mother named me Elizabeth Ann Bell. And the obstetrician, Dr. Mary Rodney, who delivered me, said to Mother and Daddy, "Well, she doesn't look like an Elizabeth to me. She looks like a Nancy." And that's what she wrote on

Nancy in her baby buggy in 1933.
Evans family album

the birth certificate. So my baptism certificate says Elizabeth Ann Bell, and my birth certificate says Nancy Ann Bell, which I always went by.

Hughes: Much better than Vernal Equinoxia.

Evans: Yes! (laughing)

Hughes: Tell us about your dad.

Evans: William Lawrence Bell. He came from an interesting family. They were from Bradford, Pennsylvania. I have books on the whole history of his family going back to the seventeen-, eighteen-hundreds. It was one of those old traditional Eastern situations that if you were a boy you went to Princeton and if you were a girl you went to Vassar. So his sisters went to Vassar and the brothers to Princeton. But he decided he wanted to go West. I think he wanted to sort of leave that Eastern culture. He went to Stanford when Stanford was just a fledgling school—Leland Stanford Jr. University way out in Palo Alto. He was in one of the first classes, as was Herbert Hoover, another future mining engineer. I think my father was in the Class of 1898. He was only 16 or 17 when he went out West to school. Their yearbook, which was only a quarter of an inch thick at that time, featured the class yell: "Ra-ra-ra, ra-ra-ree, nine-teen hundred cen-tur-y!"

Hughes: I love that kind of stuff. Stanford back then really was still on "The Farm." That's its nickname.

Evans: Yes, "The Farm." My father took German and engineering—mining engineering. And when he graduated they asked him to stay and be a professor in German, despite his youth. He was a very smart person. But he wanted to be an engineer. His father was a business person.

Hughes: What was your paternal grandfather's name?

Evans: William Weldon Bell. He was one of those people who made a million, lost a million, made a million, and so on. He was from Pennsylvania. His father had sent him off to New York to work in a bank. He was a cashier at age 16. Within 10 years, he was president. Grandpa Bell was president of the bank for many years but he had other investments as well, including rubber plantations in Peru. So my father went down to Peru and spent a great deal of time there building roads to get to the plantations, hiring native workers.

Hughes: So your father's family was well-to-do?

Evans: Yes, but my father was doing all these wonderful, exotic sorts of things. He spent a lot of time down in Mexico as well. This is all before he met my mother. We have some diaries and letters that he wrote. They're really interesting because he talks about the bandits in Peru who knew when payroll day was. He had this dry sense of humor, but he always told one story very sincerely, so I'm assuming it's true that he came across Butch Cassidy one time down in Peru. They became sort of passing friends at that moment in time. But he could have died in his encounters with bandits. My father went down to Davenport, Florida, after he'd been to Peru and Mexico. His father had bought a lot of land down there. It was just swamp land and my grandfather wanted my father to drain the swamp land for development. And that's where he met my mother.

Hughes: Lilith Jordan. What was her middle name?

Evans: It was Stoltz. And she pronounced Lilith "Lie-leth." Mother's father was a Methodist minister. And the name Lilith, as my mother used to tell me, is from the Apocrypha, which was the part of the Bible that is not usually included because of its questionable origins. Some people say "Lill'th," but she was "Lie-leth." And her sister was Eulah—aren't those unusual names!? Mother always used to say that as a child she was the typical minister's daughter because she wanted to rebel against everything. *She was a rebel.* If you weren't supposed to do something, that's just what she was going to do. She was a suffragist, too, marching for women's right to vote.

Hughes: I wish I had known her. I like everything I read about your mother.

Evans: Well, she was wonderful because she really enjoyed people. Amazingly enough, she was also extremely conservative in some ways, I mean about what you should and should not do. But she also would never pass judgment until she really got to know somebody. She was very open to new ideas, new things, anything new.

Hughes: Who are you more like—Dad or Mom?

Evans: I hope I'm a happy combination of both.

Hughes: So how about your grandmother on your paternal side? Tell us about her.

Evans: She was Mary Elizabeth Bartlett Bell. We have two volumes of records of her family going way back—the Underwood family and the Bartletts. It was a long-time New England family. There were a lot of Bartletts....All of our antecedents are British.

Hughes: I'm mostly of Welsh origin and there's a lot of Bells in Wales.

Evans: I know. Dan's family has a lot of Welsh. Evans is a very Welsh name. But we think primarily England, actually. We have a letter that's framed, hanging downstairs, that was written by the brother of a Bell who came to America in 1812 or 1814. "Dear brother," the Englishman says, addressing the letter to William Bell in Ceres, New York. There's no street address, nothing else except "America." He asked if there was work there in America for a person like him. His brother was my great, great-grandfather, who had been gone for a number of years. His brother goes on to say, "Since you left, our mother has died, our sister has…" It goes through all these family issues. "Things are very hard here," he adds. He was from Haltwhistle, Northumberland, England, which is right up near the Scottish border. So when we went as a family to visit England in 1977, we of course went to Haltwhistle. It was early April, but it was still cold; the wind was blowing; the trees were not budding leaves at all. It was bleak! But we stayed in a B&B and found this wonderful woman who just loved to know that we had family from there. She called the woman who worked at City Hall, who came right up and was eager to talk to us. Mother was with us at the time. We were sharing all the information we could and then we went out into the graveyard. It was "Bell," "Bell"—Bells were everywhere—John Bell, William Bell…all sorts of Bells. There was nothing welcoming about the town because life was harsh there, and you could see it and feel it. Just a lot of sheep herders and what have you. But there is something wonderful about being in a place where your family came from, where they had lived, worked and died for generations. At one point in time, probably in the 1950s, Daddy had read an article about this man from Haltwhistle whose name was Bell. He had started as a sheep herder and had become the headmaster of the local school. So Daddy wrote him a letter to the effect that, "Certainly we must be long-lost cousins…and congratulations on what you've done. And, by the way, since we are long-lost cousins surely you'd like to share with me some of your best products, namely Bell's Scotch." Daddy was being funny again. And back came a letter in this beautiful Spenserian script. "My dear cousin: It's a pleasure to hear from you," and on and on and on. And the Scotch became sort of the running joke between them.

Hughes: So how about mother's father, the reverend? Tell us about him.

Evans: His name was William Jordan. He was an itinerate sort of minister. My mother was born in Morland, Kansas, on Jan. 15, 1892. My father always said that my mother's father was the sweetest man he'd ever known. He was just a very lovely, sweet person. The Jordans ended up in Davenport, Florida. That's where my father came down to drain the land, and they met. I've got to get out a map and look some time because I think that's right about where Epcot and Disneyworld are today.

Hughes: Doubtless no longer swamp.

Evans: I should have that swamp land now that my grandfather owned!

Hughes: How about your mother's mother?

Evans: Hannah Pritchard Jordan. I don't know much about her.

Hughes: What's the earliest that you've traced any of those ancestors from all branches of the family tree coming to America?

Evans: We go back to the 1600s on both my mother's and father's side.

Hughes: I read a wonderful line where your mother told a reporter she could have belonged to the Colonial Dames if she'd ever applied. Was your father involved in Sons of the American Revolution or any groups like that?

Evans: No. And mother had declined the Dames, but we did go back a long way.

Hughes: But the Jordans were clearly also early arrivers in America?

Evans: Yes. But I'm not sure when my Grandmother Jordan's side of the family arrived. She was a Pritchard.

Hughes: A Pritchard? That was her maiden name?

Evans: Yes, like Joel (former congressman, lieutenant governor and great friend to Nancy and Dan Evans). And it's been a long time since I looked, but I think it was on my Grandfather Jordan's side that the ancestors in America went back to the 1600s. I'm not sure about the Pritchards. The Jordans go back to the 1600s but I don't know anything real specific about them.

Hughes: "Bell" rings in my mind as having Quaker roots.

Evans: Yes. My father's mother was a Quaker. Although my Grandfather Bell was very active in the Presbyterian Church, there were Quakers in the family—a lot of them.

Hughes: It was a pretty gutsy thing for your father to leave home and all that family and come West to a fledgling university.

Evans: Oh, yes. They all thought he was lost. But when my mother and father got married in 1918, they moved back to Bradford, Pennsylvania. My sisters, Barbara and Mary, and my brother, Bill Jr., were all born in Bradford. But my father really wanted to get into mining engineering, which was what he'd studied at Stanford, and much of mining was in the West. I don't know exactly how this worked, but he came out to British Columbia, then went back and got my mother and the children. They were quite young when he brought them all out to British Columbia. (Barbara Bell was born in 1920, William L. Bell Jr. in 1924, and Mary in 1925.) That's where the mines were, and my mother said, "We're going to be lost to the East." That was the way she worded it when she told the story.... "We'll never come back, and it will never be the same." She didn't want to leave. And then years later she'd say, "Thank goodness we left. Thank goodness we came West." They lived up into the wilds at Squam Bay, which is north of Vancouver. I always heard wonderful stories about Hong, who was their Chinese cook. Eventually they moved to Vancouver, and then to Spokane in 1931, where I was born two years later. He traveled to work on mining ventures, but Spokane was home. Daddy first came to Spokane as a bachelor in 1908 after his two years in Peru. He traveled widely to work.

Hughes: What kind of education did your mother have?

Evans: Well, she was a minister's daughter. Her older brother was a Methodist minister as well. I'm not quite sure how this happened, but while he was in school and a new pastor, she would live with him and his wife and go to school herself. So I know that she had a year at the University of Chicago. And she had a year at Purdue because that's where her brother was living at the time. I think she had another year of college, too, but I don't know where that was. It could have been in Florida. In any case, she became a teacher and a nutritionist. She taught nutrition for the schools, and she did very well because she was bright and determined.

We have some of her school papers, and I know she got *the* big award for her senior thesis, or whatever they called it, in high school. After college, she went back down to Florida to live with her parents and to teach. We have some books that she taught with, and her notes on the teaching of nutrition—classic stuff. Mother was a really good cook. She had a very good friend, Betty, who would come to visit at our house. We all loved her. She was a nutritionist, too, and ended up going to China to improve nutrition in the 1930s and '40s. But when Betty would come to visit, she would help mother with the cooking. I remember that her vegetables were always mushy and overdone, while mother always liked them sort of crisp, you know, like we all do now. So she was ahead of her time. She was a good cook, a sensible cook. But she also had a wonderful ability: At every meal there was presentation in everything. It was not fussy; it was not pretentious, but there was always her special touch. She presented things nicely, just as a matter of form, for her husband and four children.

Hughes: And did her four children appreciate that at the time?

Evans: Well, we did. I always remember that we did. Unless the kids were gone someplace or off doing things, we all sat down to dinner at the dining room table every night. And when dinner was through, my father would say, "Never a finer meal was served by a fairer hand."

Hughes: I love your dad!

Evans: Yes. Daddy was wonderful.

Hughes: Did he go by "Bill"?

Evans: Well, his old friends called him Bill, but my mother and the newer friends all called him Lawrence. His middle name. That's what his parents had called him because his father was also William.

Hughes: What was it like growing up in the Bell household in Spokane in the 1930s? Was it a busy, rambunctious kind of place?

Evans: Yes. Especially when I was really young. My brother Bill was about nine years older than I. My sister Mary was seven years older—a month younger than Dan, in fact. My sister Barbara was 13 years older. So my nearest sibling was seven years older.

Hughes: You must have been doted on.

Evans: Well, I was a spoiled brat. (laughing) I *was* doted on, and I *loved* it. I don't deny it. But it was a hard time because it was the Depression. And then my brother Bill got trench mouth, I think from drinking from a public fountain. And in those days, before antibiotics it ate away at his lower lip. So he required a number of surgeries over a period of time. And it was all a new procedure in those days. They would take skin from various parts of his body that were similar in texture to his lip—from behind the ear, the thighs, the inside upper arm. They would do a little layer at a time.

Hughes: So did poor Bill, at the worst of this problem, did he have a disfigured lip?

Evans: As a young teen, and you know how sensitive teenagers are.

Hughes: Absolutely. Acne is bad enough. Just think about losing your lower lip.

Evans: And you have no sensation there (from the grafts). He always was a slobbery kisser. (laughing) We used to tease him about it. But it didn't deter him because he was always a very popular teen. But at the time it was hard. Financially it was *very* hard for us because there was no insurance at all. It was a hard time anyway in mining—a hard time everywhere in America.

Hughes: So your dad was still working sporadically as a mining engineer?

Evans: Oh, that's all he did.

Hughes: With a wife and four kids.

Evans: Yes. Many mouths to feed.

Hughes: Was he away from home a lot?

Evans: When I was very young he was. In fact, he went back down to Mexico for a while. The story is, and I have *no* idea if it's true—maybe it's apocryphal—but they always said that he came to the door one day when I was 5 or 6, and I opened the door and said, "Mother, that man's here again." And it was my father. (laughing) But when I was older, Daddy was not gone a lot.

Hughes: So, tell me more about the siblings.

Evans: Barbara is the oldest, then Bill, then Mary.

Hughes: They're all gone now?

Evans: Yes, unfortunately.

Hughes: Where was your house in Spokane?

Evans: 521 Sound Ave. It was on the South Side of Spokane. In my growing up years, Spokane was a very nice, comfortable place to be. In those days I took the bus everywhere or rode my

Nancy at five. *Evans family album*

bike. It was a good family life even though it was, by today's standards, very simple and very easy, despite the financial difficulties at times.

Hughes: What are your most vivid memories of those growing up years—1933 to 1950?

Evans: During my early childhood, my father was working at several mines in Montana. So he would be there all summer. I'd go to visit him. Mother would put me on the train at night. We knew all the porters, everybody who worked on the trains. It was like "the friendly skies" but it was on rails. I'd be by myself, at age 6, and they'd put me in a sleeper. In the morning they'd get me up and make sure I got dressed and everything. And my father would be there to greet me at Butte, Montana. I would spend my summers over there with Daddy. They had a house up in the mountains, and I had a little Shetland pony that I rode all the time. Some great memories. There was one other family—one of my father's assistants—and he had two daughters. Both were a little older than I was, so I had people to play with. It depended on what my siblings were doing, but we spent a lot of the summers there all together, too. My sisters would enjoy being with all the young mining men, the boys at the mine.

Nancy, left, and a friend enjoying a pony ride while visiting her dad
in Montana one summer in the 1930s. *Evans family album*

My brother then started to do some work in the mines. We went for a lot
of years until the war broke out. Those were gold mines, and then in the
space of one day FDR shut all the gold mines down. No more manufactur-
ing of gold during wartime. So that was a severe blow to the family.

Hughes: Which is a perfect segue to politics. Were politics talked about
in the Bell household?

Evans: Yes. My father was not a meeting-going or church-going or "anything going" sort of person. But we did talk politics at home. My siblings, being older, had interests that were different than mine, but I would listen a lot to the discussions. On Election Day my mother would be one of the people there as a Republican poll watcher. And she went to some political meetings. Daddy didn't. But both my sisters and my brother were all active in one way or another in the Republican Party. And actually Bill ran some big campaigns for candidates. He was very active in Dan's 1964 campaign for governor. He was also an early supporter of Gov. Stassen of Minnesota when he first ran for president (in 1944). Barbara was a precinct committeewoman for a while.

Hughes: This was the Willkie-Dewey era in GOP politics.

Evans: Well, I don't remember Willkie being discussed much, but Roosevelt was. My father always pronounced it "Roose-a-velt." And my mother would say, "It's 'Rose-a-velt.'" FDR was discussed a *great deal* at the dinner table—with derision from my father. Dan's father was the same way. Daddy would be the devil's advocate and Mother would always be trying to placate everything, you know, "Now Lawrence." Everybody would enter into the discussions, so it was very much a part of our family life.

Hughes: With mom having grown up with a Methodist preacher for a dad, was going to church a big deal in the Bell household?

Evans: It was in my mother's household. Never in my father's. I don't know that he ever went to church except to see his children baptized or married.

Hughes: Did you kids all go to Sunday school?

Evans: We all went to Sunday school. We actually went to a Congregational Church, which we all preferred. That's where Dan and I were married. Many of my family's friends went to the Episcopal Church in Spokane—St. John's Cathedral. But it was not to our liking because we all sort of liked something more lively. I like a good sermon, usually one that's provocative. And I like the music. So we really chose the Congregational Church. It was very New England-ish in its essence. We had a wonderful minister too, who was very provocative at times and not afraid to try to instruct or challenge the congregation on all sorts of things. I used to play and sing in our church choir. I couldn't sing very well, but I could carry a tune.

Hughes: Nancy Bell Evans was destined to become a music teacher. Did that all start with piano lessons?

Evans: Well, yes, and we all were musical. My mother was very musical. She played the piano a little. One of my sisters had a really nice voice, and my brother had a nice voice. And he was artistic. I took piano lessons starting at an early age—fifth grade or something like that, and I moved along pretty fast. So by the time I was in eighth grade I was playing pretty well. Maybe I was a freshman in high school when I had an interesting formative experience. I don't know how I even learned about it, but they were looking for a pianist at the orphanage on the north side of town so the kids could learn Christmas carols for a program. Perhaps my mother suggested it to me. In any case, after school on certain days of the week I would take the bus to the north side of town, quite a ways north. I had to transfer buses to get there. And I would play the piano. They had a woman there who was leading the children, teaching them various songs. We worked with the kids for a number of weeks leading up to the program. I became a friend with one of the girls in the orphanage who was my age. I don't remember her name, I'm sorry to say. But suddenly it occurred to me that the program was over, Christmas was coming and she was going to be at the orphanage. So I asked my parents if I could bring her home during the holidays. And they said, "Of course," that would be very nice. That's what my parents were like.

Hughes: So, growing up in Spokane, did you do all the classic things like go to the matinees and sock hops?

Evans: I was a very typical teenager, enjoyed it all. I still have two very good friends in Spokane, and we keep in touch a lot. Being a girl was a very happy time for me. I was very active in school and I was a student body officer. I was a cheerleader. I was just a typical teenager—had boyfriends, you know, the whole thing. I really liked my music, and I was really active in that. I would play the piano for the choir, and I would play the piano for the Madrigal Singers. I played the piano for soloists. *I played the piano a lot.* I was active in the musical productions and things of that nature. We had a wonderful music teacher at that time—Cecil Enloe. Later he went to California and we were all very sad.

Hughes: Tell us about some lasting lessons you learned from growing up during the Depression.

Evans: Well, to this day I turn off the lights and scold my husband and my children for not doing so. And I always say you should turn off equipment that you're not using.

Hughes: Or as my mother would say, "We're not supporting the PUD!"

Evans: That's right. I'm sure I've carried it way too far, but I can be very cheap about things if I don't see the reason for spending money. I'm sure our daughters-in-law don't want to hear me preaching to them about it anymore, and I'm sure my sons don't either. But I just grew up in a time when you were not extravagant in any way, and it has stayed with me.

Hughes: Can you remember times during the Depression when things were so thin that you really noticed that different meals were being served?

Evans: Our meals were always just fine because Mother could take nothing and make it something. And we would always have dessert. I haven't made a dessert in I can't tell you how many years. I don't make dessert; we don't eat dessert. But there was always the regular dinner at our house when I was growing up.

Hughes: Mother probably did wonders with Jell-O.

Evans: *Of course.* And she would make pies and cakes—all of those things that I don't do. So food was never a problem—but I had several friends who always seemed to have more sweaters than I did, you know—things you compare yourself with when you're a teenager. When I went to college, the big thing there was cashmeres and pearls, and I didn't have either. So I suppose clothing was sometimes an issue.

College bound. *Evans family album*

Hughes: Did you make some of your own clothing?

Evans: *I cannot sew.* I took Sewing in school because I had to. In the eighth grade and during your freshman year, you had to take Cooking and Sewing. I practically flunked both.

Hughes: Here's a wonderful thing that you said during a 1972 interview: "My parents brought me up to believe that you could do anything you want to do."

Evans: Yes. Mother particularly always said that because she had that religious, spiritual basis for much of what she did. She was not religious in the strict sense because she accepted so many other ways of life and other people, but that was part of her philosophy—that you could achieve anything you put your mind to.

Hughes: She was a Methodist?

Evans: She was. But she was very fundamental about certain things, and there were certain things that you talked about and certain things that you didn't talk about.

Hughes: What were some of the things that you didn't talk about?

Evans: Sex.

Hughes: You didn't talk about sex with your mother?

Evans: Oh no! I learned all about sex—well, as much as you can learn—from my oldest sister, Barbara, who became sort of a surrogate mother when my mother went back to work. She was the one who would put my hair in curls as a young girl because she had time. But Mother was always encouraging. There was financial difficulty during my teens, but Mother kept saying, "Well, don't let this detour you. There is always a way to get what you want to get." It was always that way with Mother. And so when it came time to discuss going to college, which obviously was expensive, how to pay for it was an issue. And mother said, "Well, work hard, study hard. Maybe you can get a scholarship." And that's what happened.

Hughes: Before we get you off to college, please tell me more about your dad's personality. How would you describe dad?

Evans: Well, I *loved* my father. He was a terrible disciplinarian.

Hughes: Which is to say not much of a disciplinarian at all?

Evans: Not much. (chuckling) So I would always go to him first—his darling little girl—with any requests. And he would almost always say yes. I would never go to my mother first because she could say no. So I think we had a real relationship that was very special. He had a very droll sense of humor, very dry.

Hughes: What would be a classic droll thing from Lawrence Bell?

Evans: Well, Dan was telling this story to someone just the other day. He had asked me to marry him. By the way, I just found some letters that my sister had sent me when she was very ill—letters she'd saved over the years, a lot of them from me, but some from my father to her. And one of his letters was talking about this young man, Dan Evans, an engineer who was involved in politics, asking me to marry him. "She didn't seem to care much about the other proposals she'd had," he wrote—and I had had several—"but this one seems to be special." Well, I waited three days to say yes to Dan so there was something going on in my mind....At any rate, he asked, I accepted and I told my parents. So it was all set. They were coming over to Seattle where I was teaching school (in 1958) because my brother and sister-in-law were getting married. They were going to meet Dan for the first time, so I had Mother and Daddy for dinner. They come in, we meet and then my mother and I went into the kitchen. Dan was just sitting on the sofa next to my father, his future father-in-law. And my father said, "Well, young man, my other sons-in-law have had the courtesy to come and ask me for my daughter's hand in marriage." And Dan sort of stammered, "Well sir..." But my father was just putting him on totally. *Dan was squirming.* He remembers that moment so well to this day. Now, as a matter of fact I think he didn't ask Daddy for my hand in marriage because they were all in Spokane and we were in Seattle. Earlier, by the way, I was dating the son of the scion of Spokane who owned half of Spokane and both the newspapers—Bill Cowles. We were just friends; nothing ever serious. We were dating one summer when we were both in college. He came to the door to pick me up, and, looking down his glasses, my father said, "What are your prospects, young man?" I was just, "Oh, God dad!" He would do that to any man who came to the house to pick up any of his daughters. He would always have something to say to them that just jarred his daughters.

Hughes: So that's a classic example of Lawrence Bell's sense of humor?

Evans: Oh yes. And he was very smart. He would play bridge. He had three or four books going all the time. Loved mysteries; loved history; loved learning. And as I said earlier, he took German at Stanford and then was asked to stay and teach it. He also took Spanish. So when I took Spanish in high school he was my tutor. I'd go and I'd say, "Daddy, could you help me with my Spanish classes?" And he still remembered it after all those years.

Hughes: Any other role models or teachers that really stand out from junior high or high school? People who really made an impression on you and reinforced that notion—"I can be whatever I want to be"?

Evans: No, I think that was primarily family. But I had a piano teacher who was wonderful. His name was Hans Moldenhauer. He and his wife had come over from Germany. He was a very good teacher and a very good pianist. He climbed the mountains, too. His wife Rosalie also played the piano, and sometimes they would play dual pianos. He was also wonderfully understanding of a young girl who stopped and strayed and didn't practice as she should. I had talent but I didn't necessarily work at it that hard. But he pushed me and pushed me and was really just wonderful. When we were in Spokane, Dan and I would always go see him. He was so smart; he picked up on things very quickly. He had this huge collection of research he'd done on composers so a lot of it is in the Smithsonian now and also in European museums, private collections, libraries. After Rosalie died, he had remarried. And in later years, Mary, his second wife, contacted me while he was still living. They had two grand pianos as well as the piano we all took lessons on. One was a wonderful old German piano. Hans wanted to know if the Governor's Mansion would be able to use it. And I said it was a lovely, lovely offer, but the Mansion already had been given two Steinways and there was no room for any more. But as I thought about it, it occurred to me, "What about the reception room in the Capitol?" So I contacted someone and asked if there was a piano there, and if not, would the Capitol accept the gift of a very nice grand piano. They said yes, so Hans made sure that it was all fixed up and cleaned up. And then he died. Mary had it all packaged up and sent it to Olympia. That's the piano that's in the reception room now. It's a beautiful instrument.

Hughes: Do you still play the piano?

Evans: I don't. The eyes are so important that I'd have to get special glasses, which I'm never going to do. So my piano now is in my son's house here where our granddaughter is playing the piano, taking lessons. That's Dan Jr.'s daughter, Isabelle.

Hughes: So with brother Bill eligible for the draft, do you have vivid memories of Pearl Harbor Day? You were 8 years old.

Evans: No. I don't remember Pearl Harbor Day. But then Bill went in the service. He fought in the terrible Battle of the Bulge in the winter of 1944, and was injured there. In the den, my father had on the wall a big map of Europe. And he would try to follow Bill through his letters from overseas. You couldn't say exactly where you were because of wartime censorship. I followed the war's progress on my father's map. Then we learned my brother was coming through Spokane on the train on the way to Madigan Hospital, near Tacoma. So we all went down to the train station. And I still remember this gaunt young man standing in the doorway of the train on crutches. And I thought, "Oh my gosh, is that my brother?!" I couldn't believe it was, because he was so thin. He was so haggard looking. He went on to Madigan where he recuperated. Then he was discharged from the Army. Bill always said he was grateful to the Army because the

Mom leads a sing-a-long in 1967. *Washington State Archives*

(trench mouth) injury on his lip no longer bothered him. People assumed it was part of the injuries he had received in the war.

I was in the seventh or eighth grade when the war ended. I remember that vividly. I loved my brother and I worried about him during the war years. As a girl you like your sisters, but you *love* your brothers. Especially a big brother.

Hughes: He was a handsome boy, too. I've seen pictures. I didn't notice his bad lip.

Evans: He was very wonderful. We had a great relationship.

Hughes: What kind of a girl, on the whole, was Nancy Bell?

Evans: I think I was a pretty good student, but not exceptional. And I had good friends—a lot of friends. I was a happy person. And as I said, I was growing up during difficult financial times. But my parents wouldn't let that interfere with my feelings. There was no sense that I couldn't do things.

Hughes: But your brother Bill was in tremendous harm's way during the war. That must have been really hard.

Evans: *It was hard.* It was particularly hard on our parents, obviously. But I don't think I fully appreciated that at the time.

Hughes: Were you all very aware when he was injured about his condition and the kind of care he was getting? Did he send a lot of letters home?

Evans: No, not a lot of letters when he was in Belgium because he was in the thick of it. I just remember that we were so glad when he finally got back.

My oldest sister, Barbara, was married. At age 11, I was in love with her husband. I had this *horrible* crush on Bill Ludders. We were full of Bills in our family. He was a Navy lieutenant at Farragut, Idaho, and had grown up in Hawaii. He was very handsome. And of course he was at our house a lot as they were dating during the war.

Hughes: I'll bet he cut quite a handsome figure in his lieutenant's uniform.

Evans: Dress whites, and I truly just fell in love with him. When they

Nancy and brother Bill during World War II. *Evans family album*

got married I was *sad* because he wasn't waiting for me. I was the flower girl at their wedding—a very mature flower girl at 12, I believe. I look at the pictures now and I'm looking sort of sad. Then he went off to the Pacific during the war, and after the war they ended up in Hawaii. So they were away; they were not at home. And my other sister, Mary, went to Europe with the State Department and ended up living there. So she was away, too. So that left Bill and Nancy. He went to college at Whitman and then to law school at Gonzaga. So I saw him a lot more. He and I had a very special relationship.

Hughes: So now the war is over. It's 1950. You're a senior in high school. Were you asking yourself, "What am I going to do next?" Was it clear that you wanted to study music?

Evans: Yes.

Hughes: And why Whitman College at Walla Walla instead of WSU or Gonzaga?

Evans: Well, all my siblings had gone to Whitman. But the fact was, I really couldn't afford Whitman (without a good scholarship). It's a great school, but an expensive school. Even back in the day when I was hoping to go there, it was the most expensive school in the state. The tuition was $200 a semester, $400 a year, and that was *very* expensive compared to any other school in the Northwest. And then of course the room and board was added onto that. I applied to several schools and got scholarships everywhere I applied, which was nice, but I chose Whitman. And even with a scholarship, I'm sure my mother was thinking, "Oh, how are we going to do this?" But I got a music scholarship. I had to go down and play the piano in a competition for it. But Whitman still is the same way in helping its students. I could always work to help pay my way. They were very good at finding employment for students who needed help. I was an assistant to professors. I worked in the SUB (Student Union Building). I worked in a post office. I did everything.

Hughes: You graduated from Lewis & Clark High School in?

Evans: 1950. So I was at Whitman in 1950-54. It's a great school and a very pleasant town. But I couldn't get into Whitman now. *I could not get in.* It's a wonderful school, but it's also very broad because they really believe that the teachers are there to teach and not just do research. So the faculty now, as then, spends a lot of time with the students—an inordinate amount of time with their students in a very enjoyable way. And a lot of mentoring

Sister, Barbara, and nephews, John and Dick Ludders, in 1946. *Evans family album*

goes on besides the classroom teaching. So I loved Whitman, and I had wonderful teachers there, and wonderful help there, and all this financial support.

Hughes: Your major was music?

Evans: Yes. Then to be practical because I had to be, I also majored in education so I could teach. But it actually doesn't say that on my school records because at Whitman then, and still to this day, when you graduate you have

High school days. *Evans family album*

to take majors. They called it "orals and writtens." So I took orals and writtens in music, and I just didn't want to take oral and writtens in education. But I took all the required education classes.

Hughes: Any professors that still stand out in your mind?

Evans: Well, Ken Schilling, who was the head of the Music Department. By the way, my brother had sung in the choir at Whitman. He came back as a vet and graduated a year before I arrived there.

Hughes: Boy, it must have been 12 or 13 years that there were Bells there?

Evans: Well, my sister Barbara started there but she did not graduate because the war broke out. It just changed everything. My other sister, Mary, went there, but she didn't graduate either and I can't remember quite why. But later she went to WSU and did graduate. But Bill went all four years, finishing up after the war when he was older, and then I came. When I competed for and got the scholarship, Ken Schilling sent Bill a telegram, which they did in those days, saying, "Your sister was great" or something like that, which I thought was very nice. I played the piano for the choir and for various singing groups, so I knew Ken very well. I had several piano teachers who were also quite wonderful, but Ken was head of the Music Department and very supportive of me. I loved college! I had a wonderful time there. Well, maybe I had some boyfriend problems along the way, but it was great. I was president of my sorority senior year. Delta Gamma. I must tell you that having been a trustee and having the opportunity to hear so many students talk about what they're doing or what they would like to do, I'm so impressed with the poise of young women and men today. I think back on what *I* was like and it's embarrassing. I remember that the only thing that I publicly had to do as president of my sorority was in the spring when they would have a banquet that the alums put on at the Marcus Whitman Hotel. When I was president of my sorority all I had to do was to report on our successes throughout the year. Just a little talk. And I didn't think I would get through it. I remember just gulping—ah, it was dreadful—and swallowing and not being able to go on with the words. But I finally got through it. I remember somebody afterwards leaning over and saying, "Gosh that was tough, wasn't it?" And I said, "Yes, that was very tough!" It was very memorable to me because I was so bad. I could get up and play the piano. That's another thing, but to speak was a real challenge. I can remember taking a speech class because there was a requirement to take a class in another area, and none of them appealed to me except Speech. I stood up for the first time to give a little 30-second whatever it was, and giggled my way through it because the boyfriend at the time was in the class, too. So I was not and never have been a very good public speaker. But I'm better at it now than I was.

Hughes: So you graduate in 1954 with a bachelor's degree in music?

Evans: Yes.

Hughes: And a minor in education, or was it a dual track?

Evans: It was a dual.

Hughes: You get a teaching certificate.

Evans: Yes.

Hughes: So then I read that you ended up at Eastern Washington

College in Cheney doing graduate work.

Evans: No. That's not accurate. I moved to Seattle after graduating from Whitman. I thought it would be fun to live in Seattle. I came with good recommendations and I received a number of teaching offers. They came to the campus to interview. That wouldn't happen today of course. And my one dilemma, as it turned out, was that I had an offer to be head of the department of music education in Camas, Wash. I also had an offer from the Shoreline School District, north of Seattle. However, the Camas job paid probably twice as much because I would be head of the department.

Hughes: How much would that have been?

Evans: I don't know, but I think my first year at Shoreline paid $2,000 a year. Maybe $2,400.

Hughes: Of course, you could buy a new car for $1,500.

Evans: But, believe me, I couldn't afford to buy a car for several years. So I really thought about which job to take, and I said to myself, "Well, I really want to go to concerts." And at Camas they kept saying, "Well, we're very near Portland and there's lots to do in Portland." But in the end I came to Seattle. I went to Shoreline. I couldn't afford to stay in Seattle by myself, so I would live with different roommates during the school year. Then in the summer I would go home to Spokane. The first year, a friend from Whitman and I went to the teachers' indoctrination and met two other young graduates—they were from UPS—and we hooked up right away. The four of us rented a house in the University District on the corner of 47th and 17th. We had a great time because it was four of us, just out of college, living with all the college kids there. A wonderful little old lady owned the place. It's still there. It was a little bit worn, shall we say, but it worked very well for us because we all had a bedroom. And we put up a sign over our door that combined our sororities. The UPS girls were both Chi Omegas, and I was a Delta Gamma, and my friend from Whitman, Barbara Herman, was a Tri Delt. And it was "Chi Chi Delta Tri." I think that's what the sign said. Somebody came to the door one night from Pan-Hellenic, wondering if we were a new sorority on campus. We had a

Evans family album

lot of fun living there. Then the next year one of the girls got married, so we would break off and live with other people. But from then on there were usually two of us in an apartment somewhere. As for grad school, in the first five years of teaching at that time you had to take some college courses to maintain your credentials. You had to have X number of hours in the first five years. And for two summers when I went home to Spokane I went to Eastern and took classes. I got straight A's. I was more focused and it was fun being close to home and just knowing so many of my brother's friends. They became our friends. Our house was always lively. That's another thing I forgot to mention earlier: I never knew how many people were going to be at the dinner table because my brother and sisters would *often* bring people over. And my mother would say, "Stay for dinner." That was always no problem. One of Bill's friends lived at our house while he went to Gonzaga Law, while Bill was there too. And then other young people would come and stay for a period of time. So there were always young people in our house. So many of Bill's friends were veterans. They had a little more sophisticated humor. I just ate it up. I loved it.

Hughes: What an amazing experience for the Bill Bells of the world—first to have survived the war, then to be back on a college campus, getting an education and having fun. It was good to be young.

Evans: What a remarkable thing it was for our country—the GI Bill—and what it did to educate a lot of young people who otherwise would not have been able to afford it.

Hughes: It transformed a whole generation.

Evans: When I started at Paramount Park Elementary in the Shoreline District it was a brand new school. We were the first class there. So they needed somebody to set up the library. And I said, "Well, I can do that. I would love to do that." I love books. But I didn't know anything about setting up a library. So after my first year, I took a number of librarianship classes and other classes. I learned how to set up a library. I ended up doing it in two schools, actually. Another new school came along later,

Miss Bell's faculty photo. Evans family album

so I was teaching music at two schools and being the librarian as well. It was fun because they gave me a budget and I got order all these books.

Hughes: So you were teaching grade-school kids to sing?

Evans: Kindergarten to sixth grade. It was fun.

Hughes: In some respects, being a seriously trained pianist, did that seem a little bit rudimentary?

Evans: No, no, I enjoyed it. And we had an upright piano. It was a new-style school where it was sort of an H-shape with a central core and four outside arms extending out. I'd wheel that piano down into the rooms, and we'd have our music. Then I would wheel the piano into another room, and so on. One day the principal asked me to give a little talk at one of the PTA meetings. And I thought, "Oh my God, what am I going to talk about?" In kindergarten and the early grades you have a lot of noise-maker type things, like tambourines, cymbals and triangles. Very simple things like wood blocks. So I passed those out at the PTA meeting. I'd been hearing parents say, "Well, I can't sing, so I'm sure that Johnny can't sing at all." So that was my lesson for the night. I said, "Don't *ever* say to your children, 'I can't do this, therefore you probably can't either,' because you don't know that for a fact. Give them a chance."

Hughes: Robert Fulghum, who wrote "All I Really Need to Know I learned in Kindergarten," says that is the gospel truth—that children are like sponges, you don't tell them they can't do something or they won't try anything new.

Evans: Exactly. Well, at least we know that now. So I'd pass out the noisemakers and then I'd play a little something on the piano, and it made it fun. They enjoyed that, and I enjoyed doing that. Then about the time I met Dan, my nemesis each year was the Christmas program. That was just a lot of work. And in those days you used Christmas carols, religious songs.

Hughes: You could sing "O Little Town of Bethlehem."

Evans: You couldn't do that now.

Hughes: God only knows what would happen!

Evans: Absolutely. But I'd arrange it so that we would have something on the stage—a production. It was the lunchroom/auditorium/gym all rolled into one. Somehow we got all the kids, plus all the parents, in that room. I remember the first time Dan came in 1958, a couple of months after we were engaged to be married. It was quite a production. I was quite pleased with myself afterwards. And he was impressed, too.

Hughes: Hundreds of kids all whipped into a holiday production by Miss Bell.

Evans: Actually, Dan was *very* impressed. It was a lot of work.

Hughes: I love the story, assuming that it's true, that you told Dan you wanted three days to make up your mind about his marriage proposal. Former Supreme Court justice Bob Utter tells the story that the first girl he proposed to told him she wanted a week to make up her mind. And he quickly concluded that if she needed a *week*, something was seriously wrong right there.

Evans: Not a good beginning.

Hughes: So had there been other young men you were really serious about before State Rep. Daniel J. Evans?

Evans: Yes. Actually, I'm good friends with several of them still. Everybody I dated was a very nice person. I just knew that they were not what I wanted long term.

Hughes: OK, now for the record, when is it that you meet Dan Evans? I've read that mutual friends fixed you up on a ski trip. Tell us all about that.

Evans: When I arrived in Seattle, I met a lot of new people and really had a wonderful time. I had not skied before I came here. Well, once or twice on Mt. Spokane, but I was no skier. A lot of them had skied before, in fact grew up skiing. So I stumbled along, learning and trying not to fall. Actually, I learned by trying to keep up. Nobody was going to teach me, so the only way to be seen the rest of the day was to keep up with

Miss Bell with a student in 1957. *Evans family album*

Skiing at Sun Valley in 1956. *Evans family album*

them. That's sort of the way I was. And I learned to ski. The group was mostly boys and a couple of women. It was just all good friends. We went skiing almost every weekend. Then one summer one of the fellows, George Corley, was crewing on an 8-meter wooden sailboat with Dan. I can still remember George telling me, "Nancy, I've met a young man I think you should meet." Those were his *exact* words. He has no memory of it, but I do. I was really just one of the guys. That was our relationship. So they invited Dan to come skiing with us one time. Probably in January of '58. We went to Stevens Pass. There was no Crystal Mountain ski area in those days. It was all Stevens Pass and Snoqualmie Pass. I remember I had the flu one weekend. I didn't feel well, but I didn't want anybody to know it. Afterwards, coming home, we would always stop at a bar in Startup or one of those places coming down from Stevens, and have a beer. Sometimes we would stay and have dinner. One of them had a piano and I'd play the piano and everybody would sit around the table singing. We'd sing this beer song and pass the beer along. Sort of like musical chairs.

Hughes: Sort of like Beer Pong today.

Evans: Well, it wasn't that bad! (laughing) But we had a very good time. However, on that occasion I did not feel well. I was sitting all by myself at the counter and I just wanted to be alone. Dan very sweetly came over and asked if he could help. And I said, "No, thank you." Actually, I don't know what I said, but he felt sorry for me. He kept coming along on our ski trips. Then one time I fell, and he pulled me out from under a tree. All the other guys, they'd just go on. But Dan stopped to dig me out. And then he asked me out. And we went out.

Hughes: What was your first impression of Dan Evans?

Evans: My first impression was that he was a very nice person; very good looking; very quiet, and shy.

Hughes: So all the things they've written over the years about Dan Evans being fundamentally shy—

Evans: Absolutely true. He was very shy. As we started going out, there was something obviously there right away, but nothing that just really turned me on. It was just that I liked him. But every time I went out with him I learned something new about him. He was not one of these people who just came on the first time and you learned it all. I found that very intriguing at the time. I loved everything I learned. He already had done a lot of interesting things. He was an engineer, interested in politics, athletic, very competitive. He even won some sort of a prize in Toastmasters, which he joined to improve his speaking ability. And he had been with the Junior Chamber of Commerce, did the Boy Scout thing and served in the Navy. There were all these things that he'd done. He'd had all these experiences.

But I learned about them over a period of time, which was very nice.

Hughes: Was he different than the other guys you'd been serious about?

Evans: Well, yes and no. He was a little older. Most of the others had been more my age, and he had more experiences, like the war and what have you. And every time I went out with him I liked him more. So it worked out very nicely.

Hughes: That's an understatement. Did you meet Dan's folks early on?

Evans: Yes, because at that time I was living in an apartment not far from here (the present Evans home) in Laurelhurst with a college friend. And his parents lived several blocks away. Dan had a wooden boat and we enjoyed racing it on Wednesday evenings and in Puget Sound on some weekends. I learned to love sailing. And we would often go over to his house and sometimes have dinner.

Hughes: What were his folks like?

Evans: Oh, they were wonderful people. *Wonderful people.* Dan's father, Les, was very quiet but very nice. He was an engineer, too. Dan looks like his father. Dan's brother, several of his nephews and two of ours sons have just the same sort of angular face. Dan's mother, Irma, was just the most loving person I've ever known. She *loved* her three sons. Dan was the oldest. She loved her family and she would do anything for anybody. Dan didn't date a lot. That shyness carried through. And he's a little more serious than your average guy. His father was serious, too. So I think Irma was just delighted he was dating. It didn't matter what the girl was like. (laughing)

Hughes: So Irma and Nancy hit it off?

Evans: Oh, she loved it that we were dating.

Hughes: Right away did you get the feeling that you were approved of?

Evans: Immediately.

Hughes: How long did it take for Dan and Nancy to get serious?

Evans: Well, I think it was in January that we met, and then we were engaged on October 28th, 1958. And married the following June.

Hughes: How did Dan Evans ask Nancy Bell to marry him?

Evans: My sister Barbara and her husband were going to Victoria for a conference of some sort. That's Bill Ludders, the brother-in-law I loved at 11 years old. Barbara had invited me to go along. And I said, "Well, can Dan come along, too?" because we were dating at that time. And she said, "Yes, that's great." So they were up there ahead of time and staying at the wonderful old Empress Hotel. And I still remember very well that when we arrived we met Barbara and Bill and went to register. I still remember standing there at the desk embarrassed for my oldest sister, whom I loved because she really helped raise me. She's saying, "Now my husband and I had this room, but now we want to change. I'm going to be staying with my sister in this room. And this young man is staying with my husband in the other room." Well, that's the way it was. But she didn't have to go into detail!

Hughes: Too much information!

Evans: Too much information. But we had a wonderful time. I remember the Parliament Building was all lit up at night. It was a very lovely trip. We went to visit this lovely couple, Dr. and Mrs. Murphy, who lived in this lovely home, sort of like the Highlands of Victoria—beautiful big old homes. They had been friends of my parents when they lived in Vancouver. They were very British, very proper, but just wonderful. And then we came home to Seattle—came back to my apartment. And Dan said, "Well, let's go for a walk." And I thought, "Well, OK, Sunday night." So we walked up to the Laurelhurst playfield, which is just three blocks from here, and not far from where I was living at the time. There was a bench up there, and we sat on the bench, and he proposed. On Saturday night of the week preceding, I had been proposed to by another man on that same bench.

Hughes: So you were *seriously* dating a couple of guys at the same time?

Evans: Yes, I had several proposals of marriage.

Hughes: What did you tell the other guy when he popped the question?

Evans: I could hardly keep a straight face. And it's terrible to say, we can laugh about it now, but at the time it was very a heartfelt proposal. It was very sweet. And not just brief. It went on and on, and it was just lovely.

But I immediately told him no.

Hughes: I bet you handled that really diplomatically.

Evans: I did. Well, I hope I did. We were young and good friends. But then when Dan proposed a week later all I could think of was the week before. (laughing) And I was so stunned because I really had not expected it. I just couldn't say yes right then. Isn't that silly?

Hughes: What was Dan's reaction? Was he crestfallen?

Evans: I'm sure he was very disappointed. But I said, "Well, I've just got to think about it. Give me three days." We walked back down to my place, and he said goodnight and went to his apartment. I think it was probably the next night that I called my mother, which was pretty silly because they had never met him. I said, "Dan proposed." My sister Barbara had met him, of course, because she'd been up to Victoria with us. And they liked him a lot. I said to my mother, "I don't know what to do!" And Mother started laughing. And that really was an insult to me. I was very upset at the time. I said, "Mother, *don't laugh*. It's serious." And she said, "Well, of course it is. I'm laughing because how can I tell you what to do?"

Hughes: I like Mother enormously.

Evans: Very wise person. So she was no help. I just had to assimilate the whole idea, I guess. Then Dan came over Wednesday night and I said, "Yes." And I knew, you know, it was just "bingo!" It just came to me. It was a big leap. I think a lot of my friends thought I was never going to get married because in those days it's pretty much what you did right out of college. And a number of years had gone by since my college days. I was 26 when we were married.

Hughes: Dan was the real late bloomer. He was in his thirties. He's an "old" guy. But, you know, Shakespeare said, "Journeys end in lovers meeting." When it's right, it's right.

Evans: The minute I said yes it felt right. And we had a great engagement and a wonderful wedding, and the whole thing. The funny thing about looking into these scrapbooks was the elaborate engagement announcements. There are pictures of us, my friends in Spokane, girlfriends giving a shower. And then the next week there was a party hosted by Mrs. so-and-so.

Hughes: I love that classic old wedding write-up stuff: "Pouring for the reception was the bride's sister…"

Evans: The wedding was on June 6—"D-Day"—1959.

Hughes: And Dan met your folks when?

Evans: I believe it was when Bill and Tina were married in Seattle. I believe that was in November of '58. I'm referring to my brother Bill, who recently died from lymphoma, and my sister-in-law. We had lots of Bills, as I said earlier. So my folks came over for the wedding. They came to our apartment for dinner, probably the first night they were there, and that's when they met Dan—and Daddy demonstrated his droll sense of humor by making Dan squirm.

Hughes: Were Dan's folks surprised that he popped the question?

Evans: Dan tells this story wonderfully. He wasn't living with them at the time, but after I said yes, he went right to their house. They were upstairs in bed because it was 10 o'clock at night, or whatever. And I don't know if he woke them up, but he barged in and told them. And Irma was just in tears because she was so ecstatically happy. His father was pleased, too, of course.

Hughes: Did Irma Evans over the years prove to be someone who was just like a second mom to you?

Evans: Oh yes. She was so generous of herself, and everybody loved her. She was just one of those people who never said a naughty thing about anybody, who would do anything for anybody, and was just full of energy. She was just a very wonderful person.

Hughes: And Dan's dad was a lot like your husband?

Evans: Very solid, very quiet. When Dan was in the Legislature and decided to run for governor, I think his father was probably dismayed because that's a big leap, and he didn't want his son to be hurt in any way, whereas Irma just went, "Oh, that's wonderful!"

Hughes: "Go for it, son!"

Evans: Absolutely.

Top: The bride and groom, June 6, 1959. *Evans family album*
Bottom: The newlyweds toast one another as their parents look on. At left,
Les and Irma Evans; at right, Lilith and Lawrence Bell. *Evans family album*

Five young Republican state representatives in 1957: from left, Joel Pritchard, Dan Evans, Chuck Moriarity, Jimmy Andersen and Slade Gorton. *Washington State Archives*

Hughes: Apart from your Dad needling Dan and making him squirm with his droll sense of humor, did your folks love him, too?

Evans: Oh yes, they had a good relationship. Unfortunately, my father didn't live too terribly long after that. He died in 1962 at the age of 83. He was 15 years older than my mother. Unfortunately, we weren't together all that much. You're just not back and forth like you are today. To come to Seattle was sort of a big thing. Then we started having kids, which made it harder to go to Spokane, which took a lot longer than it does now.

Hughes: As you got serious with Dan did you talk a lot about his interest in politics, and his work as a state representative? He was voted "Outstanding Freshman Legislator" in 1957.

Evans: He was a legislator but he was an engineer by profession. But, yes of course, we talked about the Legislature and legislation. I met all of the legislators.

Hughes: Was that whole group of Dan Evans rat-pack guys, those bright young Republicans, already together when you met him in 1958?

Evans: Pretty much so. Yes.

Hughes: Joel Pritchard and Slade Gorton?

Evans: Well, Slade not quite yet. But it was Chuck Moriarty, Don Moos, Joel…I don't want to start naming names because I'll forget some of them.

Hughes: And Jimmy Andersen?

Evans: Andersen, yes, very much so. Tom Copeland was another one.

Hughes: I've never met Sally Gorton, Slade's wife. Is she a good friend of yours?

Evans: A very good friend, but not a close friend. We saw each other all the time during the governor's years. When Dan and I were engaged, Chuck Moriarty, Slade Gorton, Dan Evans and Joel Pritchard stayed in a house together during legislative sessions. Sally and Slade were married, so Sally stayed down there as well. She called herself the house mother. So we've always seen a lot of each other. And then when Dan, Slade and Lud Kramer were elected governor, attorney general and secretary of state, those three young Republican state officials were, obviously, very close. We used to do things together, things of that nature.

I remember when I christened a ship one time—a Washington State ferry called the *Hyak*. ...What's *very* hard to comprehend is the fact that the *Hyak* is now in mothballs! (laughing)

Hughes: Surely no metaphor for the former first lady of our state!

Evans: I certainly hope not. I was asked to have a "lady in waiting." I think that's the term they used, and I asked Pat Kramer, Lud's wife, to be my "lady in waiting." So the two of us went down to San Diego and cracked the champagne over the ship's bow.

Hughes: I've seen some of those, and sometimes it's really hard for the chosen lady to break the champagne bottle.

Evans: Mine did not break the first time. It's wired, it's scored and all of that, but you have to hit it just right on the right thing. I'm strong, and I swung very hard, but I just didn't hit the right thing. Then it did break and champagne got all over me.

Hughes: But back in 1958, you were a grade-school music teacher. You hadn't been real political. Was that something that you thought was really interesting?

Evans: Sure. Well, remember I grew up listening about politics. My parents loved to talk politics. In fact, later when she came to live with us, my mother would say, "Now Dan I think...you ought to think about this." And he'd say, "Yes, yes 'Gom.'" That's our nickname for her—"Gom." Everybody called her "Gom" because that was what her first grandchild called her.

Hughes: Is that because the kid couldn't say "Grandma" when he was a toddler?

Evans: Yes—and that kid is now a professor, and he's 65 years old; my nephew, John Ludders. He is my sister's son. My oldest nephew. But politics was interesting for me. And when I went down to Olympia the first time, they were all married. They were more Dan's age, and in that period of your life a few years make a huge difference. I was younger than they were. So they all sort of took me under their wing. And when I was dating him and then when we were engaged, I would go down to Olympia for the day and then come back home.

Hughes: Even in the beginning, Dan was more of a Teddy Roosevelt Bull-Moose kind of progressive than a lockstep Eisenhower-Nixon Republican. Is that a fair characterization?

Evans: I would never have put him in those terms (at the time) because those names were not even popping into my mind. I mean we were thinking Olympia, King County, the 43rd District.

Hughes: "All politics is local," in other words.

Evans: Yes, I think that was the dimension. But he tried to bring people together. Like somebody from Eastern Washington who might have a totally different approach to an issue. They would work on each other and take the best of each view. Of course that depended upon the issue. It's hard to generalize about this sort of thing. Dan just tried to get things done, and he was good at it.

Hughes: Did you have any idea then, on June 6, 1959, your wedding day, of what you might be getting into politically?—That in nothing flat one thing would lead to another; that he would emerge as a leader in the House and then running for governor?

Evans: Absolutely not. I wasn't really thinking beyond June 6th.

Hughes: Where did you go on your honeymoon?

Evans: We were married in Spokane. I've often said over the years that I married about five or six things. And one of the things I married was a *big* car. It was the first new car he'd ever bought—a big-finned, gold Plymouth. You know, the days of those terrible fins.

Hughes: Absolutely, the swept-back "look of the future."

Evans: And I married this sofa. (She pats a cushion) It has been recovered and restyled a number of times but it's still solid. In the beginning it was a white Naugahyde sofa. It's a Miller design, and it's been recovered many times. I also married a sailboat.

Hughes: You had a sailboat right off?

Evans: He already had it. I married that. There were certain things in his life that just came along as part of the deal. I remember that car so well. Dan thought it was just great. We drove from Spokane down to Reno and then went over to the coast, to Carmel and up to San Francisco. We stopped by to see my sister Barbara in Lake Oswego, Oregon. We took movies all along the way. That's another thing I married—a 16mm movie camera, which we took to Europe with us a year later. It was big and bulky but it took great movies. We have some great movies from San Francisco and Carmel. We have a wonderful set of movies where I was wearing a really pretty cotton dress. And I had a big straw hat. We went into a little delicatessen—that's still there actually—bought some salami, and a baguette, and some cheese, and a bottle of wine, and some Blum's chocolates. And we drove out to a place on the beach and Dan put the camera on a tripod or something. I've got this hat on and he's sitting there. And he takes a close-up of the Blum's chocolate. And then I'm slicing up the bread and putting on the salami. Then he gets the corkscrew and he tries to open the wine, but it won't open.

Hughes: This is like early Spielberg stuff! Dan Evans, the director.

Evans: Absolutely. Oh, listen, Christmas mornings with him were terrible because of the camera. All the kids had to line up for his movies. But at any rate, he stopped the camera for a moment, and got the wine open. Then you see us sitting there and eating our salami and drinking our wine.

Hughes: So did Dan say to you, "Well, someday I'm going to be governor; we'll have three kids, and we'll live in a mansion and have teas and receptions"?

Evans: Obviously not. I probably would have said no.

Hughes: "Listen, Dan, I need more than three days to think about that!"

Evans: Exactly. There was no talk of governorship. There was no talk about anything like that at that time.

Hughes: In a 1974 interview, you said, "He grew on me….He didn't come on strong…He hadn't dated all that much. The thing I remember most, other than that he was a very nice person and a very handsome man, was his intrigue. Each time I went out with him I learned something new. I saw a man of depth."

Evans: Is that what I said?

Hughes: You did. And I really like the word "intrigue."

Evans: Well, that's the way it was. Gee, what else do you have there?

Hughes: Oh, all kinds of stuff. Your life is an open book. There are no secrets from The Legacy Project. They say you're supposed to Google yourself and see what you can find out.

Evans: Nah.

Hughes: "I didn't know what I was getting to," you added. "I knew he was a legislator, but good heavens—at that time the Legislature was two or three months every two years. I had no idea he would ever run for governor, and I don't think he did either." Meantime, you're pretty soon a mom. When does Dan Jr. arrive?

Evans: November 25, 1960.

Hughes: So were you still teaching part-time?

Evans: No. When we got married I quit teaching. It's shameful, but I have never worked for money since we were married.

Hughes: Well, you have done a lot of other important things.

Evans: I've been busy, but it only costs money. We don't get paid; we pay out….But I need to tell you a story about another wonderful trip we took before our lives got so complicated. Dan was an engineer, and I think around September (of 1959) he came home one day and said, "Well, I quit my job." And I said, *"Really?"* (laughing) Or words to that effect. Then he said, "Why don't we plan a trip?" And I said, "Well, jeepers, don't you have to get a job first?" He wasn't worried. He had been working a while so he had some money. I didn't have any. I was a school teacher.

So we started planning a trip. We ended up writing letters to tourist bureaus all over Europe. We ordered a car. And on December 31st we flew to Los Angeles, saw the Rose Bowl, which the Huskies won, spent the night on the floor of the hotel room of friends of ours, Aylelne and Alan Bluechel. And the next morning flew to Copenhagen on SAS nonstop. You could have 40 pounds each of luggage. And in those days there were no backpacks or nylon duffle bags. There were hard suitcases. And we had our skis and all the 16mm film. It was so much cheaper to buy those here than in Europe. My purse was a bag that was about this high, probably plastic because that's all they had in those days, and I was going through customs carrying it on my arm like it was nothing. It weighed 20 pounds I'm sure because of all the film. And Dan wore his ski boots because of their weight. He went with two shirts, two trousers for a six-month trip.

Hughes: That's amazing.

Evans: Yeah, it was marvelous. And the only schedule we had was the pick up of the car. We booked early enough that we got a cabin with a window on a Holland America cruise ship, the *Rotterdam*. It was its second voyage. And that was in the end of May. So off we went and we skied for a month, in Europe on $5 a day—$10 a day for the two of us. The only thing that did not go in that $5 was the ski lift tickets and the car.

Hughes: What kind of car was it?

Evans: Well, you've never heard of it because we had wanted to order a Mercedes—

Hughes: I'll bet it was a Borgward.

Evans: It *was* a Borgward. You *have* heard of it.

Hughes: I'm a car guy.

Evans: And the only reason we didn't get a Mercedes was because there was none available at the time we wanted it.

Hughes: Borgward was a very good automobile.

Evans: Well, it was and it looked very much like a Mercedes. It was light blue. So we skied the month of January, and stayed in pensions (guest houses) that were wonderful, with these big feather comforters. And those wonderful croissants, and jams, and cocoa. I wasn't a big coffee drinker then. We spent $5 a day, so $10 for the two of us—three meals and a room at night. That's when the dollar was king. We lived *very* inexpensively. Then we picked up the car in Germany and started driving. We headed towards Spain where we thought it would be a little warmer. It was, sort of, and into Portugal. We just drove all over Europe.

Hughes: What a wonderful adventure.

Evans: It was a great trip. And then we came home. That's when Dan decided he wanted to form an engineering partnership with Vic Gray. And I came home pregnant with our son. I can tell you where and when, but I'm not going to. (laughing) Our son Dan knows. It was a *wonderful* trip, because we were places where now you go and it's so crowded with tourists. We stayed in a pension right on the Med in Nice and Cannes. The only place where I didn't want to get out of bed because I didn't want to put my foot on the floor was in Paris. We were in this dirty hotel on the Left Bank.

Hughes: Did you go to Monaco and down the Riviera?

Evans: Yes, we did. We just went all over....

Hughes: Then, back home, your lives grew more frenetic. A new job for Dan, and in the middle of becoming a dad, he became House minority leader at 35 after that 1960 election. All of a sudden did it dawn on you that this is heading even higher?

Evans: No. That was it. That was as far as he looked—minority leader. Well, he would have liked it even better if he had been *majority* leader. And that step up was a big thing because he was young and he was a newer member. There were others who had been there longer and deservedly should have been elected. And he respected them. So it was an interesting thing.

Hughes: Was your table talk or pillow talk often about politics?

Evans: Yes, we talked about political issues.

Hughes: Is there some issue you recall from then that really resonated with you?

Evans: I'm not sure I recall anything particular from 1960. That's a long time ago. But over the years I can remember a lot of discussions. You know, the ERA (Equal Rights Amendment). I was for that, and (legalized) abortion. Things of that nature would be of special interest, and other social issues. I'm not going to discuss with him the highway budget or how to deal with traffic. We didn't always agree on things.

Hughes: Early on, can you recall something that you really disagreed over?

Evans: No. I can't. I think he would agree that often we disagreed on things. But I've always respected his stand on an issue because his was well-thought. Mine was not always well-thought-out. He would always have thought about it—the pros and the cons. That's our thing when we talk about issues. So I always respected his views because he has an engineer's way of looking at things carefully. And oftentimes he's changed my view, but sometimes I think I've softened or brought him a little bit more my direction. Maybe not changed him but had some influence.

Hughes: Can you think of one issue?

Evans: I can't be specific. It's hard. Fifty years is a long time.

Hughes: Four years after getting married you've got two sons and Dan's star is rising. It must have seemed like your life was on a jet plane, didn't it?

Evans: Well, in thinking back on it I don't know how I did it. But, you know, at the time you just do it. And I think back to my mother's advice. She always said, "You can do whatever you really want to do if you work hard." The other important thing is that when something comes along you're ready for it. In other words, that you've done whatever you needed to do to get to the point where you're ready if there's an opportunity—if somebody says, "Will you do this?" Or, "Can you do this?" So I guess in all my growing up, the Bell household somehow prepared me to do what

I did, for better or for worse.

Hughes: Do you remember when Dan came home the first time and said, "The fellows are all talking: They think I ought to run for governor."

Evans: I don't remember that specific moment. It was in 1963. But I do remember the discussions that were taking place, and some meetings that he was going to. He'd come home saying, "Well, they're talking about this." And I'd say, "Oh God!" Initially I was very skeptical of the whole prospect. I just didn't think he had a chance.

Hughes: A lot of people felt that way. He was a dark horse—a fresh-faced dark horse, but a dark horse nevertheless. 1964 was shaping up as a Democratic year.

Evans: And I had good reason to think that way because that was the case. And, yes, I was pregnant with number two, Mark. That was my focus.

Hughes: I'd forgotten you were pregnant.

Evans: Yes, I was pregnant when this (governor talk) started. And then I had Mark in September of '63. The campaign actually was already in formation at that time. So we asked Mother, who was a recent widow, to come and stay with us to help with the children so that I could get out and about a bit. She was real reluctant to do so because she always said "I do not believe in living with my children." And I said, "Well, we're not talking about you living with us."

Hughes: Not to mention the fact that Spokane had been her home for all those years.

Evans: That's right. Dan was the one who convinced her to come over to Seattle. We had a very small house—not very far from our present house. So Mother came, and that helped. Then I was able to go out and do a little campaigning with Dan.

Hughes: "A little"? Is that by means of understatement?

Evans: No, because I still had the two kids. But Dan liked it when I could go along to things, obviously. Again, even then, and to this day—I shouldn't say this—but he's just not real easy with meeting people.

Hughes: I read that some of his staff called him "Old Gluefoot." He really is shy, isn't he?

Evans: Uh-huh.

Hughes: Is that the right word—"shy"?

Evans: Today it isn't, but at that time it was. Today it's not shy, it's just his nature. And it was his father's nature. He's just not an outgoing type of person. He *likes* people. It's not that. *It's just his nature.*

Hughes: I've noticed the gradual change since I first met him 40 years ago. He seemed to be more outgoing, more voluble when he became president of The Evergreen State College in 1977 than when he was governor. I always sort of intuited that besides really enjoying that job, he picked up some energy from being around the students and the faculty.

Evans: Maybe I was too close to him. I don't know that. But in the beginning, campaigning was not easy for him. You go into a room with a lot of people you don't know. He just couldn't go around and say hello easily. And I could do it a little more easily, for some reason.

Hughes: Did you find that after your initial anxieties it was fun?

Evans: I enjoyed it. I really enjoyed the campaigns, although they were extremely tiring and sometimes hard on

Rep. Dan Evans, R-King County, 1961.
Washington State House of Representatives

The candidate with his family, 1964. *Evans family album*

family life. And I always gained weight. You go to all those coffees where they have all those special things that the host just baked.

Hughes: And it would be really rude unless you ate them.

Evans: I don't even eat sweets much now, but in those days I certainly did. And I would come home saying, "Why did I eat that?" But there were certain communities around the state, as we got into it each time, where you made really nice friends.

Hughes: Tell me about that.

Evans: Well, just different communities that you just like, where you feel welcomed. I really enjoyed going to Bellingham because we had good friends up there. Yakima was a place we enjoyed, too. And of course Spokane, just because it was people you knew and you could renew those friendships. So the campaigns were enjoyable in many ways. Dan was always invigorated by the campaigns, but not the same way I was.

Hughes: Tell us your most vivid memories of that 1964 campaign? From the get-go, young Dan Evans was a real underdog against Governor Al Rosellini, who was seeking a third term.

Evans: But first he had to win the Republican nomination. There was one early poll, and I'm not going to tell it right; Dan will tell it right. But they took a poll, and Joe Gandy had entered the race (for the Republican nomination). Joe was extremely popular and well known because he was a business man in Seattle, and also had been one of the key people in making the Seattle World's Fair a success. And later his widow, Laurene Gandy, became one of my very dear friends because I got her to be chairman of the Governor's Mansion Foundation that I organized. But that's another story. Joe's candidacy frightened me because he had a lot of immediate popularity, and supporters, and *finances*, which was extremely important. And then there was the blond Lutheran minister—Dick Christensen. He was a very popular, well-known. So they took a poll, and I'm going to tell the numbers wrong, but the question was, "Do you know Dan Evans?— Have you ever heard of Dan Evans?"

Hughes: *Name recognition.*

Evans: Two percent had. "Would you vote for Dan Evans?" Four percent. (laughing) More people would vote for him than knew him. Maybe it was six or seven percent, but it was very low.

Hughes: Christensen ran for the U.S. Senate earlier, against Warren G. Magnuson.

Evans: That's right. And lost. But we were really underdogs. And it was

Nancy at a Republican reception. *Washington State Archives*

Richard Christensen on the campaign trail. *Washington State Archives*

a long campaign. Dan and Vic Gray had just formed their new engineering partnership and just began to work on that in 1960.

Hughes: Sure, we forget that Dan had to have a job that actually paid real money.

Evans: Exactly right. So they formed their partnership in the fall of '60 or early '61. Vic, bless his heart, was a good guy. It was hard starting out, but they got some jobs and things were looking good for the partnership when the campaign got really serious and Dan had to take time away, Vic couldn't have been more wonderful about agreeing, "Absolutely this is what you must do. And I will carry on."

Hughes: Even though Dan and Vic were just starting out together, the prospect of a governor's salary wasn't nearly as lucrative as owning a successful civil engineering firm?

Evans: Oh, absolutely not. And in fact we had the same salary for 10 years as governor.

Thanks to Governor Rosellini, I think they raised it on the day before Dan took office to $32,500. And it was that for 10 years. I can remember that.

Hughes: Speaking of money, campaigns today are obscenely expensive. But even relatively speaking back then it had to be pretty expensive. Justice Utter recalls taking out a second mortgage on their house to pay for a King County Superior Court race in 1964, the same year Dan was elected governor.

Evans: Well, Dan has said many times—and he'll say it in his book, and to you if you ever do one of these on him—he always told the campaign that he would never use any of his own money. First of all, he didn't have any. But when he would go on campaign trips, he would never use any of his own money. They had to raise it. And if they went broke, that was the end of the campaign. But there was a time when they were down to literally only hundreds left. And they made a visit to a well-known businessman in Seattle—I won't give a name, but maybe Dan would—who wrote a check that carried them through. It wasn't a huge check, but it carried them through until more money was raised. Norton Clapp, Booth Gardner's stepfather, who was a well-known businessman, was one of Dan's supporters. But there were just 10 or 12 people around the table, and Dan had a difficult time asking for money. He still does. And I think it was Norton who stood up and said, "Look, we all know what we have to do and nobody is leaving this room until we write a check."

EDITOR'S NOTE: On Oct. 21, 1964, *The Seattle Times* reported that Evans was being outspent by Rosellini by over 4-and-one-half to 1, with Evans' expenditures on track to total $100,000 from the primary through the general election. Rosellini's expenditures were on track to total $450,000, based on feedback from "advertising men."

It was a campaign that was pretty much run on 3x5 filing cards (of key contacts). They went to Pat Goodfellow, one of Dan's friends from high school who ran an automobile agency, and asked for a donation. He replied, "I can do something better. Go out in the lot and find a used car you like. I'll loan it to you." They loaned him the car. Jim Dolliver, who became Dan's chief of staff when he was governor, was the driver. Jim and Dan put *thousands* of miles on that car. I'm sure the fellow had no idea how many miles it was going to be because they drove all over the state in that car in the period of a year, year and a half.

Hughes: What was Jim Dolliver doing when he hooked up with Dan? He wasn't a legislator.

Evans: I think he was the House Republicans' attorney. So that's how he and Dan got to know each other, in the Legislature.

Hughes: Was that the two amigos right from the get-go?

Evans: *Absolutely.* Oh yes. Jim Dolliver was wonderful. And he carried me through sometimes because I would get very down. I'd say, "Oh Jim. This is not going to work." It was very hard emotionally on me at times. And he'd say, "Look, you've just got to keep going."

Hughes: I'll bet it was hard emotionally, wasn't it, to be the candidate's wife?

Evans: Oh it was. Sure. My insecurities would rise up. But they put a lot of miles on that car and drove everywhere. And it was really the two of them and a few people in Seattle. Then each community had its own leadership, of course. It was a very simple campaign by comparison to campaigns today.

Hughes: As things went along, were there new polls that showed Dan making some headway?

Evans: Oh yes. It's one of those things. Timing is everything in a race like that. Particularly because we started so early, and from nothing really, other than the support of some good people, you're bound to see some improvement. Then it got toward the end of the race, and it was Christiansen still in the lead. Joe Gandy had dropped out by that point. And it was really down to Christiansen and Dan. But we had a lot more visibility and a lot of people out there working hard. Women—young women—thought he was very handsome.

Hughes: My mother thought he was cute.

Evans: He was. Oh, absolutely. Very good looking. So it was a little scary to me at times. But I do remember the Republican Convention of 1964. Joe Gandy was still in the race. Dan's parents were there. We arrived and there was this huge Christiansen contingent. That's the part I hate about those conventions—all that hoopla. I just don't like it. I can still remember standing outside the foyer of the center. Somebody up there on the stage was announcing, "And now here we have Joe Gandy and Mrs. Gandy!" Laurene Gandy was just a lovely lady. And I can still see her, just putting her chin up saying to herself, "OK, I'm going to do this!" And here was this lovely lady walking down amid the hoopla, hoopla, hoopla. Then they announced Dan, and it wasn't quite as much hoopla. But Dan always says, "I'll never forget that when I got up on the stage and looked down, there was my father." This quiet, dignified person was waving Evans signs as big and as wildly as he could. Dan had never seen his father doing anything like that.

Hughes: That's great! A very proud father. Unfortunately, your dad was not there. He had passed away. Was your mother there?

Evans: I don't think so.

Hughes: Back looking after the kids?

Evans: Yes, probably. That's exactly what she would be doing.

Hughes: Now we're getting down to the nitty-gritty.

Evans: September is the primary. And Dan won.

> **EDITOR'S NOTE:** Evans crushed Christensen by 100,000 votes. Christensen conceded gracefully, pinning on an Evans campaign button and declaring, "My task now is to join with this man and make him the next governor of this state..." The Rosellini camp, meantime, had tried to woo crossover votes with ads that said "Thinking Republicans CANNOT: 'Go with Goldwater,' 'Crusade with Christensen'...or 'Endure with Evans.'"

Hughes: Then it's the sprint to November. Did Dan and Al Rosellini have any debates?

Evans: Yes, they had two in 1964.

Hughes: And then in 1972 there was the memorable debate when Al called him "Danny boy." We can talk more about that later. I've got an "I'm for Danny boy" bumper sticker right here.

Evans: (Laughs)

Governor Al Rosellini in 1956.
Life Magazine

Hughes: Do you remember meeting Al and Ethel Rosellini for the first time?

Evans: I had met them when Dan and I were engaged. Mrs. Rosellini hosted teas. The First Lady would have open houses at the Mansion for legislators' wives and other guests.

Hughes: What was Ethel like?

Evans: Mrs. Rosellini was a *very* nice person. Very sweet. I always liked her. And I'd met Al a few times, and he can be very charming.

Hughes: No doubt about it. And he's now 99 years old!...So when the battle between Al and Dan was fully engaged, if you ever encountered Ethel Rosellini she was always—

Evans: We were fine, absolutely fine. Both of us.

Hughes: And in the 1964 race, Al had not made the strategic mistake of "dissing" young Dan Evans, as the kids say today.

Evans: No. He was an incumbent, and he had the money, and he had a history, good or bad.

Hughes: 1964 wasn't exactly a fortuitous Republican year.

Evans: No!

Hughes: Barry Goldwater may have been the conscience of the conservatives, but Lyndon B. Johnson was on a roll. Still, was there any moment in October, despite still trailing in the polls, when Dan said, "I think we have a shot."

Evans: Well, he always was positive. He was always very good at understanding what the numbers meant at that moment in time. So he wasn't often surprised about things.

Hughes: Who was the Stu Elway of that era who was crunching the numbers for the Evans campaign?

Evans: Jim Dolliver and Dan.

Hughes: Do you recall any kind of defining moment where Election Day is a week away and you thought, "My God, we could really win this"?

Evans: Well, I don't remember the moment because it was too long ago. But Dan didn't trail in the polls after the primary so I just know that I had a feeling "this may happen." Then I think I began thinking, "But what if it does? What will I do then? What's going to happen to us?"

Hughes: That reminds me of the movie called *The Candidate* where Robert Redford is the dark horse who just got elected to the U.S. Senate in a huge upset. He's in the back seat with his Jim Dolliver and he goes, *"What do we do now?"*

Evans: Exactly. "What do we do now?" I think it's sort of that way for everybody who wins. But the one thing about that campaign that I loved was not just the people we met out in the communities; it was the people here in Seattle, our friends, and others who became really good lifelong friends, who just had the passion as well. You could just feel they were working there because they *really* wanted to be there. It was sort of like the Obama campaign—they really wanted to be a part of it. I'm not comparing Dan to Obama in any way, but this was really a mission that they were on, and they were having fun.

Hughes: Not too far-fetched an analogy, actually, for what Dan represented at that time. It was a changing of the guard in Washington politics.

Evans: And we had fun. It was *really* fun. It was so personal. And there were gatherings where we really were with them a lot—the campaign workers—and you just enjoy being together. I don't think those happen anymore. I have really good memories about that.

Hughes: Dan won by nearly 150,000 votes. On November 11, 1964, *The Olympian* declared, "State's New First Lady, Pretty, Practical." It says, "Washington's new First Lady...Mrs. Daniel J. Evans, has plenty of other attributes that helped her husband become the state's youngest governor at 39. She also has poise, a warm personality, and an interest in politics. She also has good feet and an excellent digestion."

Evans: Absolutely!

Hughes: It sounds sort of like horse-judging at the county fair.

Evans: Yes, it does. (laughing)

Hughes: "The feet, encased in needle-heeled shoes traveled the campaign trail beside those of her husband. She ate everything she was served."

Evans: Absolutely.

Hughes: "Mrs. Evans says, 'Well, sometimes I passed up the bread and potatoes at dinner but I ate all the cookies and nuts at all those coffee hours. And I gained 15 pounds, to my alarm.'"

Evans: I'd forgotten the 15, but, yes, that's also true.

Hughes: "Mrs. Evans said she enjoyed campaigning because it took her into 'every nook and cranny of this state. At first I dreaded it, but everyone was so friendly and kind.'"

Evans: That's really true.

Hughes: Then it concludes, "Nancy Evans may be the state's youngest first lady, but there will be few challenges she can't handle."

Evans: Well…

Hughes: Did you really find that people all around the state were friendly and kind?

Evans: Yes, by and large. But one of the public things that I hated and dreaded in campaigns were the parades because you'd get boos.

Hughes: Really?

Evans: Oh yes, boos and everything. And in Olympia, there's the Lakefair Parade. And when you went by a particular tavern all the tavern people would be out in front booing.

Hughes: Really?!

Evans: Oh yes! (Laughing) So Dan, bless his heart, seemed unfazed. And when the boys would come along as they grew older, they enjoyed these fairs, festivals and the parades. But it was sort of hard on them because people were booing. They'd say, "Why are they booing at my daddy?" So Dan was very clever. He said, "Find somebody on the route. For instance, see that woman standing up there looking at us. Just look at her and smile and wave as best you can and I'll bet you you'll get that person to smile." And, by gosh, that's what happened. Even I would try to find somebody to help me smile and wave at them.

Hughes: Any *one* special memory that sums up 1964 for you?

Evans: Election night.

Hughes: Tell me about that.

Evans: Well, Dan doesn't want to be with a lot of people on election night. He wants to sit and watch that television and keep track of the numbers. So conversation is not in there. And that has no exception. So my memory is that we had a room at the Olympic Hotel with his family and my family, brothers and sisters and that sort of thing, where he could keep tabs. And of course things were a little slower in counting the results in those days. And then when we knew he had won we went down to the campaign headquarters. Dan was talking with KING TV up on the stage and it was so noisy…And then the reporter had his microphone in front

Dan and Nancy on the campaign trail. *Evans family album*

of my mouth. But I couldn't hear his questions because it was so noisy. And I know I stood there looking like, "Duh." I think I was actually in a bit of a daze.

Hughes: I'll bet you were.

Evans: But I couldn't hear him and just sort of went, *"What did you say?"* It was not that my mind had gone blank. I felt so stupid standing up there. Then I was overwhelmed. In a good way.

Hughes: Did you learn anything about your husband by watching him on the campaign trail—something that you hadn't seen before? Did you see him evolve?

Evans: I did, absolutely. And you asked if we discuss issues. Well, we do in a family sort of way. But I really saw him grow with his understanding of issues in a broader sense. Being around the state so much more and talking to so many more people, getting different sides to every issue. I think he had a wonderful understanding of the major issues for our state, and he learned how to articulate them in front of people.

Hughes: As a reporter in that era, it really seemed to me that Dan and his brain trust of bright young people started to look more closely at social services issues when they got in power, and that they started growing too.

Evans: Absolutely.

Hughes: Environmental issues.

Evans: Absolutely. Environmentalism came very easily to Dan because of his old Boy Scout days. Ever since he was a kid at Camp Parsons he had been hiking in the Olympics. To this day he takes a hike every summer in the Olympics or the Cascades.

Hughes: Do you do that too?

Evans: Well, I did for many years, but I don't now because I have a foot issue. But he does still. He did last summer. So the environment was and is very important to him. But it was never defined in those days as the "environment" and "ecology," and all those words that we are so accustomed to today. So when that whole movement came along he was at the forefront because he felt so strongly about it. That was a given.

Hughes: Justice Utter recalls with horror casually dumping garbage off the back of his sailboat in the 1960s.

Evans: It's terrible what we used to do.

Hughes: In the *Time* magazine article about Dan in '68, "Gummie" Johnson, the Republican strategist, is calling Dan "Old Gluefoot" because he wasn't good at mixing with crowds. That they'd find Dan off with a couple of people and you'd be off really schmoozing.

Evans: That's what he'd do. He'd just go in the corner with a few people. He was enjoying the conversation and couldn't understand why he had to break away.

Hughes: That's funny. And then there's this 1972 piece that Joel Connelly wrote: "Surrounded by admirers, Evans looks stiff and uncomfortable. His wife, by contrast, is relaxed and outgoing. Unlike the two governors and Mrs. Rockefeller, who were waiting for people to come to them, Nancy Evans is moving around the hall, seeking people out and thanking them for coming to the dinner." This is in 1968 when Nelson Rockefeller was here to pay back a political debt to Dan for endorsing him for president over Nixon.

Evans: (Just smiles)

Hughes: OK. So there you are. It's 1964, and you're going to be

Ethel Rosellini in 1962.
Washington State Archives

Washington's First Lady at the age of 31. Does Ethel Rosellini do the Laura Bush sort of thing—invite the new First Lady over to the Mansion and say, "Here you go, kid, but the plumbing doesn't work..."?

Evans: Interestingly, it didn't happen immediately, and it's not as pro forma as the presidential thing. There's nothing written down.

Hughes: There's no reception for the two families—outgoing and incoming?

Evans: Nothing of that nature. I had been there to the Mansion a number of times to legislative functions, dinners and teas. But I didn't know what was upstairs.

Hughes: Did you have any sort of impressions of the place? "Nice old house"?

Evans: Well, yes, of course you do. It was fading elegance. Obviously it was a grand old home, and it was very exciting to think about living there. But, again, overwhelming because I had no idea, no concept of how it functions. I remember saying to someone, "I don't have a clue. Do they have towels and sheets?" Someone suggested I contact Evelyn Langlie because she lived in the Mansion for 12 years. She was widowed and lived here in Seattle. She was a lovely person. She was very nice to me and to us. She told me what she could, of how it was when they had been there, but of course that had been nine years before. Later when I got into doing research on the Mansion itself, she came down to Olympia a number of times and we'd go through the whole Mansion identifying things and what have you. But Ethel Rosellini did contact me, and asked if I would like me to come down and meet with her and she'd show me around, which was very nice of her. And I did. I went down and Mother went with me.

Hughes: Was she gracious and charming?

Evans: She was a *very* nice person.

Hughes: Any signs of Governor Al?

Evans: No. And I didn't expect any. Dan was not with me. It was just me and Mother. And we three talked. I remember meeting Lorna Leidy, who was the housekeeper at the time. Lorna stayed on with us. She became a part of the family. She was a widow, a long-time widow. Her husband had died too young. She needed to work and that's what she did. She was just a delight. She had been with the Langlies, too. But at that time they were more formal. They called her an "upstairs maid." She was working there a long time. She was elderly when we were there.

Hughes: As in her 70's?

Evans: Yes. And she would keep terrible hours, into the evenings, and up early the next morning. And I'd just often think, "How did she do it?" She was *wonderful*, just the loveliest person. We all loved her dearly. And I think that she grew to love our family, as she had the other governors' families she had worked with. At that first meeting, she showed me around and we discussed what we had to bring and that sort of thing. So that was a real help. Lorna had a house in Olympia not too far from the Mansion, so she would also go home. She was just so loving, and just took us in her arms immediately from the day we arrived. That was a *great* help to me. She arranged flowers, too. She was wonderful. There were two others over the years that we really enjoyed—Twila Ogle and Helen Wright. Both were with us quite a long time as housekeepers. We kept in touch right up until they died. They were all wonderful to work with.

Hughes: Those ladies must have really enjoyed having those three livewire boys around.

Evans: They seemed to. But I'm sure the boys were nuisances a lot of the time too.

Hughes: The first time I went into the Mansion after the Lockes moved in and I saw the play set, the trikes and the Legos it made me smile.

Evans: Well, I used to always say that I would not like to live in the

Mansion without children because it's just big and quiet.

Hughes: It humanizes the place, doesn't it?

Evans: It really does. And we determined very early on that the house was their home, and they could live everywhere. So the ballroom was a great play area *a lot* of the time.

Hughes: Any first impressions when you saw what the private quarters were like in the Mansion?

Evans: Well, It was just not our home, that's all. But right away, after the election, we were besieged by requests for entertaining at the Mansion. And I kept saying, "I don't know."

Hughes: This was before you moved in?

Evans: Yes. And I remember a request from the ARW, which is the Associated Republican Women. It was quite an active organization. Dan's mother was a member. They came down to the Legislature each year and they said they would like to have lunch at the Mansion. Let's see, the inauguration was on a Wednesday, and they wanted to come for lunch that Friday or maybe the following Monday. And like a *nit-wit* I said yes!

The Mansion ballroom in the 1960s. *Washington State Archives*

I remember that. But, at any rate, they came and we did fine, I guess. But the move was very hectic. You want to hear about the move?

Hughes: *I do.*

Evans: Well, Dan was being sworn in at noon. And the Rosellinis were still there (in the Mansion) the night before. Meantime, there was the question of the redistricting gerrymandering the Democrats were trying to pull off in the Legislature. Dan had his hands full as a Republican leader in the Legislature on the eve of his inauguration as governor. (*That was Tuesday, January 12, 1965.*)

Hughes: You're absolutely right. Dan Evans got himself elected governor right in the middle of the one of the biggest redistricting brouhahas in the history of the state, and he was in the thick of it, together with Slade Gorton, in the days leading up to his inauguration.

Evans: I probably have the wrong company, but I want to say Shell Oil maps were the maps that everybody was using to draw the new district boundaries because they were the best. Slade and Jim Dolliver were key members of the strategy team for the Republicans, together with Tom Copeland, the Republican floor leader in the House.

Finally, somebody told Dan, "Well, the Constitution says that you have to be sworn in on that certain day, but it doesn't specify a time." Dan didn't want to take any chances. If the Legislature was still in session at midnight, they were going to swear him in one minute after midnight— One of the Supreme Court justices (Richard Ott) had agreed to do it. They wanted to prevent the Democrats from jamming through their redistricting plan. Dan called me from Olympia—I forget what time it was—and said, "Nancy, you've got to get down here tonight. I'm going to be sworn in at midnight and I want you here." And I said, "I need a babysitter!" I went next door to Poagy Mallotte's.

Hughes: Poagy?

Evans: Yes, pronounced "Poe-gi." She had a little girl who was our oldest son's age. And she said, "I'll come over and stay." I was scrambling. We had two little children and a crib and the whole thing. I guess they were

Governor-elect Dan Evans joins other Republican legislators and staff members as they work on a redistricting map and discuss ways to redraw the boundaries of a contested district. **From left:** Joel Pritchard, Damon Canfield, Mary Ellen McCaffree, Dan Evans, Tom Copeland, Howard McCurdy (drawing the lines), Slade Gorton. *Howard E. McCurdy*

Editor's Note: The gridlocked Legislature was working late on re-districting on the eve of Inauguration Day. There was a "tremendous amount" riding on the issue, Copeland said in an oral history interview with the Secretary of State's Anne Kilgannon in 2007. GOP leaders believed that if the Democrats' redistricting plan was enacted Republicans would be reduced to a more or less permanent minority for the next decade.

sending a car for me, so I wasn't going to be driving. Then they called around 9 or 10 and said, "No, it's not going to happen. So you can get back to what you were doing." That was a relief, and Poagy could go back home. She didn't have to stay.

Editor's Note: Here's more of the back-story: Maneuvering like crazy to keep the Democrats from capturing the 50 votes they needed, Rep. Copeland told Dan Evans, "I don't know if we can hold the damn thing or not." The governor-elect replied, "OK, we'll go ahead and set the machinery in motion. If you guys can delay it long enough to at least get past the 12 o'clock hour, then we'll go ahead and make arrangements for me to get sworn in." Speaker Bob Schaefer "was painfully aware that he was unable to find the necessary votes to pass a redistricting bill" satisfactory to Bob Greive, the Democrats' majority leader in the Senate. Copeland told Schaefer what the House Republicans were prepared to do—swear in Dan Evans early. Schaefer said, "You're not kidding, are you?" Copeland said, "No, I'm not kidding at all. I'm absolutely dead serious. That is what's going to happen at 12 o'clock." Schaefer said, "How would it be if we adjourned right now?" Copeland said, "You've got a deal." And the House adjourned until 10 a.m. Inauguration Day.

Then the next morning, very early, we got up. I had to then dismantle the crib that Mark slept in and put it in the trunk of our station wagon. And then I had to get everybody up, dressed and fed, and ready to drive to Olympia to see Dan sworn it. So we go outside and all the neighbors were out to say goodbye. It was wonderful. In fact, I remember that the night after the election, we got home very late. The next morning the whole neighborhood, all along the street, there were just signs everywhere, which was very nice.

Hughes: But there's Nancy with the crib jammed into the station wagon, kids in her arms.

Evans: Exactly. Not feeling very First Lady-ish. So we say goodbye. And I'm putting my inaugural gown on top of everything, over the crib in the back. And the boys were all in the back seat. I drive up the hill and all of a sudden I look back and they're all yelling. Well, the trunk door was open and everything is falling out, including my dress!

Hughes: Was it hurt?

Evans: No, it was in a plastic bag.

Hughes: That would have been a great scene if you had had tire tracks over the inaugural dress!

Evans: I packed everything back in the trunk and drove to Olympia. I arrived at I don't know, maybe 11, with the swearing in set for noon. I had arranged for some high school kids to be there at the Mansion to help carry in a few suitcases and to set up the crib. Then I was trying to figure out where to put the crib and settled on somewhere upstairs. So the kids took the crib up and pretty soon they came back down and said, "We can't figure out how to do the crib!" Dan's father, another engineer, had to go up and show them how to put the crib together. Then I had to get the kids something to eat! (laughing) I don't know how it all happened. At least I was dressed. I had just worn whatever I was going to wear for the ceremony. But the kids, we had to get them dressed. And then we had to feed Mark, who was just 16 months old, and get him down for his nap because it was that time of day. And then be over there at noon. Ah, it was amazing! But we made it.

The Inaugural Ball is that night, so we had to come back and unpack—you know, with kids and all. I had somebody there to babysit because Mother was going to go to the ball. Dan's parents were there, too. But we had a dinner to go to first put on by Rainier Bank. I remember that. So that was another evening dress I had to put on. I honestly don't remember how all this worked. Then we came back after that. Mark was in bed, but Danny was up to greet us in his pajamas and bathrobe because he

Nancy with Mark and Danny at the Governor's Mansion in 1965. *Evans family album*

was 4. Then Chuck Herring of KING-TV came to the door—this was all planned—for an interview. And you had all the cables—all the gear that they brought along in those days. It was a huge undertaking. So we're sitting in the drawing room being interviewed. Dan always remembers it so well because Chuck Herring said, "And, Mrs. Evans, you are the youngest First Lady at 32." And I say, *"I'm 31."* Dan always thought that was very funny. Poor Danny, he was 4 years old and he was just so excited; his parents are being interviewed for TV.

Then Herring said, "Can I have a tour?" And, of course, I say, "Sure Chuck, come with me." So we go down the hall and into the ballroom. Danny is just running all over the place, and I'm trying to take his hand and be a mother. I can look back at it and smile, but at the time I was just thinking, "Couldn't you just stand here and be a nice, quiet little boy for a few moments?" But, no, he was very excited in this new big house, with a new big playroom that he had to play in.

Then we had decided to invite friends over to the Mansion after the Inaugural Ball. But we would do it sort of by word-of-mouth as they came through the receiving line. The Mansion staff that stayed on had prepared some refreshments. But we had no idea that the ball started at 8, I think, and we were in line for three and a half hours.

Hughes: My gosh, your feet must have been killing you.

Evans: There were so many people; we had so many friends, so many supporters. This was so exciting to them. I felt sorry for us, but worse for all those people who were getting pushed and shoved.

Hughes: Was this at the Capitol?

Evans: No, this was at the Armory, the old Armory on the East Side of Olympia. Big bare, empty room, and a stage, and we were on the stage. And, yes, my feet were very sore. And my hand was very sore. No break. We just stood there. And we were trying to remember to say "Come by the Mansion" to people, but it was noisy. By the time we got to the Mansion it was midnight and the party already had been going on for a long time! (laughing) It was shocking to me that people had been upstairs. It just didn't occur to me that people would be that obtuse.

Hughes: They'd just sort of wandered around in the family quarters?

Evans: Yes. In the children's rooms, our room, you know all over. We found this out later. So we finally went to bed at 4 in the morning or some-thing—just exhausted because it had been a *long* day. Then Dan was up a few hours later, off to go be governor. Well, I was up too with the boys.

Hughes: (Handing her a photo) I don't know if this was your first inaugural gown, but I thought it was really lovely. I love this photo.

Evans: (laughs) That was in 1973. The dress is bright red—a pretty deep, cranberry sort of red.

Hughes: Which son is this with you?

Evans: That's Danny, our oldest son. ....And those long gloves I'm wearing! I still have those gloves somewhere. So what is he—about 12? He's got a Prince Valiant haircut. He was born in '60 so this would be the 1973 Inaugural Ball. I liked that dress, too. It was bright red and very daring because the back was bare. It had a jacket. I wore the jacket for the official proceedings that took place. Then I did take the red jacket off to dance. Dan liked that too. (laughs)

Hughes: What I like is the look in that boy's eyes. He isn't looking embarrassed to be dancing with his mom. He's really proud of her.

Danny dances with his mom at the 1973 Inaugural Ball *Evans family album*

Evans: He was having a wonderful time. But Mark was not. I remember that, Mark went home early. Mark was not going to dance.

Hughes: I think a lot of little boys would be real self-conscious.

Evans: No, Danny liked things like that.

Hughes: Did you have any first impressions about the Mansion as a place to live, that when you turned on the faucets, flushed the toilet or whatever, that you were going to have some challenges?

Evans: Well, it didn't take long to discover the little idiosyncrasies that the house had. The cabinet wives—the wives of the cabinet members—formed an organization primarily to be helpful to us in any way. It was also a nice way to get together informally. They had a dinner once a year at somebody's home, a potluck, and we all came. So there was some socializing between them, getting together and knowing each other, and being with each other's families. It was very nice. I don't think a lot of that happens any more with the wives or husbands of the governor's cabinet. Another nice thing was that all of them moved down to Olympia—including people Dan did not expect to move down. Some, in fact, were people who Dan didn't even expect would say yes to his offer of a job because of what they were doing, usually here in Seattle. But they all moved down to live in Olympia and become part of the community, which was wonderful and *very* helpful.

Hughes: Son Number Three, Bruce, arrived in 1966. I'm not going to be one of those men who ask you the stupid question, namely, "Did you have your baby in the Governor's Mansion?"

Evans: You mean actually *in* the Mansion?

Hughes: Yeah, exactly.

Evans: No, no. But almost because he came so quickly. I went to the hospital, barely.

Hughes: St. Pete's?

Evans: Well, the old St. Peter's. And as quick as it was I wouldn't have made it to the (location of the) new hospital. It was one hour from the first pain to delivery.

Hughes: I think there was one child who was actually born in the Mansion. Was that a Hay?

Evans: Yes. The Hays were the first family to move in and Lizzie Hay had a child there in the Mansion, Margaret Hay.

Hughes: There you were with three young kids, being first lady. In essence you were the chief executive officer of the Governor's Mansion.

Evans: There was a budget for staff, for upkeep, for maintenance. It was all one big lump sum of money. And what I did was just continue on what Mrs. Rosellini had done in large part. And I retained their cook and housekeeper. They lived on the third floor. Then there was a person who came five days a week who was a state employee as opposed to a Mansion employee. That person came to clean and some other work. The housekeeper also cleaned, but also did flowers. Lorna was the housekeeper, the lovely woman I mentioned earlier. They were not paid a huge sum of money. And part of their pay was room and board. The third floor is a very large sort of central room and then there are three bedrooms off of it, and one bathroom.

Hughes: Do you know if that is still configured the same way?

Evans: Yes it is. But there has not been live-in help since the Spellmans where there (1981-85).

Hughes: But when Dan and Nancy and their two boys moved in, upstairs on the third floor there lived a housekeeper and a cook, who did the cooking for the family as well as special occasions.

Evans: Yes. And we had *a lot* of cooks over the years. It was difficult to keep a good cook. Some were temporary, and we knew that at the time, because I was desperate. I had some interesting people to say the least. (laughing) But most of them were quite good. We had a couple who answered an ad I'd placed. The woman came with references, and she was walking from California to Alaska with a parrot.

Hughes: That made her tailor-made for your house. You could use a parrot to go with all the other pets.

Evans: Well, she was very pleasant, she really was. She had cooked for some movie actors. She had come from the Hollywood area. And she was good and fit, obviously. But she wasn't with us all that long; she wanted to move on....Very few people wanted to come there to live. Living up on the third floor with somebody they didn't know, all that, it was *hard* for them, too. We had a lot of cooks over the years. Some were disasters and some were wonderful.

Hughes: Tell us about the wonderful ones.

Evans: Well, Elsie was one. She was with us quite a long while. She was a widow from Longview. And she had the most wonderful family in the area. She had three or four children. When she was going to be off for a long weekend, they would pick her up and take her back down to be with them. They were a *wonderful* family. And Elsie was just another grandmother in the house. She was just great. Elsie loved to bake. She was the one who started making these wonderfully shaped birthday cakes for the boys. They'd be in the shape of whatever they were into—a football player or whatever. She was so good about things like that, just a pleasure to have in the house.

Hughes: Did you have any people you hired who turned out to be a colossal pain?

Evans: Oh yes. One I fired on the spot. He was an alcoholic, and I didn't know it. He was a good cook, too. It was a shame. He was probably one of the best cooks I hired because he had really gone to culinary school. I actually had two who were dipping into the sauce. We had an important dinner party. He appeared very late, and I just said "That's it, goodbye."

Hughes: What could you pay a cook, Nancy?

Evans: I don't remember. I have no idea.

Hughes: People have the impression that if you're in the Governor's Mansion and you have a cook that you're having crêpe Suzette and prime rib every night.

Evans: No. You have to be able to buy the groceries....And I also cooked. You know, the cook and housekeeper had time off, obviously. So they would go off on their days off and I would cook.

Hughes: So you were going out and doing the shopping once a week in the station wagon…pushing a cart in the supermarket?

Evans: Yes, I bought everything. That was my decision.

Hughes: So if you were going to have a big dinner—

Evans: Well, if it was a large dinner, 50, 60, whatever people, I would not do the shopping. There would be a caterer. But that came out of the budget, too. So it was *very, very* limited.

Hughes: Did you have a separate food budget?

Evans: No. You had a separate Mansion budget. And that I could do with what I wanted.

Hughes: You could feed your family from that budget—the everyday stuff like hot dogs, pot roast, Mac & Cheese?

Evans: Yes, although we paid for part of that.

Hughes: Your spouse told me he thought you did an amazing job of running the "wretchedly decrepit" old Mansion. He was *very* praiseworthy of the job you did managing the place.

Evans: He better be! (smiling) But if I were to do it all over I would be so much more wise. Even 20 years ago I would have been so much wiser. But at the time I was not very wise about these things. And there was a very small budget.

Hughes: Over the dinner table or over pillow talk did you say, "This budget is ridiculous" and talk about cooks?

Evans: Well, it just sort of became a running joke, quite honestly. When we found some people who were good and fun to be around and could put up with our family, then things ran quite smoothly and quite nicely.…

Hughes: Was there a kitchen where you and your mom could do cooking?

Evans: There was only one kitchen.

Hughes: *One* kitchen.

Evans: Yes. Today, it's greatly expanded and modernized.

Hughes: OK, let's make sure I've got this floor plan down during your era there: First floor, kitchen, State Dining Room, ballroom, the library, drawing room. Second floor is—

Evans: Bedrooms and bathrooms and a very small sitting room for the family.

Hughes: Third floor was the servants' quarters. But there's only one kitchen. You didn't even have a hot plate so you could...?

Evans: No. When Bruce was a baby it was sort of a pain in the neck to in all hours of the night run downstairs and turn on the water to heat a bottle.

Hughes: Especially when the plumbing wasn't working well.

Evans: All that aside. It's sort of a long way down from our bedroom to the kitchen. And I remember that Ralph Davis, the chairman of Puget Sound Power & Light, sent me a hotplate, (laughing) which I used to heat the bottle.

Hughes: But typically would the cook be cooking dinner for the Evans family? You always tried to have dinner together?

Evans: Yes. And in fact I remember when Bruce was born (in 1966) in those days they had little plastic seats to carry around a baby. They were just sort of an L-shape with a leg—nothing like the car seats they have today. Bruce sat in his little portable seat in the middle of the dining room table in the State Dining Room. That's where we ate every night because there was no other dining room. And he was the centerpiece on the table at night! We would try to hold dinner until Dan got home, so we could all eat together.

Hughes: What time was that?

Evans: Often it was 7, and for little kids that's late. I can remember one of the boys when he was in grade school, maybe even later, said to me, "Why can't we eat dinner at 6 like all the rest?" But Mother and I tried to make things as routine as possible. We tried to have dinner together.

Hughes: Did you have a key role in planning the menus?

Evans: Oh yes, absolutely.

Hughes: What was the favorite dinner at the Evans household?

Evans: I don't think we had a favorite because we simply liked food.

The dining room at the Mansion. *Washington State Archives*

We ate a lot of foods. Elsie made wonderful cheese soufflés. I would find recipes and give them to the cook to try.

Hughes: Someone had a nickname. Who was "Lolo"? Was that Lorna, the housekeeper?

Evans: No. Lolo was a babysitter, a wonderful woman who baby sat the boys when Mother couldn't. Lolo had babysat for Sally and Slade Gorton during legislative sessions. That's what Sally's kids, I think, had named her. Lolo's real name was Ann Neubrech. She lived in Olympia with her husband and family. Lolo was just great because she liked our kids and she would come to the Mansion. Mother was living there but she wanted to do things as well. We often went to Seattle to the concerts or whatever. And so if Lolo could come to the Mansion it was always great because she enjoyed our kids so much. It was Lolo who gave Danny a cat we named Boots. And I said, "Oh Lolo, how could you do that!?" But Boots was a nice cat. It was black with white boots, aptly named. I'm not a cat person, but I learned to like Boots and then we got Scamper. I don't remember how we got Scamper, a *second* cat. Then Boots had babies, and we had kittens running around.

Hughes: Then there's the gerbils—

Evans: Oh God, the gerbils, yes! Which I thought were terrible. And Mother had tropical fish. She loved her tropical fish. The boys did too. And we also had turkeys and rabbits.

Hughes: How did you get turkeys?

Evans: Talk to your friend Ralph Munro about that!

Hughes: I will! *(Munro was an Evans aide who went on to become secretary of state.)*

Evans: Actually they arrived in the backyard, early on, unbeknownst to us. We woke up to the sounds of, "Gobble, gobble." They named one "Augie" after Senator Mardesich (the Democrats' majority leader)—and the other was "Lenny" after Len Sawyer, the Democrat who was speaker of the House. Those two were giving Dan a lot of trouble in the Legislature. So now we have turkeys back there. What do you do with those? I wasn't going to butcher them. We got rid of them somehow, gave them to somebody. Then we had rabbits from Easter in a little pen in the back yard.

Editor's Note: Here's Munro's story: "When Dan got ticked off about something in the Legislature that could be fixed in five minutes by Lenny Sawyer or Augie Mardesich, he would say, 'Oh those two turkeys will never get that done' or 'Those two turkeys won't be able to figure that out...' So this big party was coming up. I think it was Dan's 50th birthday. I called the Agriculture Department and asked them where I could buy the two biggest live turkeys in the state. They told me about a ranch up on the Skagit River someplace. The guy was coming down this way anyhow so he said that he would even deliver them. They were HUGE. I paid $35 apiece for them. They were there in time for the party, but Dan's plane broke down in the South Pacific someplace and everything had to go on hold for 24 hours. I drove up to the Mansion the next day in my truck and carried in four steel fence posts and a roll of chicken wire. Outside in the back yard I built a little pen. The governor was supposed to arrive at 7 p.m. from SeaTac, if I remember correctly, so about 6 p.m. I took over the two turkeys and put them in the pen along with a sign 'Happy Birthday from Lenny and Augie.' When the governor arrived, he was dead tired. But Nancy and Mrs. Bell appeared as Playboy bunnies. We had one hell of a party, then I announced that Speaker Len Sawyer and Majority Leader Mardesich had arrived to bring greetings. We all went out in the backyard to see Lenny and Augie. Everyone cracked up. The next morning about 5 a.m. my phone rang at home. It was the governor saying, 'Get those damn turkeys out of my yard!' They are gobbling like hell out there.' "

Hughes: With that menagerie at the Governor's Mansion, the footage of Michelle and Barack Obama and their girls with that new puppy must have put a smile on your face.

Evans: We had a puppy except it was never little.

Hughes: That's Peggy the Irish Wolfhound?

Evans: That's Peggy, and she was marvelous; she was a great dog.

Hughes: The pictures of that dog are pretty amazing. How did you come by Peggy?

Evans: We had a friend who was head of Pacific Northwest Bell here in Seattle. They had just bought a puppy, their second Irish Wolfhound. And then he was sent to New York to the headquarters to be vice-president of AT&T. So he called one day and said, "Would you like a puppy?" And I thought, "Oh, that is a lot to take on with everything else we've got."

Hughes: This is early in the going—1965 or so.

Evans: Yes. They lived in Woodway, up in North Seattle. And we went up to their house and there was this puppy. Well, I say "puppy," but it was never small. They had an end table by one of the sofas and she used to always go under it until suddenly she couldn't go under it, so she would carry the table with her! (laughing) They showed me a yard stick where they measured at her hip. Literally in one week she would grow that much, and eventually she was going to be "this big." And I thought, "Oh boy, that's a lot." But we just fell in love with her. And of course we said, "Sure, we'll take her." We did not name her. She was already a Peggy. "Peggy O'Neil of Glochamora," something like that. She was a pure bred. So we brought Peggy to the Mansion and she became everybody's friend because she was so friendly. Sometimes too friendly. Her tail would bruise my mother's leg because it was so big and heavy. When Bruce was a baby, she came running toward him one time and knocked the toddler right over. She would put her paws right on my shoulders and look me in the eye.

Hughes: That's a big dog.

Evans: She was a *big* dog. She was always out on the front porch greeting people. People would say, "How's Peggy?" And then they'd add, "And how's your mother? How are the kids?"

Yeah, she was a great dog.

Hughes: How long did Peggy live?

Evans: Twelve years. That's a long time for a big dog like that.

Hughes: Three livewire sons, lots of pets and Grandma "Gom." What an amazing place the mansion was. For the record, do I understand that in the beginning your mother said, "I'll stay for only six months"? Is that a true quote?

Evans: It's a true quote. Dan asked her to come live with us during the campaign, but she said, "No, I don't believe in living with my children." Finally he said, "OK. Will you come for six months? Get us through the Legislature?" And she said, "Yes. I'll come for six months but then I'm heading back to Spokane." She stayed for Christmas because that made sense. Why go home and be alone? And fortunately, there was a wonderful group of older women in Olympia. They just befriended her right away.

These were wonderful active women, some widows, some not. They enjoyed each other and had fun together. So she made, in some ways, better friends here than she had in Spokane at that time.

Hughes: Talk about Heaven sent. Who were some of those ladies?

Evans: Dorothy Donworth was one. Her husband Charles was a Supreme Court justice. Another was Miggs, the wife of Volney Gaudette, who was with Rainier Bank. She needle-pointed two pillows for us that are in the living room. Mrs. Jean Richards was another of Mother's new friends. Her husband was with the bank as well. One of my favorites was Katy Barbey. Her husband had been a very well-known Navy admiral in World War II. Every time she came she had a dirty joke to tell us. She had her eyes done at 82.

Hughes: Wow.

Evans: Oh, these were great women. And they had this Saturday lunch bunch. Every Saturday at 10 or 11 they'd go out to Arnie's at Tumwater.

Hughes: Oh, Arnold Ball. Good chef.

Evans: He was our caterer a lot. But my mother and the other ladies, they'd just talk and giggle and have a great time. So Mother made a lot of good friends and she was very busy, very active. She enjoyed having all the young people around too—Dan's friends. So she just stayed on.

Hughes: For Dan Evans, that's the flip side of the "mother-in law from hell"—to have a mother-in-law like your mother.

Evans: It wasn't that she always agreed with us. And sometimes I think it was harder for *me* to have her there than it was for Dan because we were two strong women. (laughing) And she would often say, "Nancy, I don't think he should be doing this," or something like that, and I would get very defensive.

Hughes: "I'm a grown-up now, Mother!"

Evans: That's exactly right. So we had our moments. But it was wonderful because Dan and I were gone a lot. And I know it was harder for Mother, in a way, because our oldest son at that age grew to be, sort of, you know, into mischief—not that they all couldn't get into mischief. Three

Washington's first family with Peggy, their Irish Wolfhound. *Washington State Library*

boys together get into mischief with each other *all the time.*

Hughes: Are those boys more like Dan or more like you?

Evans: I don't know. They're wonderful young men.

Hughes: What a joy for those boys to have their grandmother there for those formative years.

Evans: It worked out really, really well. Mother obviously continued to live with us for a number of years, and as she became older and more frail and dependent on them, the boys took over the role of what she had had with them as young boys. They took care of her....But having my mother at the mansion was a *huge* help and it really is what made it possible for me to not go crazy. (laughing) And she was also very sensible. Any sensibility I have I learned from her. She was very practical, and when I wasn't around she tried to keep things orderly, as much as she could with the kids. So she was a lifesaver.

Hughes: Your dad was in his fifties when you were born in 1933, wasn't he?

Evans: Yes. He was 55. He was a very proud man, my mother said, and she was not jubilant!

Hughes: That's hilarious. I remember my mom and my Aunt Phyllis were both pregnant at about 43 in 1954. And I can still see my mom and my aunt sitting in her kitchen. They were both smoking up a storm—both pregnant, smoking. My aunt was drinking a can of Oly, and they were just sitting there in their shorts and smocks, both huge with child. How things have changed. Nobody thought anything of smoking and drinking during pregnancy.

Evans: No, of course not. I didn't smoke then, but that was very typical, absolutely. Speaking of being fat and pregnant, I was huge.

Hughes: For the record, I didn't say anything about you being fat and pregnant!

Evans: But I was huge with Bruce, because he was a 10-and-a-quarter-pound baby. He was tall and big, and he was *late*. It was August and it was *extremely* warm and hot. And I remember I was sitting upstairs in the Mansion in a shift that I had that fit me, just a sleeveless cotton thing that just went straight down. And Peggy was in heat. The trooper called up and said, "Mrs. Evans, Peggy got out!" So I went out. I was in bare feet. I still remember this so well. …I was on the east lawn, way on the east side of the capitol, over by Capitol Boulevard, chasing this enormous dog, "Peggy! Peggy! Come here, Peggy! *Peggy!*!" And Peggy was just—she was free. Of course, no dog could handle her, she was so big. No *male* dog around in the neighborhood. And there I was, furious, uncomfortable and chasing her around. And she wouldn't behave. And off the freeway came my husband and (his State Patrol aide) Bill Lathrop, who was driving. It was on a weekend, Sunday afternoon I think. Dan saw me and rolled down the window and waved. And they right went on. And I was *so* mad at him! When he came strolling in, I said, "Didn't you see the turmoil I had out there?"

Hughes: That's just too good to be true.

Evans: There was no dignity! Me pregnant chasing the dog in heat.

There was no State Patrol guard post when the Evans moved in. Note the "Caution, Children at Play" sign to the right. *Washington State Archives*

Hughes: Where was your mother?

Evans: Well, she might have been someplace. I don't know where mother was or where the boys were, I have no idea.

Hughes: How old was mom at this time? She might have helped you chase Peggy.

Evans: She lived to 94. *(Editor's Note: Lilith J. Bell died in 1987.)*

Hughes: Was grandma there at the Mansion for the full 12 years Dan was governor?

Evans: Yes, and then at Evergreen when he was college president, the full six or seven years.

Hughes: That's a lovely story about the role reversal and the boys taking care of "Gom."

I forgot that the job of being president of The Evergreen State College came with a house as well. I always liked Mike Lowry's line when he greeted editors and publishers at the Mansion, "We're enjoying public housing."

Evans: That's what we used to always joke about. We always live in "public housing" wherever we go.

Hughes: In the Governor's Mansion, is the master bedroom something special? Is there any special bedroom like the Lincoln Bedroom at the White House or fascinating lore associated with a particular room?

Evans: Well, the bedroom we had is not the Governor's Bedroom now. It's all been redone since we were there. I think of the new Governor's Bedroom that we enjoyed for a year.

Hughes: What a gyp! You did all that work, then you moved out.

Evans: I know. It was so pretty. And the fabric was just gorgeous. It was a nice room.

Hughes: I understand that one hot summer's day you were scooting around in shorts when you encountered some touring taxpayers who just wandered in.

Evans: The front door was open so I could get some cool air in. And of course we didn't have the guards like they do now.

Hughes: And no air conditioning?

Evans: No. And I was just coming down the stairs and here were two people standing inside the house. And I was startled: "Oh! Can I help you?" And they were very nice. They said, "Well, we thought this was open and can we just tour?" And I said, "Oh, I'm sorry. No, you cannot because our family is here." They were very nice, and very embarrassed. I felt sorry for them because I knew that they were feeling silly. They just wandered in.

Hughes: I gather that you really tried to make that a normal kind of place so the neighborhood kids could come in and they could play trains and race cars with your boys.

Evans: Oh yes. You talked about seeing Legos at the Lockes—We had Legos in the Ballroom and those fast tracks that go around, with the miniature race cars. But I would tell them one thing: "Boys, no basketballs, no footballs in here." Well, by golly not too long ago I came across a picture of our eldest son with a basketball in the Ballroom. I had said, "Only Nerf balls." Well, it was not. It was a real basketball. But by and large there were toys everywhere, and tricycles. They were all in there. Danny, our oldest son, was in a Cub Scout group, and we had the Christmas party at the Mansion.

They sang Christmas carols. It was fun. Yes, we did all those things.

Hughes: Well, you were remarking that there wasn't a State Patrol cadet guardhouse down at the end of the drive in those days. What kind of security did you have then?

Evans: When we first moved into the Mansion it was not long after John Kennedy had been assassinated. So there was a new awareness of issues of that nature, sort of like what happened after 9/11. And we had two children. The yard was large, so there's a lot of places to get lost. On the side of the house there is a grassy area and then quite a bank that goes down to the water. We actually set up sort of a large play pen. There was a fence on that grassy area, which was silly because we never really used it much as it turned out. But at the time we thought they could play out there together and occupy themselves, and leave toys out there. There was one retired policeman, I believe he was, who they brought in during the day for some security. There was no guard house. What security there was used the bathroom down in the basement. Then the State Patrol became involved as this awareness grew.

Eventually they had a cadet for security. Then they had two of them. They would take shifts. In the back of the house there was a garage where we kept our car because we always had our own car as well. Then they built a little annex off of that for security. Years later, we learned all the tricks that our boys played on them, and all the things they taught our kids, which we had no idea about at the time. They were all kids, you know. These cadets were all 19, 20 years old. Six feet tall, but they're young and having a good time.

Hughes: So, could you still get in the car and drive down to the Thriftway?

Evans: Absolutely. I did that a lot.

Hughes: And how about if you wanted to go off on a weekend? Did you have State Patrol security?

Evans: It depended on what we were doing. Will Bachofner was the chief of the State Patrol for many years. And right after the election—the next day practically—he assigned Bill Lathrop to be Dan's driver. Bill became Dan's best friend. He was wonderful. He and Dan hit it off right away. Bill was just so painstakingly helpful, and careful, and so honest. He would do it like it's got to be done, but he also would just do everything possible to accommodate us in every way. And then they assigned a patrolman for my use. A year later maybe. But if I was going to Seattle, which I did a fair amount for functions, then I would be driven. I can remember getting into the car—the same car that Mrs. Rosellini had used. I was sitting in the back seat and riding home to Olympia. I happened to look over there on the upholstery that was behind the side window, and here are all these corsage pins stuck in there. You'd get a corsage wherever you would go, and you'd get in the car, and you'd take it off.

Hughes: That's funny.

Evans: But I would just hop in the car and just go. If we'd go to a friend's house for dinner, we would just drive. But they were fussier about Dan, understandably, so he did not drive himself. They said, "What if you're in an accident?" Obviously, being governor, you would be on the front page everywhere, even if it's not your fault, all those complexities. So he was driven everywhere. We went up to Crystal Mountain to go skiing every other weekend pretty much in the winter time. And they wanted somebody to be driving because we would get home late from skiing on a Sunday night. So one of the State Patrolmen learned how to ski, and of course he loved it.

Hughes: That's tough duty.

Evans: But if we would go on vacation they wouldn't come with us at all. When our oldest son was in kindergarten, one of the men who helped clean the house would drive him up to school. But then the kids got older and walked to school. That was not an issue. It was just nothing like today. Will Bachofner, the chief, called one day and said, "Mrs. Evans, can I come over for

Chief Will Bachofner.
Washington State Patrol

lunch someday?" And I said, "Sure." He added, "With you and the governor?" And I said, "Sure, come on over." We were sitting at a little table in what's now the library—a card table—and he said, "I need to talk to you about your security. Mrs. Evans, we really would prefer that you just not hop into your car and drive wherever you're going." And I said, "Well, I can't do that. I just can't do that. I know you feel responsible, but I'm going to go wherever I want to go."

Hughes: And he never really tried to countermand that?

Evans: He couldn't.

Hughes: Will Bachofner was a good guy, by all accounts.

Evans: He was wonderful. By the book. Everything was by the book.

Hughes: I'm told that the chief hardly ever drank. And yet he'd prowl around town at night during the Legislature, from the Tyee to downtown, just to see what was going on.

Evans: I think probably his one vice, if you could call it that, was horse racing. I don't know that he gambled that much. But he loved the horse races. And he had a wonderful wife.

Hughes: In 1965, when you and Dan moved into the Mansion, you were quite a young woman. And your whole era as first lady was a transitional time in the way women felt about themselves and asserted themselves, and some of the trappings of what we used to call "society." *The Aberdeen Daily World*, the *Tacoma News Tribune*, every paper, had a "society" section. There would be a lot of detailed write-ups, even in small dailies, about guilds and sororities and all that sort of thing. One of the controversies I remember that really burbled in the early 1970s was courtesy titles. When the longtime society editor of *The Aberdeen World* retired and a new woman came on—a much younger woman—she decided it would be a lot more egalitarian if "Mrs. Daniel J. Evans" became "Nancy Evans." Some women were just enraged. They liked going by their husband's names. We got a lot of flack over that.

Evans: I'm sure you did.

Hughes: Did you see some of that in the expectations for what you should be—and in your own feelings about yourself?

Dan and Nancy try out the governor's chair for the first time. *Washington State Archives*

Evans: Well, then as things changed even more I became just "Evans." "Evans" did this, and "Evans" did that.

Hughes: Is that jarring at all to you?

Evans: No, not really. I think at the time I was part of that transition. I was brought up with the notion that you called older people "Mrs." or whatever courtesy title.

Hughes: So until you got to really know her, would you have called Mrs. Joe Gandy "Mrs. Gandy"?

Evans: Oh yes. And she was that kind of a person, without knowing it.

She was not trying to be that way at all, but she was a very proper person. Later, we were "Laurene" and "Nancy." But always older people were "Mrs." or "Mr." by and large. But I wanted to be called Nancy because I was younger.

Hughes: The times were a-changing.

Evans: Well, for the most part…And I said, "Please call me 'Nancy,'" when they kept calling me "Mrs. Evans." It just seemed easier—and easier to talk that way somehow.

Hughes: Beyond the volunteers and good Republican cabinet wives, did you have any kind of help in keeping up with correspondence? Like a deputy press secretary who would help you?

Evans: Well, when I first arrived there was nothing. No help of that kind. But it didn't take me very long to realize that I needed somebody. I had in those days a lot of requests for recipes. Every organization was putting together a cookbook. We had a lot of, "What's the governor's favorite whatever?"

Hughes: What was his favorite recipe?

Nancy examines a new cookbook. *Washington State Archives*

Evans: Oh, I don't know. But they would suggest an area. And so I put together a fair amount of those. But I was getting a lot of requests for use of the Mansion, or asking me to go someplace. So finally a woman from the governor's staff would come over twice a week for an hour or two. And we would sit upstairs in a tiny little sitting room and she would take notes. That went on for a year, maybe two years, and I thought, "This isn't going to do it." So I insisted that I had to have some help. And we got, from the state, a half-time secretary. That's just what I needed. She ended up working pretty much full-time, but they paid for half-time. She was great. I had two of them. But the one I had for a long, long time, Warrene Graves, was unflappable and always worked more than her half-time pay allowed. She was very easy to work with. Her husband was a patrolman.

Hughes: Was Neil McReynolds the governor's press secretary from the get-go?

Evans: No. He was the second.

Hughes: Who was the first?

Evans: Wayne Jacobi. He wrote for *The Seattle Times*, I believe. He was there a couple of years, and then Neil came on, and then Jay Fredericksen.

Hughes: So over the years, you got to visit the White House, and Pat Nixon and Betty Ford both visited you at the Governor's Mansion. Did they tell you any stories that the White House wasn't really all it was cracked up to be either?

Evans: No, you didn't get into that sort of discussion. Besides, they keep very good care of the White House. ...I remember visiting when the Nixons were there, but particularly it was the Johnsons who would open up the White House more when they had dinners there. We were allowed to go upstairs into the private quarters.

Hughes: I read that about Lady Bird (Johnson). Very hospitable.

Evans: And we did go upstairs. I remember one time it was so surprising to me because we were on our own. We would just wander. Obviously if the door was closed you didn't open it. But I went into the Queens' Bedroom, where many royal guests have stayed, and then the Lincoln

Bedroom. I was in the Lincoln Bedroom all by myself because nobody happened to be in there at the time. I remember thinking, "This is wonderful just to be in this room all by myself." I just stood there for a minute, then quietly went around the room and looked at everything and tried to put it in my mind as a picture. So that was fun.

Hughes: Meantime, back home in Olympia, when did you finally get some traction in making the Legislature understand that this was not a very satisfactory living arrangement?

Evans: Well, something *had to be done.* Dan tried to get money for a significant remodel, and the addition of some private spaces. They hired an architect, put a design together. I believe it was a very good design. Then the numbers came in and the Legislature wouldn't do it. Dan afterwards regretted not having been stronger on it and insisting. But it just didn't happen.

And then as things got worse I thought of the idea of forming a foundation and doing it privately—not the remodel of the house, but furnishings, that sort of thing. I visited Don Foster, a lovely man who had the Don Foster Gallery down in Pioneer Square. (Now Foster/White Gallery.) He and Dick White had a lot of wonderful artists they represented. He suggested I contact Jean Jongeward, the best interior designer in Seattle. He said, "You've got to have her" because she was really talented. I called her and said, "We can't pay you a lot of money" and all of that. So we worked out a deal. She volunteered her time and very often gave us her (wholesale) prices on things.

Editor's Note: When she died in 2000 at the age of 83, *The Seattle Times* noted, "Jean Jongeward, the elegant designer whom clients and colleagues called 'Seattle's queen of design,' built a national reputation for originality, patronage of local artists and decades of influence in Northwest homes and businesses. Largely self-taught, with a background in accessorizing model rooms for the old Frederick & Nelson store, she worked with top regional architects and helped establish the Northwest style."

Jean was very generous. She was very, very good. So for starters she redid Mark's room, which had been flowery for one of the Rosellini daughters, as well as Bruce's room. In 1965 when we moved in nothing major had been done in large part to the Mansion since it opened all those years ago. Much of the furniture was the furniture that Mrs. Hay bought in 1908 from Frederick & Nelson. It was late Victorian style, so it's heavy. The State Dining Room was furnished completely in this furniture. Mrs. Rosellini had bought a few other pieces, like in the drawing room there was a little settee that was a little more modern—not contemporary, but newer, sort of Italian-style almost. And I know this because, as I mentioned earlier, Mrs. Langlie came down to visit me and we went around and identified pieces. Governor Hay's daughter also came down. She didn't grow up in the Mansion, because she was grown when her father was elected governor, but she had visited her parents. And then Mrs. Rosellini also was very helpful in identifying things of that nature to me. So I did a lot of research. The wall-to-wall carpet that was in the front hall and going up the stairs was the same that had been put in in the '30s by the governor from Spokane, Clarence Martin.

I can remember our oldest son, Danny, when he was in about the second grade had a friend over who lived in the neighborhood. I did not know it but the boy's father was a carpet layer. I was standing there, and the boy said, "Gee Mrs. Evans, you need to get my father over here." And I said, "Why?" And he said, "Your carpets are really old! Look at your stairs, how worn they are. He'll lay some nice carpet on those stairs." You know, the edges were all white with threads.

Hughes: What did you say?

Evans: "You're absolutely right. I'd like to do that."

Upstairs, on one end of the house, there were two bedrooms, the governor's and the first lady's, originally for Mrs. Martin. It was done in pink brocade, silk brocade, with light blue fringe, only it had all faded to grey. That became Bruce's room. It had a dressing table with a curtain and a tall white 18th Century-style highboy with painted flowers. It was lovely.

The foyer of the Mansion in 1970. *Washington State Archives*

The room had a fireplace, too. But everything was very faded. The threads were worn on the bedspread. So things like that had not changed over the years. There were three other bedrooms at the other end and then one in the hall.

Hughes: So everybody had a bedroom.

Evans: Oh yes. They all had bedrooms. And those rooms had been redone for the Rosellini children. One was very flowery, and one was for their youngest son, Albert, so that was sort of a boy's bedroom. Then there was another room that was sort of flowery, too, and that was Mother's. It was a big bedroom.

You asked earlier about some of the things that led to discomfort. The heating system was very bad. There were two thermostats in the entire house. One was in the State Dining Room—and I say the "State Dining Room" because that's what we called it, but there was no other dining room.

Hughes: Is the State Dining Room the one that has the little balcony for musicians?

Evans: No, that's the Ballroom. It's just behind that. The other thermostat was in the hallway on the second floor. And when the Cabinet Wives that I discussed earlier would come over and help address all our Christmas cards—we sent out several thousand every year—we'd all freeze. All those names and addresses were on card files, 3x5 cards. And one of the women would organize it all. Then we would set up tables in the Ballroom.

Hughes: I like the Christmas card that shows your three boys sitting on a driftwood snag with their legs dangling.

Evans: Well, that's one of our favorites. My mother was shocked that we would print that picture with the holes in the knees of the jeans. That was up at Dinner Island in the San Juans. And there were lots of logs, and it was just a picture we just happened to take one day.

Hughes: I think they look like real kids.

Evans: Well they were—they were real kids. ...But we would be addressing Christmas cards and we'd plug in the coffee pot. We had big 50-pot urns, and that would blow a fuse and then the heat would go out, or the electricity would go out. So we would unplug the coffee pots and go down into the basement again to change a fuse. The women would all be sitting in their overcoats because it was so cold. We took pictures of them. Then we would plug in the electric heaters, and that would blow the fuses

Governor and Mrs. Daniel J. Evans

Bruce Mark Danny

Dan and Nancy's 1972 Christmas card. Grandma "Gom" thought it looked bad that the boys' jeans were patched. But Nancy said it showed they were real boys.
The Legacy Project collection

again. I mean that's the way life was there. For the first couple years we lived there, all of us had colds—all of us just all the time because we were living in this cold old house. And then at one point in time something happened to the plumbing and when you would sit on a toilet the water was warm.

Hughes: Well, at least that had to be pleasant! (laughing)

Evans: You could warm your bottom! (laughing) So there were a lot of maintenance issues that had not been taken care of either, over the years.

Hughes: Looking back, in 1974 you were telling the AP, "The first two winters we literally froze."

Evans: Well, that's a little dramatic. But it was cold.

Hughes: Then you recalled Dan climbing onto the roof on Christmas Day 1973. Is that a true story?

Evans: That's a true story. Water is pouring into the ballroom. All our families are there. We have lots of kids and lots of people, and it's just pouring in. He was telling someone about that not too long ago. And as he said, dumb him, he went up there and was looking around, trying to figure out where it was coming in. But then he thought later, "It doesn't come in this way, it travels." It was actually coming in from the dining room area and then over into the ballroom. We had buckets all over. It was just pouring down. And of course this is Christmas and nobody is around that you can call.

Hughes: You've got a leaky roof, a creaky staircase and the threadbare carpet. Did you ever grab some legislators and legislators' spouses and say, "For Pete's sake, we need to do something here."

Evans: A little later I did.

Hughes: But early in the going you made do.

Evans: You go with what you have.

Hughes: What was it like working with Jean Jongeward?

Evans: We got along *very* well. But we had our fights—not fights, but disagreements about things. She was not always practical, as designers can be very easily. It's understandable. And I kept saying, "Jean, we've got thousands of people who are coming through here every day. We've got to be practical about fabrics and treatments and different things." It wasn't so much style we disagreed about, it was practicality. I remember she was so excited one day. We were in the drawing room and she had some sample fabrics for the drapes, which the state was paying for, as well as (samples of) the tassels that went on it. And she was very excited because she finally found what she had been looking for, and she spent a lot of time looking for these things. Dan came home, probably for lunch. She was starting to tell him about the drapes, and he was just aghast at the cost. I had been not discussing it with him because I knew he would blow a stack. He asked, "So how much is one of those tassels, Jean?" And she told him. I forget the cost. And he said, "And how many are you going to use?" I could see the wheels turning in his head, "And that's X thousands of dollars." Then he said, "We can't do that, Jean!" Well, we worked it out.

Hughes: Sticker shock.

Evans: Yes, *oh*, big time. . . . Then eventually we did our bedroom as well, and that was a very pleasant change. But then the public rooms in the Governor's Mansion just needed a lot of work. . . . There was this dark green wall-to-wall carpet as you walked in that went all the way to the ballroom and up the stairs with the thread showing on the risers. Then hanging on the doors that went into the ballroom were these very, very faded pink silk drapes.

Hughes: How ghastly.

Evans: They *were* ghastly. And then in the ballroom on each of the doors and the windows were the same things. Over the Palladian window at the end of the ballroom there was this heavy pink brocade cover. It was all done in the 1930s. And there was all this fringe.

Hughes: Who knows how much dust was in all that stuff.

Evans: Exactly. It was dirty. And then there was the State Dining Room. There was no place to eat other than the State Dining Room, other than a little butler's pantry that was off the kitchen where there was a round little white table that had been painted many times. There were three chairs in there because four wouldn't fit. That's where we ate breakfast. Family dinners were in the big State Dining Room, which is a very large, formal dining room. And so there were a lot of things that needed attention. And we needed a more comfortable living room. That's when Dan first talked about an architect—Ibsen Nelsen was his name. We hired him and he drew up a wonderful plan (for renovation of the Mansion). Unfortunately the Legislature didn't provide the funds. And we often think it would have been *so* much cheaper if they had approved that plan (in 1966).

Hughes: Did you have some pretty strong ideas of your own about design and decorating? Is that something that sort of came naturally, that you knew what you liked and then you got smarter?

Evans: I got smarter, that's for sure. But I certainly wasn't knowledgeable. But, yes, I knew what I liked and didn't like. I had some ideas. But from working with the architect earlier I also learned about the style of the house and things of that nature. And I continued to learn a lot as time went on.

Hughes: I'll bet that was really a lot of fun for you.

Evans: Well, it was. So then I decided to form the foundation. But who to pick to head it? I talked to some people who suggested Laurene Gandy, who I told you about earlier. Her husband had dropped out of the 1964 governor's race to back Dan. Laurene was fairly recently widowed. I had met her and knew her, but only slightly. So I asked her if she could head the foundation. She said she had to think about it, which I understood. Then she accepted, and she turned out to be just the best choice I could have made because she was very wise and she had great taste and knowledge. But she also had time for the project and she knew people. Jean drew up drawings of the sort of furnishings we were looking for. Then Dan and I started thinking about trying again to have the house remodeled at the same time. But the foundation was organized before the redo of the Mansion. It was functioning well. Laurene Gandy and I put together sort of a dog-and-pony show. That's what we called it. We drove to Spokane, drove to Yakima, all different places talking about the project, making friends and putting together a group of people, especially trying

Sitting room at the Mansion. *Washington State Archives*

to build support in Seattle, the I-5 corridor here. Then something would come along that was just wonderful and we'd say, "Look at this! Isn't it exciting?" And then something else would come along to keep us going. We kept finding wonderful things and gaining momentum. But I knew right from the get-go that I could not be the one who would say yes or no to donations of furniture and artwork because people were coming to me and saying, "Well, I have this wonderful little glass dish," or this lamp, or whatever. Somebody else would say, "Well, I have Aunt Sophie's tablecloth that would be just perfect!" So we set up a committee of people with real knowledge of furnishings to handle acquisitions or "acceptances." And we also organized the foundation it in a way that the first lady is only an honorary member. I didn't want to be the one who was saying no or always making the big decisions. The foundation had to be something that would last after I was long gone. For the acquisitions committee, we had a wonderful woman in charge of that, Marie Edwards. She used to be the buyer for the Old World Shop at Frederick & Nelson's. She was very knowledgeable, and I also enjoyed her tremendously.

Hughes: Were there any furnishings, any paintings that were really special from the original Mansion collection?

Evans: There really was not a lot. The paintings were mostly prints. And there were a few nice pieces of furniture, but not very much. The furnishings were primarily this late Victorian style and none of it really fit the Georgian design of the house. We decided the State Dining Room furniture was worth keeping. It was all Frederick & Nelson furniture from the original 1908 purchase. The table itself would have been so hard to replace because it would have been so expensive—just because of the size of the room and the size of the table. We decided just to keep that room the way it was because it was so completely furnished. As nice-looking as it was, the furniture that Mrs. Rosellini had brought in did not fit in any way to the house. Marie and Jean went to Washington, D.C., Philadelphia and New York together to visit dealers and look for antiques with the money that we were raising.

Hughes: Nancy didn't go along?

Evans: Oh, no, no, no. Just the two of them. I didn't have the expertise at all. And when they came home they had things they had acquired and pictures of things they wanted to acquire. So we could show people, "We need X number of dollars to buy this. Would you be interested in making a donation?" That sort of thing. On the trip, they purchased some light fixtures with crystals on them to go on the mantel and on some tables, and one of them arrived missing some crystals. So we called back to see if they found the crystals. They had, but they also said, "We just got this call from a customer of ours in Connecticut." She had a lovely demilune (crescent moon-shaped) server, and she told the appraiser, "I'd like to give it to some worthy organization that is poor." We certainly qualified as a poor foundation at that time. And he said, "Well, we just had two women in here from the State of Washington," which to her was probably—

Hughes: The Wild West!

Evans: Exactly. And he said, "They might be interested in it." So they contacted Jean or Marie and sent this picture of a gorgeous piece that was by far the loveliest thing that we had seen. We said, "We'll take it!" It now sits just off the entry hall in the Mansion. John Seymour was the builder— a very prestigious cabinetmaker. It's all inlaid. It's lovely.

Hughes: I wonder what that's worth.

Evans: Oh, quite a lot, I'm sure. But they really were very successful in what they found back there on that trip. Those are the pieces that are in the Mansion now. And their value has increased tremendously.

Hughes: Don't you love watching "Antiques Road Show" with those obligatory moments when the appraiser says, "Do you have any idea what this is worth?"

Evans: Yes, exactly. "I paid $300."…"Well it's $30,000 now!"

Hughes: Back to architecture and engineering: Tell me about the celebrated "Dan Evans & Sons" tree house at the Mansion. Where was that located?

Evans: Well, as you approach the Mansion, up the right side of the drive, right at the top of the drive there was a big, old wonderful maple tree. I think the residue is still there. Mark was about 5 when they built it, so

Dan's second inauguration in 1969. Mark had broken his leg while skiing. Looking on, at left, is Grandma "Gom"—Lilith Bell. *Washington State Archives*

they were about 2, 5 and 8—something like that. And Dan thought, "Oh, we'll build a tree house." Because it was one of those wonderful forked trees. Dan loves projects like that. So they all worked on it. It turned out to be a *really* expensive tree house. But, boy did they have fun. We put some boards, lathes on the trunk going up one side so they could step up to it. But it also had a trap door with a pole running to the ground. So you could go that way or you could put the trap door up. One weekend, I remember *very* well—the kids were playing in it. The trap door was open and Mark fell down and cracked his head. Everything happened on the weekends when the doctors are not around. We dashed to the hospital. He had a big gouge, and blood was all over. I was holding him in my arms and Dan was driving furiously to the hospital. It ended up causing some sort of nerve damage. He was having some trouble coordinating for a while. Not really too visible, but a problem. So we ended up making a number of trips to Children's Hospital in Seattle. It worked its way out with no residual effects, but it was very expensive treatment. But they all had a lot of fun with that tree house. When Governor Ray moved in, she took it down almost immediately.

Hughes: We'll skip ahead for a moment to 1976. Did you have any meetings with Dixy when she and Marion Reid, her sister, were getting

Governor Dixy Lee Ray.
Washington State Archives

ready to move in? Dixy wasn't married, so her sister was the "first lady."

Evans: Oh yes, I met with Marion.

Hughes: So Marion came by, but not Dixy Lee?

Evans: Not at that time. I was there once, maybe two weeks after we were out of there. The Governor's Foundation wanted me to come back and do some tapings. It put together a film. And I said, "Well, I'd be happy to if Mrs. Reid would be happy to let me come." So that was fine, and I went down, and we did the tapings. And I think we were through and it was getting to be noon-ish. The governor was coming home for lunch, and Marion invited me to stay for lunch, which was very nice.

Hughes: Interesting. Dixy had her beloved dogs. That poodle that Dixy Lee Ray had was not a nice dog in my experience.

Evans: No, it was not a nice dog.

Hughes: It peed all over everywhere.

Evans: *Everywhere*. The rugs—the poor Foundation people, they were having such troubles with the carpets. I heard all about it.

Hughes: What was your impression of Dixy Lee Ray?

Evans: She was an interesting person. And certainly a well educated and smart person. But for some reason, despite the fact that Dan had not run against her, she did not like my husband. And that became very obvious. And I've never figured it out. And Dan doesn't know exactly why either. Dan did some very nice things for her in a parting gesture. He sent a bottle of champagne sitting in ice in the silver cooler on a silver tray from the silver service from the *USS Olympia*. The silver service resides in the Mansion. It was to be there when she arrived in the Governor's Office with a personal note of good will. I said, "I wish you wouldn't do that," not because of her but because I didn't think the silver should be out of the Mansion. Well, he did have the champagne delivered and there was no acknowledgment by her. Everything that he tried to do nice was just dismissed. And we don't know why. There was no reason for the animosity. We never understood it.

Hughes: How strange. That's very sad.

Evans: It is sad.

Hughes: Dixy just had a tin ear when it came to politics. She might have been brilliant but she was not a good politician.

Evans: Well, I think that there were things maybe in her life that impacted that. I don't know. She had lost touch with the ability to work with people and to respect people. But we never understood, and it was disappointing, frankly.

Hughes: At the Mansion did you have a number of overnight guests who were dignitaries?

Evans: The house, until we redid it, was not equipped for guests.

Hughes: Interesting that Harry Truman stayed there overnight all those years ago.

Evans: Probably there was not a (deluxe) hotel in Olympia at that time....But in our era we had the Tyee, which was pretty spiffy and fairly new. But we had family visit us—a lot of family. Every major holiday we had both the Evans and the Bell families. People would come from wherever, Idaho, Oregon, and they would come and stay with us, particularly at Christmastime. We would just put all of the children up on the third floor and give our kids' rooms up to whomever.... However, I was reminded of one house guest when we were down in Olympia in February (of 2009) when Bill Gates Sr. was receiving one of the awards—

Hughes: The Medal of Merit.

Evans: Dan had suggested him as a recipient. He's a very good friend, and we wanted to be there. When we were walking over to the Mansion afterwards for the reception, I was walking over with Trey and Libby, Bill's son and daughter. I'm sorry...I'm referring to Bill Gates III. We call him "Trey."

Hughes: I don't know Bill Gates III.

Evans: That's the head of Microsoft! He's Bill Gates III.

Hughes: He's not "junior"—he's the "third"?

Evans: Our friend Bill is "Bill Jr." His famous son is Bill III.

Hughes: I did not know that.

Evans: Now they call Bill Jr. "senior." But Trey has been "Trey" since he was a child because he had the same name....In fact when people today are talking about Bill Gates, I don't think of Trey, I think of Bill, his father. My mind goes to Bill and not to Microsoft. He has become "senior" now to separate himself from his son.

Hughes: I met the father, the son and the new Mrs. Gates at that reception.

Evans: Mimi.

Hughes: She was very down-to-earth, and I thought that Bill, the dad, was absolutely old-shoe charming.

Evans: He's wonderful. He's accomplished so much in his career and yet, is so down to earth and such a good friend.

Hughes: It was the first time I'd ever met "Trey."…He seemed like a classic computer guy.

Evans: Really? I'm so used to being around him because we've known him since he was a child. We've been really good friends for a long time.

Hughes: So when this kid was buzzing around underfoot, could you see signs that he was a genius?

Evans: You knew that he was different, and he was discussing very heady stuff at an early age—absolutely. But anyway, we were walking up the driveway to the Mansion for the reception for his father. We were identifying ourselves to the cadet, and Trey said, "Nancy, do you remember when I was a page down here?" I'd forgotten about that. He was selected to be a page in the Legislature, and so Mary, his mother, called and asked if he could stay with us. And I said, "Sure." When Trey mentioned it, it came back to me, and I said, "I *do* remember. You came down with Paul Capeloto." The Capelotos are part of our bridge club, and they're all neighbors. They grew up together here in Laurelhurst. And Trey said, "Well, Paul was only here a week. I was here *three* weeks."

The thing I most remember is that at that time we had one empty bedroom. Paul and Trey shared a double bed for a week. We didn't see a lot of them because they were over in the Capitol a lot. But I remember one night we were sitting upstairs in the tiny room that was the upstairs sitting room at that time. It was literally a room about 12x12. Not big enough for a sofa. It had a love seat, a TV and a couple of chairs. That was it. We were sitting up there watching TV. And Trey came up the stairs and popped his head in the door. I said, "Hi Trey, come on in and sit down." And he said, "Thanks. But I'm going to go to my room because I'm not allowed to watch TV during the week." Mary Gates was sort of the family disciplinarian.

She did not want to have him watching TV. My kids are like that now, but actually we didn't watch that much. It wasn't a big thing in those days with our family. But I remember looking at my family and thinking, "Oh my goodness—here we are on a weeknight watching TV," and Trey went off to his room. But then as we were walking up the driveway to the Mansion, Trey said something else that I had totally forgotten. He said, "You and Dan left and went somewhere, and I was alone in this Mansion." The whole family left. I guess we went on vacation. "And so I was alone in the Mansion with the help for a week and a half."

Hughes: What a great story. So, what kind of a kid was the future Microsoft billionaire?

Evans: He was interesting. A very smart young man. I can remember one night we went over to Bill and Mary's. We were all going out to dinner or something. Mary wasn't quite ready. And Mary said, "Trey, why don't you tell Dan and Nancy what you've been doing." So Trey, Dan and I are in the living room. He was in about the sixth grade, seventh grade maybe, and he stood up and he said, "Well, my friend and I have decided to form a group that will get together and discuss issues that are happening in the world today. And each week we take a subject and read about it, research it, and then discuss it."

Hughes: Did you turn to Dan that night and say, "Trey is going to be really somebody some day"?

Evans: Well, you knew that he was. I also have many memories of the wonderful bridge club we were in. Mary and Bill Gates founded it before I knew them—sort of out-of-college, newlyweds. These were all married people. I think the club started as four couples, just two tables, and it evolved over a period of years. (Future U.S. Senator) Brock and Betty Adams were part of that bridge club early on. Then people would move. Brock went back East, and people moved to California, or whatever. Then they'd bring another couple in.

Evans: We did not know these people back then in the early years of the club....But in the mid-'60s we were up at Crystal Mountain, and they all were up there skiing, the members of this bridge club. They had rented some condos—very small ones—and they invited us to join them for dinner. Bill and Mary's condo bedroom was like ours. It was two bunks and a trundle underneath, so three bunks on each side and then maybe four feet in between them. So we all sat on the floor because that was the only place that we could sit for dinner. We put down towels and sat around. We knew them by now, but we weren't part of the bridge club, and didn't even know much about the bridge club. It was after that, I think, that the bridge club people who didn't know us were just seeing if they liked us. It was like rush at sorority. Before long they asked us if we would like to join. And we said, "Yes, we would love to" because we loved to play bridge. There ended up being 12 us who would get together once a month at everybody's home. We would rotate around....We were all good friends. And you'd draw for partners. You never knew that evening who your partner was going to be—your husband, or another woman, or a man. Then we would total up the score at the end of the evening. And then we'd have dessert and coffee and go home.

It got so that some of the same people were always winning and some of the same people were always losing. Then on the fifth month the losers would give a dinner for us all. Every time we came to play bridge we would bring five dollars. Bill Gates had a sock that he would bring and the money would go into that sock. The losers would take that money and have dinner for the rest of us, the other 10 people. So it was a lot of fun. We really became very, very, very good friends, all of us.

Hughes: It's really easy to see that with Bill Gates Sr. He put me at ease instantly and we were meeting for the first time.

Evans: Oh yeah. He's a lovely, lovely person. He truly is. At any rate, I need to finish this story that I started....It's just been in the last two years that some of our members have died. Mary Gates died, and then when Mimi married Bill we always had an extra because she doesn't play bridge. But it always worked out because some would be traveling. And we didn't do the five dollars anymore because it would hardly cover the wine. So we just did the dinners and we tried to do different things. We had some that were just absolute classics. One that everybody remembers was a treasure hunt in downtown Seattle. It was absolutely wonderful. Bill Gates and Barbara Frederick, who is one of my dear friends, put it on because they were the losers.

But we got these same people losing and winning so we finally went to a handicap system that would equal us out a little bit more. It worked pretty well, actually, and we all had our handicaps. However, just in the last two years it's become very difficult for some of us to play bridge. So we have now, very painfully, sort of quit our bridge club. We don't play bridge anymore. It was just too hard. But we still have many of our old friends, dear friends. When the new museum opened, Bill and Mimi hosted the bridge club, and we all went there for a private tour. Then we had dinner in the restaurant afterwards.

Hughes: You're talking about the Seattle Art Museum?

Evans: Yes. And we've been to the Air & Space Museum because one of our members, Bill Helsell, is on the board there. And Barbara Frederick and I put together an outing to see *To Kill a Mockingbird* at the Rep. You know, we're always looking for things of that nature that we can do to- gether....So that's the story of our bridge club. We were in existence for a *very* long time, and with many of the same people throughout that time.

Hughes: Like "Trey," when your three boys were growing up, did they talk politics too? Were they interested in that, in terms of breakfast and dinner table talk?

Evans: Well, you've got to remember that when we left being governor our oldest was only 16.

So, yes, we did talk about politics. But you just can't do it all the time. I'll tell you what we talked about the most, and that was sports. Especially by the time we got to Evergreen, I had quite a household of sports fans. Well, mother was still with us, but there were the four boys—Dan and the three sons. Sports was just the talk every night because they *all* are big sports nuts.

Hughes: What's their favorite sport?

Evans: Our oldest's would be football because he played football in high school. They all like football. But, you name it, they like it. And I thought to myself one night, "I'm tired of listening to sports. I want to talk about something else." I saw in some magazine some word game. So I remember that I served dinner, then I sat down at the table and said, "OK, tonight we will not discuss any sports. And here is a word game." And I passed around pencils and something on paper. "This is what we're talking about tonight," I said. So we sort of started out and there was a lot of lethargy there—not a lot of excitement. They sort of stabbed at it and tried to be good sports. But pretty soon I thought, "No, this isn't working." I gave it up.

Hughes: Let's talk about the 1972 campaign when Dan was seeking a third term. You were there that fateful day when former governor Al Rosellini called your husband "Danny boy." Tell us about that.

Evans: Well, I don't remember a lot about the details except that it was a big crowd. It was at North Seattle Community College. And I just remember standing there, watching it all unfold, and when I heard Governor Rosellini refer to Dan as "Danny boy" I remember just thinking, "Oh, that's it." I just knew right away that was a mistake.

Hughes: *Big* mistake.

Evans: Yes, a big mistake.

Hughes: Did any kind of look come across Al's face, like he knew he had made a faux pas?

Evans: No, because he repeated himself. He said it again. He actually said "Danny Boy" 12 times. I'm sure he rues it to this day.

Hughes: I'll bet he does. That would be an interesting thing to ask him about. Now over the years, when all those former governors get together, I wonder if time has pasteurized out the old wounds? Do you think Dan and Al have ever talked about that sort of thing?

Evans: I don't know. I don't think they've gone back and rehashed it all. There's no sense in that. I think they just look at things today and what needs to be done today. And it would only be between Dan and Al because they ran against each other a couple times. But let's see, Booth defeated John Spellman, so I guess there could be (some baggage). But neither John nor Booth are the kind to do that. Several years ago when Booth was having his early difficulties, we became really good friends. The phone would ring at 6 or 6:30 in the morning and I knew who it was. I would pick up the phone and just say, "Hi Booth." Because with Parkinson's you often don't sleep well and you wake up very early. He would just call, and we would chat. We've become very good friends. We've also become very good friends with the Lockes, Gary and Mona. All of them. I think it's all in good feeling—goodwill, among all the former governors.

Hughes: You said that Ethel Rosellini had been really gracious to you as a young first lady. Is there sort of an unspoken rule among political women that your spouses could be involved in the hand-to-hand combat, but that women are going to be more civil to one another and sort of talk about kids and all the logistics of maintaining a home?

Evans: I don't think there's an unspoken rule. I just think it's sort of good manners. We're not fighting each other. The spouses—the wives—in this case, had no animosity. In fact, probably quite the opposite because we knew what the role entailed, and the difficulties, and responsibilities—and we appreciated that.

Hughes: Interestingly when Dan was going for that third term, in mid-October the polls, however reliable they were, had Al ahead, didn't they?

Evans: Periodically. Well, you know, as an incumbent what you're doing is more in the papers and people are more aware of it. And they'd sort of forgotten some of Al's peccadilloes, I suppose. And in fact we laugh about it now. Dan's been out of office a long, long, long, long time. And if all the people who come up to him and say, "Oh, I wish you'd run again," or, "I should have voted for you"—if they actually had, we would have won by a landslide!

Hughes: "Where were you when we needed you?"

Evans: Yes. They just forget the bad and think of the good, which is nice.

Hughes: What was the biggest and most memorable event that you had—sort of the be-all, end-all during those 12 years at the Mansion?

Evans: Oh, we had so many. I remember the first big legislative party we had that first year in '65, and I had never done that before—Where you invite the legislators and their spouses, and the cabinet members and their spouses, and the Supreme Court justices and their spouses, and office staff and their spouses, and the state elected officials and their spouses, to dinner. And I had been to one with the Rosellinis, so I had an idea of how it worked. But it's a huge crowd and everybody comes because it's during the legislative session. There was sort of a play room downstairs. Not a huge room, but I had movies going down there—a film of some sort. The scenery of Washington or something. And then we had a buffet, and a bar. We put awnings around the outside of the porches and heaters to heat it up so the bar could be out there. We had dancing and a band and the whole thing. I remember I was very nervous about that because that was a *big* production to put on. We did that, of course, every two years. We had two Christmas parties with a lot of friends and some officials. We had parties two nights in a row. That was one of my highlights because we really had a good time. And the house was all decorated. It may have been our next-to-last Christmas there.

Hughes: Did you do anything special for the holidays? Did you and Dan ever dress up

Evans family. *Washington State Archives*

in costumes for trick-or-treaters like Mike and Chris Gregoire and Gary and Mona Locke?

Evans: We did do the trick-or-treater thing. Absolutely. Jones was the name of a gentleman who worked at the Mansion and had worked there for several years before we arrived. It was his idea to put a ladder up with a sheet over it on the porch that faced the Capitol. Then we put a pumpkin that we would carve on top of that. And he had this blinking bulb that he would put in there. And all the trick-or-treaters, in those days, came right up those steps and up to that porch. Dan and I would dress in something. We had a lot of trick-or-treaters at the Mansion. Our kids would go out trick-or-treating in the neighborhood.

Hughes: Was there a cadet guard post down there by then? Or could anybody just walk up?

Evans: In the beginning, there was no gate, no fence, no nothing.... There had never been anybody down at the driveway while we were there. It was in the back of the house.

Hughes: Did you say anything special to your three boys growing up that harkens back to the kinds of things your folks inculcated in you, both sets, that they had these extra responsibilities because their dad was the governor and their mom was the first lady?

Evans: I don't think we ever put it in those terms. But we always considered it a privilege, and we always wanted them to be respectful of others who didn't have those opportunities. I hope we taught the children that. I think we did.

Hughes: What kind of boys were they?

Evans: They were very normal—full of mischief. And they're all different, of course. The boys couldn't walk by each other without punching, you know. As they got into their pre-teens and teens, they couldn't go through a door without jumping up and trying to touch the top of the door—for years!

Hughes: Some place in the Governor's Mansion are there any pencil marks on a door jamb that indicate the kids' heights?

Evans family collection

Evans: I hope they've all been painted over by now. There were a lot of nicks and bruises that the house got from our boys' activities. But then, we were just people. During the first six months we were there it was very busy because it was a legislative session. And in those days it was 60 days in the odd year. But we had *tons* of tours and teas. The first ladies for years had always had—every Wednesday—"at home" they would call them. That's a very old fashioned custom: "Mrs. Daniel J. Evans will be at home from 2 to 4 P.M."

Hughes: And if you couldn't stay or the lady of the house wasn't there, you'd leave a calling card.

Evans: Yes. But that (leaving a card) was sort of gone by the time we were there. Through the course of the first month—the first few weeks really—I realized that a lot of the people in the community of Olympia had never been in the Mansion. The mayor's wife, for one, and others I would meet. So I sent the invitations to the spouses, because this was a women's thing, of all of the officials of Thurston County and the city offices and the county offices and the service clubs and all that sort of thing, and opened it up. We ran out of cookies at the first event.

Hughes: I bet that made a big hit.

Evans: It was a good thing to do, but it really jammed us up. In those days, they called it Children's Orthopedic Hospital, which is now Children's Hospital. And once a year in May I had a tea at the Mansion to benefit the hospital. And because people were curious about us many people came. The first year always has the most interest in your administration. I forget how many we had for the first one. But it was a *hot* day. I remember that. And we stood at the front door greeting people. It just was huge! So that first June, Dan said, "Well, let's look at the guest book and see how many people have signed." And we had had 10,000 people that we had fed something to. So these are not just people who came in to tour or for a brief meeting. It was 10,000 people in six months.

Hughes: Every time I go to the Mansion I like to look at Harry S. Truman's signature. And you said that one of the boys wrote his name in the guest book. Which son was it?

Evans: Danny. Our oldest because he was old enough to write.

Hughes: You found out he had written his name in there?

Evans: A lot! (laughing)

Hughes: So it's Harry S. Truman and Daniel J. Evans Jr.

Evans: Well, he didn't go back to those pages (where Truman signed). But as you kept turning the pages they had his contribution. He had signed his name several times.

Hughes: I want to ask you about a story I heard about the Evans kids turning up in their jammies on the musicians' balcony during a fancy dinner at the Mansion.

Evans: Yes. (smiling) That happened. It was during a Japanese trade mission, and it was one of my disasters. They had just arrived in Seattle, I think. And then they bused down to Olympia for a dinner. So they were tired. And I made a mistake with the dinner. I had been to Japan, but I just wasn't smart enough to (plan the menu accordingly). At that time, many dinners featured prime rib. That was sort of a luxury, you know. So that's what we had.

I can also remember that we were trying to find some little gifts for them because they're so wonderful about gifts of some sort. I tried to find some little inexpensive items—we had no budget for any purchases—some little something that we could put at their places that would be reminiscent of their trip to Washington State. And somebody said, "Oh, we've found it. It's just great." They were little carved and painted totem poles, and they weren't expensive. And I thought, "Oh, that's perfect." So they brought them over. I turned one over and they were made in Japan!

Hughes: Of course!

Evans: So that went out the window. I don't know what we ended up with. But our guests all came down, and in those days we had long cocktail hours. It was a way of entertaining that I inherited and that I carried on. We got better at it later on, shortened them oftentimes.

Hughes: Today it would be called a wine hour. The alcohol content of the wine is a lot lower than the martini.

Evans: Well, we served juices and other things as well because that's really primarily what they drank. But it went on too long, you know; it just went on too long. Then we sat down in the ballroom for dinner. And I looked around and realized nobody was eating the meat. The Japanese people were not eating. The Americans were, of course. They just went through their plates. But prime rib was not something very appetizing to the Japanese. Some of them ate some of it, or picked at it. But a big piece of rare, red meat is not to their liking. Then I noticed that everybody was sort of giggling. And I thought, "What are we giggling at?" And I noticed

A reception with Japanese Prime Minister Eisaku Sato and his wife, Hiroko Sato, November 12, 1967. *Washington State Archives*

they were looking up. I looked up and there were our boys, standing at the balcony looking down. They had been put to bed but they were not *in* bed anymore. All the people thought it was cute, of course. And so I went up and took them and put them back up in bed. *(see photo on page 124)*

Hughes: Did your boys ever do any von Trapp children kind of parlor tricks—have a little musical or anything like that?

Evans: No, no, no.

Hughes: Never played guitar?

Evans: Not with anybody around, no.

Hughes: Those kids just look so normal to me. That's an amazing achievement that you two pulled off.

Evans: Well, they're normal in good and bad ways.

Hughes: Sure. But most people would think that there would have been a lot more problems with the kids putting on airs or saying, "My old man's the governor..."

Evans: I'm sure they did that. I'm sure they tried that—particularly the oldest and middle son (Dan Jr. and Mark). The youngest one (Bruce), I just think he sort of just tagged along, went with the flow for a lot of it just because he was so much younger.

Hughes: Yeah, he's the classic kid brother, isn't he?

Evans: Exactly. I recall that Danny was selling cans of honey-sugared nuts for the YMCA or the Scouts—they were really good too. I think it was for the YMCA because he was doing swimming there, or something, taking swimming classes. And he went over to the Governor's Office. Well, of course, who is going to say no to the governor's son? And then he went around to Lud Kramer's office at the Secretary of State. He went around to all the places he knew, and he was selling all these nuts. I wasn't really aware of it. Finally, I found out and I called up and I said, "Tell everybody they *do not have to buy* these nuts from this child."

Hughes: That's funny.

Evans: He was taking advantage. I think probably he went there because he knew the people; he didn't really think it was taking advantage, but he actually was.

Hughes: So could the boys just walk in and see their dad?

Evans: Well, not that casually. You know, they were busy, too. They were in school and what have you. But they would go over there occasionally. And they had fun around there. When they were very young, shortly after we moved in, on the backside of the Capitol there were steps that lead up with marble sides that they would get on and slide down. It just made me very nervous because there were sharp edges everywhere and no sides. They just thought that was such fun. And I really worked hard at telling them they could not do that.

Hughes: Is it true, as it has been written, that Nancy Evans once delivered her son's *Olympian* paper route one day?

Evans: Well, I don't think it was just one day.

Hughes: Really? Which son was that?

Evans: This is Mark, our middle son. He was very enterprising. He was the one who would save his money and be careful about how he spent it. I won't go into comparing children. But what was he, 11 or 12? Something like that. And so he decided he wanted a paper route. But occasionally he was sick, and I'd fill in. Dan did it too, at various times. We knew the route. It was down towards town, part commercial, part residential. And Mark was young, you know, and he'd sort of forget sometimes. We'd get the complaint that "We didn't get our paper." And we'd have to run down there and deliver a paper. Dan was helpful because he got a clipboard and made a chart, a map, or a list on how to proceed through it. Then he put see-through cellophane or something over it to protect it from the rain. After that we didn't get so many complaints.

Hughes: Now that's what I call management expertise.

Evans: Yes. And Dan and I both filled in when necessary. But Mark did it, and got his money, and saved it, and it was good.

Hughes: You know, I keep thinking: Nancy Bell grows up in Spokane during the Depression, with a great mom and dad, and a loving family, and she has a lot of common sense. Then she's a music teacher. Then six years later you're first lady. Did you learn all this management moxie to run that Mansion through on-the-job training?

Evans: I think so, yes.

Hughes: Well, you did manage those Christmas pageants at school.

Evans: Yes I did!

Hughes: I read that you, and I think Dan, too, are both people who like to read in bed and stay up late.

Evans: Yes. Still. I cannot go to bed and turn off the light.

Hughes: Are you reading a book or are you watching Jay Leno?

Evans: Usually the TV isn't even on. We read and do *New York Times* puzzles, or Sudoku.

Hughes: Were there a lot of times during those 12 years he was governor that Dan would come home and say, "You're not going to believe what they did to me today"?

Evans: Well, yeah, occasionally, sure. Sometimes we'd have those discussions—not necessarily in bed.

Hughes: What time were you getting up in the morning if you're staying up late?

Evans: Fairly early because the kids went to school.

Hughes: I found out that you are a good writer.

Evans: No, I'm not!

Hughes: Well, in 1966 you wrote a really good piece for *Puget Soundings*, whatever that was.

Evans: Oh, that was sort of an eight-page paper, a weekly. And it was like what you might find on the Internet today—like "Crosscut," which I subscribe to.

Hughes: Well, I thought you wrote a really good piece for *Puget Soundings*. It says, "When asked what it was like to be the wife of the governor, I used to reply that it's really no different than being the wife of any man. I now have changed my answer and say that it's really no different than being the wife of any hard-working, never home, usually tired, sometimes depressed, responsibility-laden man. And I have no doubt that in these modern times most wives would include themselves in that that same category." And then there's this wonderful story you tell: "Almost every morning when my husband is breakfasting with our two sons and is about to leave for the Capitol, our youngest son Mark, who is two-and-a-half, asks, 'Are you going to the capitol daddy?' And Dan replies, 'Yes.' Knowing that the next question will be, 'Are you coming back daddy?' It sounds a little fatalistic, but I'm sure it must seem to Mark that his daddy does not come back for many days, as often he does not return until long after the boys are in bed. And sometimes, of course, he does not return for several days. And then I think, 'What a shame he can't spend more time with his father.' Only to be caught short as I'm preparing to go somewhere and Mark asks me, 'Are you coming home mommy?'"

Evans: Aaahhhh. (smiles at the memory)

Hughes: And you said, "Don't tell me I'm gone that much, too."

Evans: We're going back east to visit Mark and Bruce in a couple weeks and I should take that back. Mark works in Boston. His wife did too when she was working. And he's an hour plus each way, on the train. And then he drives from the station home. And he gets home at 7:30, 8, 8:30, *always*. And I should remind him of that. He's repeating (what his father and mother did).

Hughes: Tell us about that first big trip that you took on your own. If I recall correctly the Legislature was in overtime in 1965 and Dan couldn't get away to go.

Evans: It was a wonderful trip, but I didn't want to go alone. It was a trade mission to Asia, and it had been planned for some time. I think the

HOME FROM THE WARS

A cartoon from the 1960s. *Washington State Library*

planning started with Governor Rosellini because you have to notify the countries you're visiting, and all that. It takes a lot of time. And we had both planned to go. My brother, Bill, at that time was working with the State Department of Commerce. So he was going too. And he was taking his wife, Tina, my sister-in-law. We were like sisters. And we also took Mother. We paid for that. We knew it would be a treat for her. And Dan's parents came down to Olympia to the Mansion to stay with the kids. Dan couldn't go because the Legislature just wouldn't adjourn. I was young and had never been away on a trip like that, and certainly never away from my children for three weeks. I did not want to go without Dan. I remember I was just distraught. And he said, "No, you go, and you'll have a good time." And then the question was "who was the leader of the delegation?" No, not I.

Hughes: Really?

Evans: It was sort of a quiet duel between the Mayor of Seattle, Gordon Clinton, and Lud Kramer, who was the Secretary of State. It was very important mostly to the Japanese when we were in Japan, to know who the leader was because that's the person you defer to and you sit at the right place at the tables, and on and on—all the protocol that was involved. And they didn't quite know what to do. I feel sorry about that in retrospect. But at any rate, I went off on this trip with the delegation, and of course had a marvelous time.

I became *very* good friends with Governor Kanai of Hyogo Prefecture— that's our sister state—and Mrs. Kanai. I had some memorable side trips with Mrs. Kanai, who spoke no English. She was just the most wonderful woman. I just loved her. We had an interpreter who spoke beautiful English and who had spent time in America, so understood Americans. They were both so dignified in their carriage and everything they did. And they loved Mother and Tina. So we three women went along with them on side trips. I remember the beautiful garden in Hyogo, in Kobe, where the azaleas and the rhodies were all in bloom. They had this tea ceremony. If you've ever had a tea ceremony you know they're a wonderful, beautiful thing to watch, but the tea is just terrible. It looks like split pea soup, but tastes awful. Mrs.

Kanai at that time had to be in her sixties, and I was so much younger, but we corresponded until she died. She learned to write a little English on her Christmas cards. Enough to say, "Hello…" But at any rate, Mrs. Kanai had knelt down at the tea ceremony. And the woman who was the interpreter knelt down. I knelt down for a while. And Mother said, "I cannot kneel." My mother was in her seventies. And so she said, "You'll just have to excuse me." That's the way Mother was. And of course, Mrs. Kanai couldn't have been more charming. She said, "You sit however you want." But they all kneel. So mother sort of just did this thing, sitting like this. And we watched, and it was a wonderful thing to observe this ancient ritual as this tea master was doing the tea ceremony for us. Pretty soon, however, I'm numb—totally numb from the waist down. I finally said, "Mrs. Kanai, forgive me, but I can't kneel any longer." It was an hour, hour and a half, and these two women were kneeling the entire time because they had done it from childhood. We were all just in agony. Pretty soon I'm like this (fidgeting). So I remember that very well. But they were wonderfully gracious. A lot of wonderful little things happened on that trip. But when we came to Hong Kong, it was near the end of the trip, and I was very lonesome for Dan and the children. There had been an earthquake (back home). Well, that scared me.

Hughes: That was a big quake in 1965.

Evans: Absolutely, yes. Now we think nothing of calling home, from wherever we are. Well, in those days it was just not like that. And I didn't have the knowledge even to figure out how to make a long-distance call like that. But I wasn't the first to hear of the earthquake. So somebody in our delegation called home and found out that everybody was fine. I got a chance to talk to Dan briefly, but I was practically in tears. And of course the hotel room was full of people. But there we were in Hong Kong, and I was going home early. My brother Bill had had to go on and do something—so Mother and Tina were staying a little longer than I was.

Before I left, Dan and I had gotten traveler's checks. We split them up. Each of us had signed half. So now I went off with only half of the traveler's checks. The delegation has disbanded, so to speak. I take a taxi to the airport, and I have all these gifts because everywhere we went we were given something, including a bottle of sake. Some of them were little things, some were *not* so little. Also, I had gifts that I was taking back to people. So I go to check in, and my luggage is over weight. I have way too much. I'm standing there in Hong Kong explaining to the fellow at the Northwest Airlines desk that these are not personal things; these are gifts that were given to my husband, who is an official, but is not here, blah, blah, blah, blah, blah…. I had bought Dan a very expensive Bolex 8mm movie projector. This was my gift because we had an 8mm movie camera in those days. I was carrying that as well, and it was big and heavy. I was distraught because I didn't have the money to pay them this extra amount (for being overweight). I called Tina and Mother at the hotel and said, "Do you have any money?" Well, they did, but of course they were getting short, too. It was all traveler's checks in those days. So they came out to the airport early. Tina who had grown up in Italy—she was beautiful, just gorgeous—took charge. She comes out there with her bundles of things, and her sake. She was so much smarter than I am because she said to the (airport counter staff), "Here, can I give you the bottle of sake? Will that take care of it?" Well, of course, that took care of it!

Hughes: Adventures in Diplomacy 101.

Evans: But it didn't occur to me! So I got on the plane and flew off with all my stuff. But now I'm down to zero: I have no money. I have a ticket and that is it. We go to Tokyo before flying to Anchorage, before flying to Seattle. We had to change planes, and I'm walking off the plane in Tokyo, saying to myself, "Oh, please, please, *please* don't ask for any more." I saw a man standing at the bottom of the ramp, a long hallway, and I think, "Oh please, are you from Northwest Airlines? Are you looking for *me*?" And he comes up and says, "Mrs. Evans?" I said, "*Yes.*" And he said, "Come with me." And everything was fine. So then I sat there for the change-over, and got on the plane to Anchorage feeling so relieved because now I'm going to be heading home and I don't need the money.

We landed at Anchorage to get fuel and I went into the airport to call a college friend who lived there. I bought *The Seattle P-I* and took it with me on the plane to read. Finally, I get on the plane and open the paper, and I read, "Governor's son seriously ill and in the hospital." And I couldn't speak. I just could *not* speak. The stewardess came over and said, "Is anything wrong?" I couldn't speak and I was just (motioning)…I remember just pointing to the article and finally I said, *"That's my son."* So they stopped warming up the engines, or whatever they were doing at that point. They brought a car out and took me back into the airport so I could call home. I called Dan's office collect. Ruthie Yoneyama, who was a wonderful, wonderful receptionist, answered. Everybody liked Ruthie, and still do, because she recognized everybody's voice.

Hughes: The trait of a great receptionist.

Evans: Oh yes. It didn't matter who you were, she knew you. But Ruthie says, "Hi Nancy." Then to the operator, "Will we accept a collect call?" She was being funny. "I don't know." And I said, *"Ruthie,* accept this call!" And she said, "OK." I said, "Put me through to Dan," who was *also* being silly and saying, "Well, I don't know. You're calling collect." And I said, *"Dan, how's Danny!"* Well by that time he was out of the hospital and home. And he was fine. It was some strange virus or something. And I was just trembling and in tears. But everything was fine, I found out.

Hughes: Three weeks on the road and you pick up *The P-I* and read this shocker.

Evans: Dan didn't know why I was calling, or anything about this article in the paper. So I felt better after that call. Then they took me back out to the plane and we took off and came to Seattle.

Hughes: It was pretty uneventful after that.

Evans: (Laughing) Yes, it sure was. That was my three-week adventure. That was my foray into diplomacy.

Hughes: Have you been to Russia?

Evans: Yes.

Hughes: I haven't been to Russia but I've been on delegations welcoming Russian ships. The obligatory thing is to drink toasts, and if you try to keep pace with them they'll drink you right under the table.

Evans: Well, there's a secret I learned on one trip. When we first arrived, it was lunch, and there was this round of the vodka in little shot glasses. You don't want to drink it down because when it's empty they will replenish your supply. It didn't take us long to realize that when they come around you put your hand over the glass because they're actually pouring water into the hosts' glasses and vodka into your glasses.

Hughes: Did you ever get served anything that was just incredibly ghastly that your hosts expected you to eat—watching closely to see how you handled yourselves?

Evans: I remember it was that first trip to Japan. It was the Bank of Tokyo dinner, and they served many courses. One was a fish. A *whole* fish. A little fish, like a smelt, but it was bigger than a smelt because I love smelts. Mrs. Kanai, bless her heart, was sitting right here on my right. They were all eating the whole fish. And I said, "Mrs. Kanai, I cannot eat the head." And she said, "I perfectly understand. It's like when you serve whole chickens. We don't like whole chickens." Now they like pieces of chicken, not the whole carcass. Just eating a whole roast chicken is very bad to them. In China there were a lot of (unappetizing) things we encountered. I loved a lot of the food, but a lot of it was parts of the rooster that you don't want to know about. One time when we were in Pakistan there had been an avalanche so we couldn't go back to our village on the road. That's a whole other story. But I'm sitting, on my own, in this little village way up high in the mountains because Dan had gone up to the border between Pakistan and Afghanistan.

Hughes: What year was this?

Evans: This was in the 1980s. And man walked by carrying a whole cow's head. He had been to the market and he was carrying this home for dinner.

Hughes: Yummy.…Well, let's talk about domestic relations. Dan was the keynote speaker for the 1968 Republican National Convention in Miami Beach. That must have been incredibly exciting. Before that, had you met the Rockefellers and Reagans or the Nixons?

Evans: Oh yes, we had. Each year the governors had a governors' conference in D.C., in January or February. Then the president had a dinner for the governors and their spouses. So we had been there and had met them. And on other occasions too, campaigns or whatever. Dan would go back to meet with them on different things.

Hughes: So you met the Reagans and the Rockefellers?

Evans: They had been governors together, so we met them a lot.

Hughes: Anybody who really impressed you?—where you thought, "Here I am. Nancy from Spokane, and we're traveling in some different circles now"?

Evans: Sure. We met people with capabilities and intelligence—the ability to do things and enact things. They got to where they were for that reason. Each year there would be a (national) governors' conference; then there was a Western Governors' Conference. The Western governors tended to be closer because they had similar issues, water and land, that sort of thing. We became really very good friends with about four or five governors. In fact we would all get together on different occasions.

Hughes: Who were some of those?

Evans: It was the governors of Wyoming, Utah—Republicans *and* Democrats by the way. They weren't all one party—Idaho, and Oregon.

Hughes: Paul Laxalt of Nevada was in office then. Was he an impressive guy?

Evans: He was. And we got to know them. He went on to serve in the U.S. Senate at the same time as Dan, and Paul's wife Carol came to the Senate wives' functions.

Hughes: So you met the Reagans early on there, too?

Evans: When they were governors together. Dan was elected in 1964 and Reagan was elected in 1966. You know, Washington is one of the few states that elects governors in presidential years.

Hughes: At that 1968 convention there was already the buzz about Reagan as a potential presidential candidate. What was your impression of Ronald Reagan?

Evans: Reagan was very easy to be around. He was very no-nonsense, very pleasant. He wasn't full of himself in any way. He was very nice to be with, and everybody liked him—Republican/Democrat, it made no difference. He was just a very likeable person.

Hughes: How about Nancy Reagan?

Evans: She was a little more up tight. But she was always very nice to me.

Hughes: Tell us about this photo. Nancy Evans is wearing a very sensible Red Cross smock, and Nancy Reagan looks like she's wearing a Chanel suit that probably cost about $10,000.

Evans: That's exactly what it is. Well, Dan was in the U.S. Senate and the Reagans were in the White House. Every year the First Lady gave the Senate wives a lunch at the White House. And in return the Senate wives—organized initially as a Red Cross group, which was sort of a misnomer—gave the first lady a lunch. It took a lot of planning. I learned a lot. Some of these women were just remarkable in what they would put together. I'm not a party planner. They were. They would get donations for good causes. I couldn't believe the things that they found and got stores to give. I mean it was amazing. This was at the Botanical Gardens and it had a French outdoor theme. But Nancy and I were old friends because we had known each other as governors' wives. But I had this Red Cross outfit. You could either buy the dress or you could buy the apron. Well, for $2 I bought the apron. I wasn't going to wear the cotton Red Cross dress ever. We were supposed to wear whatever

Two Nancys: First Lady Nancy Reagan poses with Nancy Evans at a Congressional wives luncheon in 1986. Nancy Evans felt silly wearing her Red Cross volunteer's apron, while the First Lady was dressed to the nines. *Evans family album*

Nancy with other Senate wives on Nancy Reagan's
First Lady's Luncheon committee, 1986. *Evans family album*

Red Cross thing we had, and then of course we would take pictures with
the First Lady. I was giggling because I felt so silly in that dumb outfit.

Hughes: I don't think I'm telling any tales out of school when I tell
you that Jay Fredericksen (the governor's press secretary in 1973) told me
that one time you told him you thought it was a little bit over the top the
way she looked at Ronnie, like he sort of walked on water. I mean they
were gaga in love.

Evans: Oh absolutely. And you knew that it was very real. But you're on
the stage so much in front of people and you listen to your husband speak
so many times. I could give Dan's speeches—I'd heard them so often. But
you have to look somewhat attentive, and she always seemed to overdo it.

Hughes: Of those people you met at the governors' conferences, who
were the most enduring of the friendships—people you really felt like you
could really let your hair down around?

Evans: The governors of Idaho and Utah, who were both Democrats,
(Cecil Andrus and Calvin Rampton) were very good friends. And in
Wyoming it was a Republican, Stan Hathaway, and in Oregon, Republican
Tom McCall, who we enjoyed knowing.

Hughes: Speaking of nonpartisan, in the same era in our state, it was the Jacksons and the Magnusons—two Democratic powers in the U.S. Senate. Did you get to know them as well?

Evans: Yes, we did.…Helen Jackson and Jermaine Magnuson. I remember one time, it was during one of the governor's conferences in D.C., and Mrs. Magnuson very kindly invited me ahead of time to have lunch with some friends. I thought that was very nice. I think we had lunch in the Senate dining room. I'm not sure about that. Then we had a private tour of the National Cathedral, which was lovely because some of these women were not only members of that church—that's where large events happen in D.C., funerals and other events—a few of them had done the needlepoint on the kneeling benches. So we had a really wonderful tour of the building. And then, she had a car and a driver because of Maggie's role in the Senate. I remember we were driving up on the north side of the White House and Bobby Kennedy was walking on the street. He was going to get a cab and go back up to the Capitol. We stopped and she said, "Bobby, do you want a ride?" And he said, "Sure." So he got in the back seat with me and we went up to the Capitol. He was very pleasant. Little things like that happen a lot when you're in D.C.

Hughes: Did you kind of just take that in stride or did you ever find yourself star-struck?

Evans: Sure, you get star-struck but it doesn't stay with you for long. King Hussein of Jordan was just one of the most charming men I've ever met. I was star struck!

Hughes: Speaking flawless English, with a gorgeous wife.

Evans: And I had lunch with him when Dan was in the Senate. His wife was in America at the time we were in Jordan. He was just one of the most charming people I've ever known.

Hughes: I heard his son interviewed on NPR the other day and he sounds like he's out the same bolt of cloth.

Evans: Absolutely. Well, it was interesting because one of his younger sons—Queen Noor's sons—was with him at this lunch. He was probably five or six years old, and he was just the most *delightful* little boy. "Giggle,

giggle, giggle." They sat right next to me. It was a very informal lunch. Very nice. He was just the most charming man and so nice to talk to. Here was this father and his son having the best time at this diplomatic lunch. It was in a minister's home so it wasn't in a hotel or some official place. They were avid skiers, so we talked about skiing. He would look right into my eyes and say, "Well, ma'am." Everything preceded by, "Well ma'am." So that lunch was a highlight in my life because of the king and his presence, but also his wit and his humor and his obvious love for his son….His eyes never left your eyes. Paul Newman was one of those. He never took his eyes off your eyes when he was talking to you. He was not looking around to see who was there. He was looking at you, which was very disarming.

Hughes: Do you remember when it was that Dan got the word he was going to be the keynoter for the 1968 National Republican Convention? That was a big deal. He's on the cover of *Time* magazine.

Evans: Yes, it was a big deal. He was very pleased to be selected and spent a lot of time on the speech. Normally he would write his own speeches…

Hughes: Really? Dan Evans would write his own speeches?

Evans: Yes. He had very few written for him, very few. It's a full-time job now. But Dan didn't have a speech writer. A lot of his talks were in Seattle. And he would sit in the back of the car on the way up, with a piece of paper and just make notes. He could do that very well. But for that keynote speech, and for like the opening of the Legislature, he would have some help. The person who helped is still a very good friend of ours—Jim Lane. He was in advertising, with a big firm. He went back to Chicago, Australia, and back to New York, then retired back here. But he wrote well. For that one (the keynote) Dan had help and input. As it turned out, that was the one National Republican Convention that I went to—and I would *never* go to another one.

Hughes: Because?

Evans: Well, I think they've changed, but it was just over the top to me. There's just all these people in these silly outfits, and silly hats, and silly buttons all over, and fans and feathers—you name it, banners and signs.

Hughes: The $64,000 question is whether you got any special allowance from the Republican National Committee, like Sarah Palin, when Dan was the keynoter?

Evans: No, no, no...

Hughes: No clothing allowance?

Evans: No, no. No money for clothes. I can remember once when mini-skirts were everywhere. So that was then?

Hughes: 1968.

Evans: But I didn't like mini-skirts. And Dan hated them because he'd stand up at the head

Dan makes the cover of *Time* magazine.
The Legacy Project Collection

table of whatever, giving a speech, and he'd say, "It's terrible. You don't know where to look because women, and even older women sometimes, are sitting in a way that they shouldn't be sitting" in mini-skirts that were riding up and what have you. But it wasn't for me. But sometimes I did sort of (wear a shorter skirt) because you feel old if it's down here (motioning to below the knees). So I was wearing one sort of just above the knee. And my picture was taken and it was in the paper. I was at the Mansion greeting somebody. And a man—*I know it was a man*—sent it back and drew a line where my skirt line *should* be. And he said, "This is where your skirt should come to. Not up to where it is. And it's shameful that the governor's wife would wear that." And most women were up to here, you know. So I wasn't that immodest.

Hughes: The '68 convention is in Miami, isn't it?

Evans: This is in Miami, and I'm not a fan of Miami. But there was a lot of stuff going on. It was just crowds, crowds, crowds. And Dan gave his speech way too late at night. We had been sitting in this hot room all day long with the speeches droning on and on and on. The speech was delayed for West Coast audiences, so the conventioneers were tired, restless and noisy. Actually, it was a good speech to the television audience, but in the convention hall itself people were talking and it was noisy. *(Editor's note: There were 17,000 people in the Convention Hall.)* And I'm sitting there and thinking, "Be quiet and listen!" It was a speech that was praised by a lot of people, a lot of the press—the *national* press. He got a lot of good press on it. But the *local* press (got a different impression) because on TV they'd shoot around the room to show the women with these silly hats on doing silly things. Then they'd go back to Dan for a few seconds, before showing images of some men doing silly things.

Hughes: I picked up on a piece that Dave Brewster wrote in 1972 in the *Argus*. He was recalling the 1968 convention and "The Perils of Political Virtue": "Scene: The Beau Rivage Hotel, Miami Beach…It's 1 a.m. and Dan Evans sits in his hotel room shortly after giving the disastrously over-rehearsed keynote address that put the convention to sleep." The story proceeded to talk about Dan's decision to endorse Rockefeller for president when most everyone was telling him the political thing to do would be to endorse Nixon. I sent a snippet of this story to Dan, and l think I sent it to you.

Evans: Yes, you did.

Hughes: Dan told me, "David Brewster's article…is partly accurate but with a high percentage of fiction."

Evans: I remember I read it to him, but I can't remember now what was wrong about it.

Hughes: Well I think it was the part about the "disastrously over-rehearsed keynote address."

Evans: Well, if you read it you would think it was good, because he was talking about things that now are still issues. And he was looking ahead about what we need to do about civility and shared goals. It was really quite forward looking for the Republican Party at that time. But it was 11 o'clock at night back there and it had been a long day.

Evans: As for "over-rehearsed"—he had 20 minutes in the auditorium for the first time using a Teleprompter. Those were very new in those days. And he had never used one. So he had a little time to practice on that, and that was it.

Hughes: Brewster also wrote in that same piece: "This is the archetypal Evans' moment revealing the perils of political virtue. As Evans sounded out the room, the advice to endorse Richard Nixon was unanimous. That afternoon Nixon's staff had informed the Evans men that the Washington governor was high on the list of vice-presidential prospects *if* he endorsed Nixon. Typically, Evans kept his staff in the dark about his decision and retired at 4 a.m. The next morning Evans picked up a stack of telegrams from the financial backers for his own 1968 re-election campaign. They said one thing: 'Go for Nixon. A shoo-in, or else.' A few hours later Evans announced his endorsement of Nelson Rockefeller, arguing simply that his keynote address had named domestic matters as the nation's top priority, and Rocky was stronger in this suit.'" Does that jibe with your memories?

Evans: Mmmhhh.

Hughes: Before Dan decided to endorse Rockefeller, another progressive, did you talk about that a lot? Did he say, "Oh Nancy, they're telling me I could be vice-presidential material."

Evans: Being vice-president had *nothing* to do with it. It was purely philosophy. He did not support Nixon and he did like Nelson Rockefeller. It was as simple as that.

Hughes: But the hubbub over the possibility of a vice-presidential spot. Is that something that you talked about?

Evans: Well, yes, you can't ignore it. It happened again in 1976 when Jerry Ford was president and that got a little further along, actually. In fact we were vacationing in Montana with our sons at a friend's cabin up in Glacier Park—a grade school friend of mine. Pretty soon a plane was coming into where we were—and we were *remote. (GOP operatives were arriving to check out Evans as a possible vice presidential candidate.)*

Hughes: I'd forgotten that the boomlet for Dan as a vice-presidential candidate was a lot stronger in 1976 with Gerald Ford than in 1968 with Nixon. Did you get to know the Fords pretty well?

Evans: No, not real well. You don't get to know any of these people really well. But we certainly had pleasant times together.

Hughes: But there were Secret Service people sniffing around, doing the obligatory background checks, vetting Dan as a possible running mate for Ford?

Evans: He was asked to put together his background, which he did. That was not an easy task. We read in the paper that Steve Ford, the Fords' youngest son, said he was for Dan as VP.

Hughes: To me, it's quite remarkable—whether it was 1968, '72 or '76—that Dan didn't end up on the ticket. The only thing he didn't have going for him is that we're not exactly a populous state.

Evans: Well, I think that's a big issue. We're not Texas. We're not New York. We're not California.

Hughes: No, it's not Kennedy needing LBJ to help carry Texas, a crucial state.

Evans: And we don't carry that many electoral votes and the whole thing. I know that when Bob Dole was chosen as the vice-presidential candidate Dan said, "I know I'd be a better candidate than he is." I ended up liking Bob a lot. But at that time when he was chosen he was very sarcastic.

Hughes: Sharp tongue.

Evans: We traveled with him later when Dan was in the Senate and he was not that way. But earlier we went to some things for him here and there, and he just turned me off. And the voters too, obviously. I don't think he helped the ticket at all. I think Dan probably might have been a better choice.

Hughes: Would Dan have taken that if offered?

Evans: I think so. Sure. The vice-presidency would have been a wonderful experience, absolutely.

Hughes: FDR's first vice-president, John Nance Garner, once remarked that the vice-presidency "is not worth a pitcher of warm spit."

Evans: "A pitcher of warm spit"—that's right.

Hughes: Actually he didn't say "spit." They bowdlerized that a little bit….One of the great political parlor games is "there but for fortune." Spiro Agnew, who got the spot on the ticket with Nixon in 1968, turns out to be a tax cheater.

Evans: Yeah, he was a disaster.

Hughes: And Richard Nixon is bugging phones and keeping an enemies list. He resigns over Watergate and Agnew is gone, too. Did you ever think about that, I mean…

Evans: "What if?" you mean?

Hughes: Well, "what if?" indeed. Dan could have been president. It could have happened to you, and you're so *normal*—the only way you've ever been. How refreshing it is to find out that Nancy Evans is just really Nancy.

Evans: No other choice.

Hughes: Not a choice. And why is that?

Evans: You say "Nancy is Nancy." Well, that's who I am.

Hughes: I know, but I've interviewed Nancys who are no longer Nancys because they became celebrities.

Evans: Yes, well, you know it's a danger. It's easy to get absorbed in whatever life you're doing without remembering how you got there—why you are there. It's very easy to do. I know when Dan was in the Senate and we moved to D.C. there were a lot of social things going on *all* the time, particularly with the Senate. And it's very formal there. Women dress up *all* the time. I had to buy new clothes. And it's very hot and muggy. But there were a lot of evening social affairs and what have you. And the Senate wives get together. And there's a lot of deference paid to elected officials back there, to senators particularly. And I say particularly because there

Nancy and Dan on the campaign trail. *Evans family album*

are 535 members of Congress and 100 of them are senators. You go to a lot of embassies and on and on and on and on. So you can quickly forget who you are and where you come from. And some of them do. It's understandable. I tried very hard *not* to. It's always been what I prefer to do. But my oldest sister, my *wise* older sister Barbara, came back to visit one time and she could see all of this going on. And she said, "Don't let yourself get so involved and forget who you are and why you're here." And I said, "Well, I hope I don't." She said, "Well, I can see that it would be easy for you to get that way." So I tried very hard not to. . . . But it's just so insidious that you're not even aware that it's happening to you. You just expect, "Of course I can do that. I can do whatever I want because my husband is a U.S. Senator." So I was often surprised at some of the senators' wives who were there for a long time—some are still there—and what services they expected to have provided for *them* in the Capitol, for instance. And *they* were not the senators.

Hughes: I got the feeling from the times I was around Mrs. Jackson that she was a lot like Nancy Evans.

Evans: Helen Jackson is a lovely, lovely lady—a lovely person. You're right.

Hughes: Speaking of remembering who you are and where you're from, Jay Fredericksen told me that on the first trip he ever took to New York with you two when he became press secretary that the Rockefellers had you and the other Republican governors and spouses up to their penthouse. And the next day when he saw you he asked, "What did you think?" And you said, *"They've got a Picasso in the bathroom."*

Evans: Oh, and they had a Leger just painted on the wall. Not a framed Leger but just painted on the wall over the fireplace. Art was everywhere. It was absolutely stunning.

Hughes: Jay also said you were showing him some of the gifts you received from the Rockefellers, and there was a Steuben glass in the shape of a salmon. Later, he said he and Don Moos were walking down 5th Avenue and happened to pass the Steuben shop, so they went inside to check out how much a piece like that would be worth. It was about $5,000.

Evans: It's a couple thousand. It's in the living room.

Hughes: Was there any prohibition against keeping gifts like that?

Evans: No. Those were not state funds. This was a Republican conference and it was a gift from them.

Hughes: From Rocky and Happy.

Evans: They could afford it. But we would have to have donations to buy gifts when we entertained because we didn't have personal money. Those gifts (from the Rockefellers) were lovely and certainly more expensive than what we would normally receive. In some states they were very small tokens of appreciation, something that was typical of the state or whatever.

Hughes: Ted Agnew was governor of Maryland at the time. Did you meet Agnew?

Evans: Oh sure.

Hughes: Did you have any kind of funny, fleeting feeling about him?

Evans: No. And I liked his wife very much. She was very nice. But, no, you don't get to know them that way and you don't know what's going on behind the scenes. (With Agnew) nobody did. But I don't know that he was one of our favorite people. I didn't know him that well. But she and I talked.

Hughes: He came and visited out here, didn't he?

Evans: Yes, in fact he came to the Mansion in 1971. He had been over in Dan's office and Dan said, "Would you like to come over to the Mansion and say hello?" He said, "Sure." So I told the boys that they were coming over and could they clean themselves up a little bit and come and meet the Vice President of the United States. Bruce was about 4 years old. So Danny and Mark did. They cleaned up. And they came down to meet Agnew. And whoever was there took pictures, and they said hello. Well, Bruce was not going to come down, and I thought, "Some day you will want to say you met the vice president." So I went upstairs and said, "Now Bruce..." And he had on this little short suit and knee socks, blazer jacket, all dressed up. Bruce is an easy-going child, the third child. He was always a *delight* to bring out; a wonderful sense of humor—he has it to this day. But he *just did not* want to do this. I sort of insisted. And there's this picture of this little child. Ted Agnew is leaning over and shaking hands and Bruce has these tears just rolling down his face. He's crying. That picture was in the papers all over the country the next day.

Hughes: I think the kid was prescient. He probably knew that Spiro Agnew was a problem.

Hughes: So, how about the Nixons?

Evans: We saw a lot of the Nixons over the years.

Bruce balks at shaking hands with the vice-president.
UPI, Washington State Archives

Hughes: Tell me about that. What was that like? All the things that you hear about Richard Millhous Nixon, the secret man. Did you get any glimpses into that?

Evans: I think so.

Hughes: Tell us about that.

Evans: Well, we were just having this conversation recently with some-body here who worked with him. He was just a loner type of a person. He was very serious. Not easy with people. Never. Dan had worked quite a lot on different things with him—commissions, meetings and different issues over the years. We were laughing the other night just talking about this. He always asked us the same thing. We would see him in July at a governor's conference, or we would see him in October at something. It didn't matter. We'd go though the receiving line, or be at the White House. He'd say, "And how is the skiing? How is the Evans' skiing?" Even if it was the middle of July—because when he saw us it would click: "Ah, the Evans. They ski."

Hughes: He probably had 3x5 cards with notes on every governor.

Evans: So he was not one for casual, light conversation. But Pat Nixon, on the other hand, was a lovely, lovely lady. She came to the Mansion one time.

Hughes: Yes, there's a nice picture of that. You know, no matter how hard one's heart was about Nixon—that scene of poor Pat, Julie, and Tricia looking on as Nixon addresses the White House staff on the day of his resignation was heart-rending. Even my mother, who didn't like Richard Nixon at all, had tears of sympathy in her eyes for poor Pat.

Evans: I felt badly for her. It was very hard on them, obviously. But she was a great person, and I invited some friends—four, five or six people over to meet her at the Mansion—and we were having coffee and tea in the afternoon while the president and Dan were meeting. I remember that Gummie

The Nixons at daughter Tricia's wedding. *Nixon Library*

Johnson's wife Betty couldn't get a sitter at the last minute for their young-est, who was Mark's age. So I said, "Just bring her along. That will be fine." The little girl—she was 4 or 5—came in to the drawing room where we were. There were strange people there, and she was just squirmy. And Pat Nixon said, "Come on over here." She picked her up and put her in her lap and talked to her. The Johnsons' little daughter was very happy and that worked great. Pat Nixon was just *very* easy with all of us. She was very pleasant. Quiet, but very nice person.

Hughes: I met Betty Ford. She was really charming—a real down-to-earth person.

Evans: She is. They all (first ladies) were in their own way. These wom-en are admirable people who have gone through the wars of campaigns and are living with a president, which is probably not the easiest thing in the world. And they often have to make their own way.

Hughes: They've all pretty much been a Nancy Bell from Spokane at some time, haven't they?

Evans: Absolutely, which reminds me of some things I want to make sure we talk about, because it is part of my life. It's about other things I was involved with in Olympia. But one thing I really think is very important, and it's one of the things that made what we have done doable.

Hughes: At the Mansion?

Evans: *Everywhere.* And that is that Dan is first and foremost a family man. I mean family is extremely important to him. A lot of people say that…but for him it was extremely important. And the beauty of the gov-ernor's job was that he could schedule things. So if there was something really important that was going to be taking place—some family event or some child's game—if at all possible he would be there because he could change his schedule accordingly.

Hughes: I saw Dan at a lot of high school football games.

Evans: We went to a lot of games—a lot of baseball games, soccer games, you name it. We would take the kids to a lot of different things. Sometimes they weren't too happy to be going but we just felt it was

First Lady Betty Ford has tea with Dan, Nancy, two of the boys, and Grandma Lilith Bell, right. *Evans family album*

important for them to be part of it. That's extremely important to em-phasize because it was very helpful to me—reassuring. And to him, it *really* was important.

Hughes: And you're right across the street from his office.

Evans: He would come home for lunch.

Hughes: Another good reason why it was so important to keep that Mansion.

Evans: Yes. It was very convenient, that's for sure. But the other things I wanted to mention are some things that I was involved with. Obviously forming the Governor's Mansion Foundation was probably the most sig-nificant thing that I was involved with and the instigator of, but I was in-volved with a number of other things. One was the State Capitol Museum. It was more active then. They had more of a collection. Now some of these things are up in Tacoma at the State History Museum....But they were doing good things. And all the first ladies at that time had given (the museum) their inaugural dresses, like the Smithsonian, does with the presidents' wives. And they were always on display. They had arts events. We were there a lot for events. I don't know if that still happens. I thought it was important to have tours, and docents. They didn't have a docent program. And I had been involved somewhat with MOHAI (the Museum of History & Industry) here in Seattle. They had a docent program. So I had invited a couple of friends over to the Mansion, together with the head of docents at MOHAI, to talk to us about forming a docent group. She was very helpful and made several trips to Olympia—in fact, all on her own, to help me. So the three of us put together the docent program called ASCM—the Associates for the State Capitol Museum. We wanted "Associates" because this was not a women's thing. This was men and women. We got a group of volunteers, and they were there at regularly scheduled events, and they would lead tours.

Nancy plays the piano for a sing-a-long in 1970. Dave Potts, *Seattle Post-Intelligencer, MOHAI*

Hughes: That was just invaluable, wasn't it?

Evans: It was. But it's no longer in existence. There's no ASCM any more, but it carried on for a number of years. And in fact a few months ago I found down in the basement the book of minutes, the organizing of this group. But at any rate, I felt good about that program because it got people involved with the museum itself. And it brought more people there to learn about our state's history. And I thought it was a good thing.

Hughes: When you moved into the Governor's Mansion and really got into your job, you already had an interest in history, but being involved with the museum really made your pulse quicken, didn't it?

Evans: Yes, I enjoyed that experience. One of the other things I was involved in was the Governor's Festival of the Arts. That was Lud Kramer's baby. He started it (in 1966), but I was very active with that. We put together a series of events—three or four concerts a year in Olympia theaters. And we brought musicians and other artists from elsewhere. That was hard because you had to get somebody who was coming from (a performance in) Seattle or Portland, who was willing to come by Olympia, too. We had Pearl Bailey and we had the Danish pianist.

Hughes: Victor Borge.

Evans: Victor Borge! Oh, he was wonderful. And then afterwards we would have a little reception for them at the Mansion. And Borge came out to the Mansion. Pearl Bailey came out, too. This event went on for several years.

Hughes: Olympia was kind of a backwater then.

Evans: It was very much so. There was no Performing Arts Center.

Hughes: Where would you have those performances?

Evans: At a movie theater. So, we had the Governor's Festival for the Arts for a number of years, and POSSCA was also formed then—Patrons of the South Sound Cultural Activities. They still have POSSCA events every two years, I think. It's like PONCHO in Seattle. Over the years that auction has raised millions and millions of dollars for the arts.

Hughes: I thought it was originally for Children's Hospital.

Evans: No. It was organized (in 1963) to raise money for the arts. What does it stand for? It's "Patrons of Northwest Civic, Cultural and Charitable Organizations." And they're having a little difficulty right now just because of the money situation with the recession. But they have huge, huge auctions. I thought that that would be a great thing for Olympia. We invited our friends who had started PONCHO to come down. We met with a number of people in the Mansion ballroom and they talked to us about how it's done. We got organized and did it initially every year. Then I think it went to every two years. They had it at Tyee or some big venue, and raised a lot of money for the arts.

Hughes: I remember vividly covering the Legislature in 1968, and in terms of cultural events and arts, Olympia didn't seem to be any more special than Aberdeen.

Evans: Well, we were struggling. Another thing I got involved with and helped bring to Olympia was Planned Parenthood. There was a group of us. We brought down the director of Planned Parenthood in Seattle, Lee Minto, and then Suzanne Cluett, who was her assistant. That was hard work because it took money and lots of planning. They came down to Olympia once a week for a while for a 7 o'clock meeting, helping us to form the Planned Parenthood group there.

Hughes: Was there any kind of family planning clinic here before that?

Evans: Nothing. There was nothing of that nature. We hooked up eventually with Shelton as well.

Hughes: By the way, it was really interesting to me to read Dan's really gutsy statements in opposition to the death penalty in the 1960s. He and Justice Bob Utter, whom Dan appointed to the Supreme Court, were absolutely kindred souls when it came to the issue of capital punishment.

Evans: Jim Dolliver was that way too, although he wouldn't be talking about it that publicly. When I was teaching school toward the end we decided to take the fifth and sixth graders who were bright, and have a special class, one class a week. I taught it in the library. So I had maybe 12 or 14 kids who were really bright and really good students. I decided, because it was an issue at that time, to discuss the death penalty. I'd say, "Well, let's have a debate." Then we invited the superintendent of public instruction and the school principal, to observe it. And the kids debated the death penalty. This was fifth and sixth graders.

Hughes: Well, your husband and Bob Utter and, to a slightly lesser extent, Jim Dolliver and Charles Z. Smith were among the most articulate and outspoken opponents of the death penalty.

Evans: Dan felt very strongly about it because I can remember discussing that with him. Periodically these cases would come to the governor's desk. "Would he sign a death warrant?" He couldn't do it. He just said, "How can I sign this, sending somebody to the chair." Do we still do the chair?

Hughes: No, we hang people or give them a lethal injection, but that's being challenged right now.

Evans: At any rate, he just could not do that. I agreed with him whole-heartedly on that. It was very hard for him because it was so personal. He was the person making a life-or-death decision.

Hughes: Talk about where the buck stops.

Evans: Yes. So that was a big issue in his life.

Hughes: My mother was really passionate about that landmark 1970 campaign for abortion rights in Washington State. (Referendum 20) Where did you come down on that?

Evans: Well, I can't speak for my husband, but I always felt it's a woman's right, prerogative, to make that decision.

Hughes: I appreciate you not speaking for Dan, but did he take a stand on that as well?

Evans: I agree with him when he said, "Nobody likes abortion." It's not something we would ever choose. But it has to be something where the woman makes that decision.

Hughes: Hillary and Bill Clinton said, "It ought to be rare and safe."

Evans: Yes. Exactly. And people forget what it was like in those days. Girls, a lot of girls, but women, too, were going to backwater places and there were a lot of permanent injuries, even deaths. All sorts of things were happening. We forget how it was. I was reminded of that era during the campaign last fall, and particularly around the time of the inauguration of President Obama. They had so many clips on the news of civil rights issues back in the 1950s, '60s, and '70s. I was very much aware of that situation, but we tend to forget what a terrible time it was, particularly in the South—but everywhere. How could we have treated people that way in this country? I feel the same way about the women and what was happening with the women concerning (back-alley) abortion. So we were both very much in favor of it (abortion rights) but it's not something we would want to do personally.

Hughes: That was really a gutsy thing for you to do at the time. I remember the battle lines were *really* drawn.

Evans: It gets to be a very emotional issue. There are people very rigid on one side, and very rigid on the other side. But there are a lot of people who are in the middle. And it *is* an emotional, *personal* thing. And I just don't think it's anything that anybody can dictate.

Hughes: My mother always told the story of having a college roommate in 1932 who was scarred for life with a back-alley abortion and never could have children.

Evans: Yes, girls taking the initiative themselves and doing damage. So those things were important to me. And there's one other thing that I don't know if we're going to get into and that is our Vietnamese family.

Hughes: Let's talk about it right now because that's a wonderful story. Was it Ronald Reagan who said that California didn't want to accept any more Vietnamese refugees?

Evans: No, it was Jerry Brown, when he became governor of California.

Hughes: Tell us about that. What did Dan and Nancy Evans say about that?

Evans: Well, it's interesting because when Dan became governor (in 1965) the governor of California was Jerry's father—Pat Brown, who was a good governor; a very good leader—forward thinking and everything. Then (in 1975) along came his son, who got a little extreme in various things. Dan heard on the radio one morning that Jerry Brown did not want to accept the Vietnamese refugees into California and when Dan went to the office that morning, I think it was Ralph Munro who said, "Look what's happening down there. It's terrible!" And Dan agreed immediately. So he sent Ralph down to California to Camp Pendleton to look into it and see if we could bring some of those people to the State of Washington. And that's exactly what happened. And of course now we know what it was like for these people because they had left Saigon in the clothes on their backs, and they came to California where they were put into sort of this large camp, warehouse sort of a thing, wondering what was going to become of them. Ralph did a terrific job of putting together the plan to bring them to Madigan (at Fort Lewis). And Dan and I went up to greet these people. It was a huge, swarming group of these Vietnamese people—cold, shivering. Then we tried to find families who would sponsor them. Many of them were sent to live with people for a time until they were settled and got jobs and could communicate better.

We got a letter from our friend Colin Nguyen just yesterday.

Hughes: My Vietnamese is fractured. Is it pronounced "New-gen"?

Evans: You pronounce it "Win." Actually, I don't think I have ever said it right, but they let me get by.

Hughes: Well, the story gets better because among the people you greeted that day was a young Vietnamese man, Chuong Huu Nguyen, and his pregnant wife, Xuan Hoa Pham, and their five children. The Nguyens were so touched by your gesture that when their son was born a few months later they named him Evans.

Evans: Correct, yes!

Hughes: And when Evans graduated from the University of Washington in 1998, I understand that Dan was in the audience. Were you there, too?

Evans: I was, but Dan was up on the stage. He was a UW regent. But a lot goes on before that: Yes, we met Colin, who is the father—he and his wife both assumed American first names—and his wife, Mary, and these wonderful five children. There was no contact for a time. So then we finally received a letter from Evans inviting us to come to his school in Renton. The papers were there and they took our pictures. That's when we first met Evans. He was this cute little guy. Then we started getting together with the family periodically, for lunch usually. We would take them someplace, and it was wonderful to watch because Mary, the mother, spoke very little English. She was shy—a shy Asian woman. Colin speaks pretty good English now, but it was very hard to understand his English back then because of his accent. Dung, the oldest child who has taken the name Rochelle, and the other children were the interpreters for the parents and for us. It was wonderful to see this family of six children. I think when Rochelle came to the states with her family she was 15 or so, and she took responsibility for the kids a lot. There was no hesitation about speaking up and talking because everybody would listen politely to everybody. That doesn't happen in our family, or a lot of families, you know. People talk over people. But that did not take place in this family. Everybody listened to everybody.

So, now we still get together. We don't do it as often because everybody is so busy. When we went to D.C., we did it less, obviously. But we would always do it at Christmastime because we usually would be back here. It has just been such a joy for Dan and me to watch this family grow and mature and become wonderful citizens. Rochelle, the oldest, is a dentist. They *all* went to college. They all graduated and did very well, many of them with post-graduate degrees. When we were in D.C., Rochelle came back because she was taking classes at Harvard, I think, and visited us. One went to MIT, one other went back to Harvard as well; one went to Stanford. They have just done *so* well academically, but they all received their bachelor's at the UW. They are such wonderful people, and they have a lot of fun together. They're a joy to be with. Our sons hate to hear this

Dan and Nancy with their namesake immigrant son, Evans Nguyen. *Evans family album*

because they say, "All you ever do is talk about the Nguyens!" They're just joking of course. But two of those children, Ailien and Dung/Rochelle, are dentists. And Quang has a great job. He travels around the world. He's married and had a new baby in March (of 2009). And Quyen works for Scansa as a project manager for construction projects.

Hughes: How about Dan's namesake?

Evans: Evans travels to China and all over the world. He's worked for Fluke and now he's working for another company. They hired him away. He does very well. And he has a new baby, too.

Hughes: We've got to scare up some pictures of Evans with Evans.

Evans: We have pictures. I'm forgetting one of the kids. I've got the two boys, Quang and Evans. And the other girl is Phuong, or Madeline, who just got married a year and a half ago and she has a new baby. Everybody is so happy and they're all doing *so* well. She loves not-for-profits. She decided that's for her.

Hughes: You've got some extra grandchildren, Nancy!

Evans: Yeah. They are really great. And Rochelle (Dung), the oldest, she's a very serious young woman. She has her own dentistry practice; works very hard. She had four children, and they're all doing *very* well. The youngest is 3. They are just a great family.

This letter just came yesterday because I just had a long conversation with Colin on the phone two days ago. He said, "I'd like to show you my grandchildren," so he sent pictures of the new grandchildren. Trevor is a good scorer in his class. He's the oldest grandson, and is also their second Math Olympiad winner—just last week. "I wish you very good health," Colin writes. "The last 34 years…April 23, 1975, I brought my family and my younger brother's family into Saigon Airport. The C141 left there before midnight and stopped by the Philippines to a bigger jet plane, Galaxy C5, to Guam. We arrived at the destination on April 24, 1975."

Hughes: Wow, what a story!

Evans: Yes. It's a wonderful story. We love this family.

Hughes: That reminds me that Dave Ammons of the AP did an interview with you and Dan when you were getting ready to leave the Mansion. The story said you had 24 red leather scrapbooks that you kept that were just full—

Evans: Probably, but *fake* leather.

Hughes: OK, fake leather. You said, "Dan and I have been scrapbookers ever since we were children." Is that right?

Evans: Yes, I have a scrapbook. In fact, Dan reminded me the other day it's in the front hall closet in a box. Someday I should get it and throw most of it away.

Hughes: Oh no, don't do that! Give it to us. We'll put it in the Archives. Do I read correctly that you got to have dinner with the Queen of England?

Evans: No. But we met her and Prince Phillip.

Hughes: What was that like?

Evans: Well, she's just what she appears. She's very gracious. It was actually during the Bicentennial Celebration in Philadelphia. And she brought their yacht *Britannia* over.

Hughes: You didn't take *your* yacht?

Evans: *No.* (laughing) But it was interesting because the Governors' Conference was in Hershey, Pennsylvania, to tie into the Philadelphia activities that year, in July. So we took the boys back. We took a couple of weeks, rented a car and drove through New England, where I had never been. The Montreal Olympics were going on at the time, and there were great stories going around: "Well, we might be invited to meet the Queen and the Prince." So the women were scurrying about. Did they have hats? I never wear a hat. Bought a hat once and wore it for my farewell from our wedding reception, and took it off and never wore it again. I don't *like* hats. But women were going out and buying hats. And then, lo and behold, *we* were invited. So then we had to get the protocol sheet on what you do, what you don't do, what you wear, and on and on and on. We helicoptered over to Philadelphia, I remember, and went aboard the *Britannia*, which was lovely of course. And the Queen was very pleasant. We all stood around and she moved around talking and introducing herself to people, and the Prince as well. We chatted. It was very impressive.

Hughes: You didn't mess up and hug her or anything like Michelle Obama?

Evans: No. I did not do anything like that. But later when we were in London for a meeting there was a reception at one of the breweries. I think it was one of the Prince's breweries. And T.A. Wilson was there. He was the chairman of Boeing at the time. And T.A. came over and said, "I want you to meet Prince Phillip." Well, we had met him but nobody's going to remember that. So T.A. took us over. T.A. was always very easy and very Northwesternly.

Hughes: That's a wonderful way to describe it. "Northwesternly." I like that. I think you just coined something.

Evans: (laughs) He took us over and introduced us to the Prince: "Senator and Mrs. Evans." And just without thinking I said, "How do you do?" and held out my hand. And if you notice his hands are always behind his back. They never moved. And I just thought, "Well, *come on,* you can shake hands with me." I didn't say anything of course. But I felt so awkward.

Hughes: You're not supposed to touch The Royals.

Evans: Well, I think she would. In fact my memory is that we did shake hands—the Queen and I. But he was not going to bother.

Hughes: When Michelle put her arm around the Queen's waist, the Queen put her arm around Michelle's.

Evans: Yes, she did.

Hughes: I thought that was one of the greatest moments I'd ever seen with Queen Elizabeth. It was just wonderful. She's loosening up.

Evans: I think she probably loves affection like everybody. But in deference, the British of course just never would do that.

Hughes: Let's get back to life at the Mansion. When the kids were growing up at the Mansion you did a lot of stuff. You went bicycling and hiking. Did you literally bicycle around town and play Pickleball all the time?

Evans: Oh yes. We built a Pickleball court in the back of the house.

Hughes: I'm told that Joel Pritchard invented Pickleball.

Evans: Joel Pritchard, Barney McCallum, and my brother, Bill Bell. They were on Bainbridge. The McCallums and the Pritchards had places very near to each other. They were good friends and Barney worked for Joel. The Pritchards and McCallums grew up on Queen Anne and were long-time friends. And Bill Bell rented a house on Bainbridge. Joel Pritchard actually had two houses—his parents' house and his house, and the parents weren't there then. So Bill would be coming home from Asia, wherever he was living at the time, Indonesia or Australia, and they'd rent the house and stay with their kids. So here are all these young kids running around. The Pritchards had four and Bill and Tina had three; the McCallums had two or three. And they were saying, "There's nothing to do!" You know, like children always say. And here they are right on the beach. Well, Joel used to play badminton and they had an asphalt badminton court in the back and a net. So they looked around and they found some whiffle balls and ping pong paddles, and that's the way Pickleball started. The story is that the height of the net was Joel's hip bone. And it just got going. All the guys invested some money into it. But Barney's son sort of took it on as a business and broadened it, marketed it and put together a professional sort of game that you could buy. Pretty soon we were getting stories back from all over the world where Pickleball was put in. Bill and Tina, when they were living in Indonesia, had one built in their yard and would invite all these dignitaries over. They ended up playing Pickleball. About a year ago, in fact, I was watching the "Today" show, or GMA (Good Morning America) and, by golly, they announced, "In the next hour we're going to talk about a new game called Pickleball." Well, of course, it's not a new game. It was around in the '60s. They had a demonstration in the studio. It's a great game because it doesn't take up a lot of space. Anybody can play it, but not everybody can play it really well. It's very challenging if you play it really well.

Hughes: Was Joel good at it?

Evans: He was *very* good. Joel was a good athlete. We all got really pretty good at Pickleball.

Hughes: Rest in peace, Joel Pritchard. He had to be one of the sweetest, brightest men I've ever met. Was he a dear friend of yours?

Evans: Joel was a very special friend, yes. Like a brother.

Hughes: So the future lieutenant governor invented Pickleball and you had a court at the Mansion?

Evans: We did. We built it sort of late, in the '70s, and we lit it so we could play it at night. The state didn't pay for this. We did. And we would have people to dinner, just friends, and then we'd go out because in the evenings it was so pleasant. There was a hedge that sort of protected it from the wind. And we'd play Pickleball. Dan and the kids played it. We were often asked to donate things to charity, to auctions like PONCHO in Seattle. And we often would say "Dinner at the Mansion with Pickleball," or a picnic or something. We enjoyed it.

Hughes: And bike riding, too? I saw pictures of everyone on bikes.

Evans: We all had bikes.

Hughes: Did you used to ride all over Olympia?

Evans: Yes, but the kids more than I did.

Hughes: I don't know why I'm so amazed by that. I guess I keep thinking of my visits to the Mansion in recent years. I noted that there was more security, which meant life at the Mansion was way different for the Locke kids than your boys.

Evans: It has changed dramatically. It's understandable, I guess.

Hughes: I remember that your husband denounced the right-wing John Birch Society in no uncertain terms. *(Editor's Note: The governor called Birch Society members "false prophets, phony philosophers, professional bigots.")*

Evans: Early on.

Hughes: It was in 1965. A couple of years ago I was with Dan on a panel discussion at a Mainstream Republican convention. Dan was incensed over the Geneva Convention violations and constitutional right deprivations by the Bush Administration. He really spoke his mind. In the wake of the controversy over his statements about the John Birch Society, did you ever have any security fears for the kids?

Dan and Nancy at a press conference around the time the Legislature finally appropriated money to remodel the mansion. *Evans family album*

Evans: Not for the kids so much. At various times my secretary was cautioned not to open certain letters, or how to open them if they felt like it was something (ominous)—a pipe or pencil bomb, or some poisonous powder. We got threats periodically. Most of them turned out to be insignificant in that the person was loony or—I guess that's not very professional.

Hughes: Actually, it's a good word. "Loony" is an underused word.

Evans: Well, sometimes it was people who were just mad and didn't word it very well. But I remember there were a couple of incidents where we were cautioned for a period of a day or two. They would follow this person and watch this person; then everything would be OK.

Hughes: Anything disquieting around the kids at all?

Evans: I don't think so. No.

Hughes: So you always felt it was safe—that you might have been Washington's first lady but your kids got on their bikes and pedaled down the driveway, off to see Timmy around the block?

Evans: Pretty much. I would hope they would tell me where they were going.

Hughes: In 1973, the Legislature finally approved money ($600,000) for the renovation of the Mansion.

Evans: And we had to move out of the house for a year while they gutted it.

Hughes: Where did you live?

Evans: Well, we went house hunting for a family of six for a year, fully furnished, and there just was very little available in Olympia at that time. We were just all over the place trying to figure out what we were going to do. Finally somebody came up with the Ingham House, which was located where the Visitor's Center is now. It's a lovely Georgian home that Dr. Ingham had built many, many years before that several families had lived in. Then the state bought it and it was sitting there being used as an office. So we went over there and looked. It was a wonderful house, but they had put in those egg-carton light fixtures on the ceiling, and it was all desks and chairs and awful—that sort of thing. But they decided that we could fix it up a bit. So we did. We did some drapes in the living room and dining room. We brought the furniture over from the Mansion that would fit. It had four bedrooms. On the third floor, it had sort of an attic with the slanted ceiling and wooden paneling. That's where the two older boys slept. It was great. It had a bathroom. And it was still in the neighborhood so the kids didn't lose their friends and could still walk to school.

Hughes: And their Dad could still walk to work.

Evans: Sure. It all worked out very, very well, and it didn't cost a lot of money. So we lived there for a year while they were gutting the Mansion. I mentioned the two thermostats that were in the Mansion. And the one that was in the State Dining Room, on the main floor, we found out it actually controlled the heat in the basement and the second floor. And the thermostat that was on the second floor in the hall controlled the third floor and the main floor.

Hughes: That made perfect sense, didn't it?! I don't know why you hadn't figured that out earlier.

Evans: They fixed the plumbing problems, and upgraded the electricity and all of that. They found that, actually, when the house was built, it was just the posts on the floor. There wasn't a lot of concrete in the basement.

Hughes: So it was like gutting the White House in the Truman era.

Evans: Yes. They found a lot of stuff, including some wonderful little old whiskey bottles that went to the museum.

Hughes: I love it when stuff like that turns up. Anything else?

Evans: We found some papers and things. But we added on two guest bedrooms and some bathrooms. The place needed more bathrooms. I remember very vividly an incident when we first arrived (in 1965) and opened

Renovation finally gets under way in the Mansion. *Washington State Archives*

up the house for weekly tours, which had never happened before. The retirement homes found out about it. They're always looking for places to go and things to do, and we had busloads come to the Mansion. But the first time this happened a busload arrived and they couldn't get up the driveway because it curves too much and it's too narrow. So they had to park down below somewhere. These were generally elderly people, and they had come from Seattle. I was always at the front door to greet people, and they all wanted to go to the bathroom: "Hello, I'm Nancy Evans" and they all said, "*Where is your bathroom?*" Well, there was one bathroom off what is now the library, which used to be a little green room; that's what we called it.

Hughes: So the public bathrooms at the bottom of the stairs weren't there?

Evans: No. There was one bathroom on the main floor. There was an old bathroom downstairs, and then there were our bathrooms upstairs. They found them all! You know, nature calls. We learned our lesson. After that they always had to stop at the Capitol first before they came over to the Mansion. In the renovation, we added public bathrooms on the main floor and downstairs for the men.

Hughes: Is it a true story that what really precipitated you drawing the line in the sand over saving the Mansion was a visit with Art McDonald of KOMO-TV in 1966?

Evans: Yes, that's all true. He literally just came to the door one day— knocked on the door, rang the doorbell. And he said, "Nancy," because we had known each other before, "Were you aware that the Capitol Committee is discussing what to do with the Governor's Mansion?" The Capitol Committee is composed of the governor, the lieutenant governor, and the commissioner of public lands—so it's Dan, John Cherberg and Bert Cole. And I said, "No, I really wasn't." Art said, "Well, there is some interest in tearing it down and building the office building that would be identical to the one on the other side," which is what the original Capitol campus plan had. The Mansion was built only because of the Alaska-Yukon-Pacific Exposition that was coming to Seattle.

Hughes: Exactly, in 1909. A huge event for Seattle and the whole state.

Evans: They had to have a home for entertaining. But I told Art, "They can't tear this down! There's too much history here. It's a lovely old building, and we're a young state and we need to preserve our history." And I went on like that. So Art left and went over to the Capitol, and Dan happened to be having a press conference. He said, "Governor, I just was visiting Nancy and she said she's definitely against it. What do you think?" And Dan said, "Well, I guess I'm against it too." (laughing) Words to that effect: "If she's against it, I'm against it." He's well trained.

Hughes: I think this is a good marriage! This guy Evans was real smart on his feet.

Evans: He knew when to accede to my wishes. So, in a way, that was the beginning because the talk (about tearing down the Mansion) was always there—for several years—and Bert Cole was very serious about this. He thought it should be a "modern home on the point where the parking lot is." He added, "And think of the view you'd have." And I said, "Yes, but think of the history you'll lose here." There were members of the Legislature who were not in favor of this plan (saving the Mansion) and did their best to axe it whenever they could. One was Slim Rasmussen. He became my nemesis.

Hughes: He was the tough ol' Democrat from Tacoma. He was a lot of people's nemesis.

Evans: Yeah, and he wasn't in favor of anything we suggested. After we moved back in, in September of '74, the Mansion was open to the press for a tour, and I was showing them around. And when Slim came over, I took him by his arm and said, "Let me show you around, Slim." I was showing him all the rooms, and the furnishings and what have you. Then he said, "Well, you've done a wonderful job here." And I know it was hard for him to say it. I felt very pleased that he had come over.

Hughes: Earlier, some architects did a study for the House Capitol Committee and said the Mansion was "not architecturally wonderful and historically ancient."

Evans: Yeah. That's what they said. (smiling)

Hughes: Was it you or Dan who said, "It's a lot more ancient than a new one would be"?

Evans: I don't remember. But it sounds like something I would say. I remember when we went to England I told Jean Jongeward and the Foundation people, "I'll look around." And I remember I got a list of antique stores to go to in London. I went to this one and told them what I was doing. I said, "I'm looking for some possible furnishings for a home for a governor in the State of Washington. And we're looking for furnishings that are old—early 18th, late 17th Century." And he said, "I'm sorry. We don't have anything after 1650." I was in the wrong store, obviously.

Hughes: For the record, did you have bats?

Evans: Yes. I think everybody who lived there did.

EDITOR'S NOTE: In 1997, Governor Gary Locke awoke one night to find a bat circling the bassinet of his 4-week-old daughter, Emily. He chased it out with a dust mop, but as a precaution, the governor, his wife Mona and the infant received rabies shots.

Hughes: At the Governor's Mansion 100th anniversary celebration last October, someone told this story that Jean Gardner came down the stairs one day and there was a bat hanging off the chandelier. She screamed, "Booth, do something!" And he says, "I'll go get a cadet."

Evans: That's a true story!

Hughes: She wanted him to do the manly, hairy-chested thing—swat the bat for her. But a good manager delegates.

Evans: I remember it was in the spring of 1965 and we had a dinner party. It was my first sort of real dinner party with friends, including Bill and Tina, my brother and his wife, who came down and other friends from Seattle, maybe 10 or 12 of us. And I'm standing in front of the fireplace because the fire is going and it feels good. Everybody is happy and I'm thinking, "This is really fun." And I look right through the hall and I see something flying around the ballroom. So I went quietly over to Dan and said, "I think there's a bird in the ballroom." One by one we sort of went in there. Well, it was obvious it was not a bird. Pretty soon, all of our friends have brooms or mops or something and were trying to swat it away.

Hughes: Gary and Mona Locke had nine bats in 13 days. You never had anything like that, did you?

Evans: Well, we had a lot. It's seasonal. They would come and do their thing, and then they'd leave. They're very important to have because they eat all those bugs, but I did not like bats.

Hughes: Among the fellows who volunteer to do research with us is one who is an aficionado of furniture, and he says there's some really lovely Duncan Phyfe furniture in the Mansion.

Evans: Yes, the piano.

Hughes: The Steinway has Duncan Phyfe legs?

Evans: No, the piano in the drawing room is Duncan Phyfe. And the sofas—one is a Sheraton and one's a Phyfe.

Hughes: That's some really valuable, wonderful stuff, and all that was donated?

Evans: Well, purchased with donated funds.

Hughes: Do you have any idea, when things really got going with the Foundation, what kind of war chest they had for acquisitions?—What some of those really nice pieces would have cost?

Evans: Somewhere in my files I have a list of all the prices. Some of those pieces were eight, ten, twelve thousand dollars—pieces that now would be thirty, forty, fifty-thousand dollars. But that was a lot of money in the 1970s.

Hughes: Absolutely. And it was a masterstroke to get the first lady out of the loop for saying yes or no to what you would accept in the way of donations.

Evans: When I traveled around for other purposes, very often people would come up and say, "Well, I have this wonderful cranberry glass that's so pretty." And I'm sure it was, but it was not appropriate for the Mansion.

Hughes: So, you've finally got this place all fixed up. It's now pretty wonderful. When you moved in a decade earlier it was "wretchedly decrepit," as Dan put it. And now you make the decision not to seek a fourth term. Was that something Dan and Nancy really mulled over together and concluded, "It's time to go do something else"? He probably could have had a fourth term.

Evans: He had asked my counsel on that. We had discussed it somewhat. I was always reluctant in these situations, because they came up several times in our life, about trying to affect his decision. I always felt that it should be his decision. Consideration of our family had to be part of it, but whether he would or would not was really his decision to make and not mine. He was tormented about that. He really wanted to go on. In my heart I knew it was not the right thing to do. I just knew it. I think that you get tired and you don't realize you're tired. But he wasn't tired. He was always energized. He *loved* being governor and he loved this state and the people. He was very sincere and earnest about all of that. But I just knew that with four more years, he would not be quite as aggressive. He would work hard as always—but maybe not as innovative, perhaps. But I didn't tell him that, obviously. And I still remember when he told me his decision. I think it was during the Legislature. I had one of my teas going on or an open house. I was standing by the front door and he came in the front door, which was a surprise, at 2 or 3 in the afternoon. And he walked right by me and whispered, "Come upstairs with me." Just like that. I thought, "Wooooooo!"

Hughes: This is a little bit out of the norm?

Evans: *A bit out of the norm.* So I excused myself and went upstairs to our bedroom. And it was very difficult for him, but he had decided not to run. And he wanted me to know. He was very sad, very teary.

Hughes: There's an interview you did with Dave Ammons in 1974. You said you'd actually had some mild opposition to Dan seeking a *third* term.

Evans: Yeah. Each time.

Hughes: And there's this quote: "I think it's only natural that a woman, a wife, wants to try to get back to a more normal existence." Then you added, "But any good wife will tell you, you usually let the man do what he wants."

Evans: Did I say that? Was that me?

Hughes: It has quote marks around it.

Evans: OK. I wasn't sure. It does sound like me.

Hughes: But for your three sons, well, the Mansion was the only home those boys had ever really known.

Evans: That's correct. That was their life.

Hughes: So how old are the boys in 1977 when you left the Mansion?

Evans: They were 16, 13 and 10.

Hughes: Before Dan made up his mind, were there family meetings on the topic?

Evans: No. Not then. No, it was not their decision to make.

Hughes: You were talking to Ammons again as you were packing up, sharing your memories.

Evans: Gee, he was a real nuisance, wasn't he? I'll have to tell him that.

Hughes: There's a picture of Ammons in there (the scrapbook) with a beard. It's one of the worst beards I've ever seen. It's a really bad beard. Dan, on the other hand, had a really great beard. Why did Dan Evans grow the beard?

Evans: I remember that very well. I don't remember the year, but it was late in the governor's office, probably '74 or maybe '75. Before he had always felt that he could not be away from the office for more than a week. So when we got away it was for maybe a week. Suddenly I think he thought, "Well, maybe I can be away a bit longer." So we took a three-week vacation. We went hiking and we went yachting up into Canada. It was just a great, great getaway because phones were not an issue. I forget all the things we did. But the beard started when we went away. He had a heavy beard. He's like Nixon. I mean when he shaved he had a 5 o'clock shadow at 5 o'clock, even when he was young. So he started to grow that beard. We ended the vacation to visit Danny who was attending the Boy Scout Jamboree in Idaho. Dan kept the beard to show him. And I abided it. By the time we got home he had a pretty good beard. And he said, "Well, I think I'll just keep going."

Hughes: It was luxurious; it was dark.

Evans: Well, it was dark but as it got longer there were two white streaks on his chin, which often happens with men. I've noticed this on men's beards. So he went on, growing this beard. In his scrapbook is a letter he got from somebody who said, "I always knew you had skunk blood in ya!"

Hughes: Was that somebody being funny?

Evans: No. No. And he got a lot of mail on the beard. It was split 50/50, and most of the 50s against were women, and most of the 50s for were men.

Hughes: And the first lady wasn't much for the beard either?

Evans: No. They were itchy. Let's face it. So then I remember we were up at our condo at Crystal Mountain—our "luxurious" condo. Actually, the square footage of the condos was 520 square feet. There were two rooms, three bunks, trundles.

Hughes: This was like the size of Happy Rockefeller's bathroom, and without a Picasso.

Evans: Oh yeah. But we loved that condo. We had that for years. We were up there every other weekend skiing. And you know you put on your parka, your goggles, and your hat and nobody knows who you are. It's a great getaway—no phone, no TV. And then we'd be standing in line to get on the chair-lift and Dan would say something. And everybody would turn around because his voice was so distinctive. I kept saying, "Be quiet!"

So we were up there at the condo. It was New Year's Eve, and we'd been out partying and the kids had been out playing. We all went to bed late. And Dan and Mark were the first ones up. The rest of us were in the other room, sound asleep. So Mark took (Polaroid) photos of Dan as he started shaving it off. So that he would first have less beard, then sort of a Van Dyke, and finally he just had the moustache. And then finally he shaved it all off. On Sunday mornings Dan would make breakfast, like a lot of fathers do. And nobody said a thing. I swear an hour went by before I finally said, "You shaved your beard!" We didn't even notice.

Hughes: That's funny. Steve Excell, who was John Spellman's chief of staff, sent us looking for a famous photo of Dan getting his hair cut by a guy who I assume is the legendary "Rags" Thornton, Olympia's celebrity hair stylist of the "Shampoo" era.

Evans: Yeah, he was. Rags was a character. He was fun.

Hughes: There's a photo of Dan looking at a *Playboy* centerfold while getting his hair cut.

Evans: Oh really? Really? *Well, why not?* But for heaven's sake, who puts those things in the Archives?

Hughes: Steve Excell. He's the assistant secretary of state.

Evans: So that's what he's doing.

Hughes: He's a hoot. And talk about institutional memory.

So, this series of pictures with Dan doing the Fu Manchu and the Smith Brothers, and then maybe a little Groucho thing—the whole thing about Dan Evans being the "straight arrow" guy doesn't acknowledge that there's sort of mischievous side to him, isn't there?

Evans: Oh yes, he actually has a very nice sense of humor. Very nice.

Hughes: Any kind of pranks that he's pulled?

Evans: Oh yes, and he's actually pretty good at that. And sometimes in his speeches, he could never tell a joke, but he tried. And I'd keep saying, "You don't laugh at your own jokes." And he'd be laughing at what was coming and he wouldn't even get to the punch line. But he was very good at one-liners. They would just come to his mind. He could do that very nicely.

Hughes: Do you remember a great one-liner?

Evans: No. I mean they were just—

"Rags" Thornton, Olympia's celebrity hair stylist, gives Dan a trim.
Washington State Archives

Hughes: Droll?

Evans: Yes.

Hughes: Your dad was good that way, too, wasn't he?

Evans: He was *very* good that way, yes.

Hughes: So, they must have gotten on really well—Dan and Daddy.

Evans: They did. They weren't together as much as I would have liked because as I said, my father, unfortunately, died shortly after we were married, and they lived in Spokane.

Hughes: He must have been really proud of what Dan was achieving as a young legislator. He would have really got a kick out of Dan being governor and seeing you in the Mansion.

Evans: Oh yes.

Hughes: I love the picture of you on your wedding day with your dad looking so classically "dad."

Evans: *Yes.* (smiling)

Hughes: Was there one moment during all the times you were following protocol, being first lady and trying to be just you at the same time—was there any embarrassing moment where you would have liked to crawl under the table and died?

Evans: I can't tell you what it was, but I know there were because I remember feeling that way a number of times—well, not a number, but more than once....I really don't remember. Probably in the back of my brain I've hidden them away—but I know I sometimes would say things that I should never have said. I can do that.

Hughes: I like that about you.

Evans: Well, no, it gets me in trouble.

Hughes: You told Ammons about times you were jawboning "some of our 17th Century legislators on your favorite causes when they visited the Mansion." And then sometimes after the guests had left Dan would say to you, "Did you really have to buttonhole that one?"

Evans: Yeah, I'm sure I did.

Hughes: That would have been Slim?

Evans: Well, there were other issues—social issues—that I would get involved with.

Hughes: Tell me about that.

Evans: I can't. I just know that there were. Abortion might have been one of them; the ERA perhaps.

Hughes: I can still see my mom wearing her red-and-yellow "ERA Now" button.

Evans: That was a very important vote, issue, and disappointing that that didn't pass.

Hughes: Well, it carried the day, finally. The amendment finally carried, didn't it?

Evans: No.

Hughes: It didn't in Washington State?

Evans: Oh, in Washington, yes.

Hughes: As usual, the females in Washington State were way ahead of the nation.

Evans: Of course.

Hughes: Just like votes for women.

Evans: Absolutely.

Hughes: We're about to have an amazing 100th anniversary of women's suffrage in our state.

Evans: Is that right? I told you earlier that my mother was a suffragist as a young woman in Chicago.

Hughes: She really was a dedicated suffragist, wasn't she?

Evans: Well she was. And she worked at Hull House, which is in Chicago, for a while as a young woman. That's the one Jane Addams founded.

Hughes: Remind me: What was she doing in Chicago?

Evans: She was going to the University of Chicago for a year and living with her brother.

Hughes: Did she talk fondly about those days?

Evans: Yes. And she always felt that it was a wonderful experience for her—a very good education.

Hughes: Please tell us the story about her getting angry over the hearing aid business while she was living with you at the Mansion.

Evans: Well, like so many elderly people, she had trouble with her hearing. I can still remember, particularly at the dinner table, I'd get up and I'd want something and I'd go to whisper to her—"Mother," whatever. And she'd say, "Nancy, you know I can't hear out of that ear." So I'd go around to the other side. And that's when I was young. So she had a hearing problem, and she got hearing aids. That was in the 1960s.

Hughes: And they were big and clunky.

Evans: Hearing aids were not like hearing aids today. And it was her issue. Because oftentimes she was in a crowd of people at the Mansion, and it's really hard to hear in a crowd. It's just a babble of noise. Dan didn't realize it at the time when he became governor, but he quickly found out that there were several hundred commissions. I think some of them have since been sunseted, but there are still a lot of commissions. At that time, there was the Mattress & Bedding Commission. They were supposed to inspect hotels and motels and whatever. And there was a Hearing Aid Commission, so Dan said, "Ah, I'll put Gom on that commission." I would run into people who were on the commission, and they said, "Your mother is just a breath of fresh air. She comes in and tells it exactly like it is. And she tells the manufacturers what for."

Hughes: That's *great.*

Evans: So Mother enjoyed that experience. I thought Dan was really brave to put her on there.

Hughes: Tell us about any other trips that you got to take during those 12 years as first lady that were really memorable?

Evans: Any trip I have is memorable. (smiling)

Hughes: Did you ever get to take the kids?

Evans: No. Not all three. When they were older we took each child on a trip. Most of them were to Japan. Most of the governor's trips were to Taiwan, Hong Kong, the Philippines, and there was a memorable trip to

Grandma's 80th birthday at the Mansion brought out all the Bells. *Evans family album*

China in 1974. Well, the first trip to the Soviet Union was an official trip. Alaska Airlines was inaugurating a non-stop from Anchorage to Leningrad, and they invited the governor of Alaska, the governor of Washington and other dignitaries. One other time, we flew on Aeroflot in the Soviet Union.

Hughes: That must have been a little bit white knuckley.

Evans: Oh, it was. But it was fascinating. I remember that we were flying somewhere in central Russia, and all of a sudden we were getting lower. And Dan said, "Geez, what's happening?" Pretty soon we were landing in a field. And the captain comes on and what he said was translated to us that we had to land: "Ladies and gentlemen, there is fog at the airport and we are landing at an alternate field," which was just grass. We're sitting in these tiny little seats. I remember it was very warm. To travel in those days, I was wearing nylon and polyester, and I think I had a sleeveless knit top that was polyester. I still remember thinking, "If I don't move I won't be as hot." And all of a sudden down the aisle came this couple, carrying their bags. A trap door opened in the floor of the fuselage, and the ladder goes down, and down they go, and they're running off. They're near home, so they just got off right there in the field.

Hughes: Unreal.

Evans: And I remember another flight where sitting across the aisle from me was a gentleman carrying a bag of oranges. And airfare was so inexpensive for Russians that he would bring the bag full up, sell them, then go back, and make money.

Hughes: Please tell us what's occurring here in this picture. It looks to me that this is an industrial-strength Scandinavian clothes dryer of some sort. And here's Senator Warren G. Magnuson and Dan and Nancy.

Evans: "Tuborg" it says. Danish. Isn't that a Danish beer?

Hughes: Tuborg *is* a Danish beer. Duh! Why didn't I think of that?

Evans: It's a vat where they make beer. That's what that is.

Hughes: You're looking like you're really interested.

Evans: Oh, I'm trying. (laughing) That was marvelous trip because we

At the Osaka Expo with Ambassador Toru Haguiwara in 1970. *Washington State Archives*

flew all the way across the Soviet Union and came around the other side and came home. That was another inaugural—an SAS inaugural from Seattle, their first nonstop to Copenhagen and the Scandinavian countries. The Magnusons were on that trip.

Hughes: My entry in the caption contest for the Tuborg photo has you saying, "Living with four men, this could actually handle their gym clothes." But that won't work if those are beer vats instead of clothes dryers. So was Jermaine Magnuson typically on these trips as well?

Evans: She was. She was on that trip I'm quite sure.

Hughes: Did you know Warren Magnuson really well before Dan went to the Senate?

Evans: Well, Dan knew him better than I.

Hughes: He was an amazing character, wasn't he?

Evans: Well, yes. He was fun to travel with. They were great people to have along on the trip. I remember on the flight over we had caviar. They wouldn't stop serving caviar, and I *love* caviar. And I ate my way through Scandinavia eating caviar trying to learn to drink aquavit, which was terrible. And that was a briefer trip. The Alaska Airlines to the Soviet Union

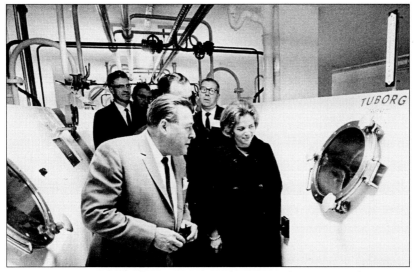

Senator Magnuson and Nancy peer into a beer vat. *Washington State Archives*

was a longer trip, a couple weeks.

Hughes: Have you seen pictures of Warren Magnuson when he was a young man?

Evans: Good looking. He was a dashing bachelor for many years.

Hughes: I read a book about JFK that said the only politician who rivaled JFK for the ladies was Warren G. Magnuson.

Evans: Oh yes. He was very charming.

Hughes: And, meanwhile, Scoop Jackson was Mr. Square.

Evans: Scoop was a Scandinavian, very quiet.

Hughes: So, let's get back to 1977: You're getting ready to move. You got the Mansion fixed up and filled with lovely furniture. Dan's made his decision; he's teary eyed. You're both looking at your scrapbooks. And it's time to go. When did Dan get the overture to become president of The Evergreen State College? In one of the articles written around this time, you said you thought a college job would be really great, that it would really suit Dan because he is "a great teacher."

Evans: Well, over the years he had *often* spoken to classrooms or groups of young people from kindergarten on up. He loves kids. When we're standing in line somewhere, at the grocery store or whatever, and there's a child around, he'll talk to that child and try to get him to smile.

Hughes: So this guy is not really as shy as he's cracked up to be?

Evans: Well, he's always liked children. And I've always thought he was extremely good at explaining things to classrooms or groups of young people without talking down to them.

Hughes: Another thing that shows you have really good instincts: The guy you decided to marry turned out to be a great dad as well.

Evans: Oh, a *wonderful* dad. So I always thought that maybe he would enjoy teaching. Not in engineering because he was passé by then. So that was in the back of my mind, not knowing what he would do or what he wanted to do.

Hughes: Were there other opportunities that came along about that time, other offers?

Evans: There were. There were all sorts of offers. But I think the Evergreen presidency was especially appealing since he had been involved with the college from its inception. Dan thought it was a wonderful institution, but it was having difficulties—a lot of difficulties then because of the legislators. Many of them did not think it had been worth the money, and did not like what they were doing there. I remember one time when he was president, I was somewhere where there was this discussion going on. And they would say, "But look at the way they dress. And they all have dogs." And I said, "When was the last time you were at the University of Washington?" "Well, I haven't been there…" "Well, go over there sometime and see what the kids look like, and whether they have dogs," because, of course, they did.

So I think Dan's choice of becoming president of Evergreen was very timely because he had the presence and the stature with the legislators to try and convince them that this was a worthwhile school, a good enterprise, and something that was good for the state and good for education. Then of course some student would do something dumb.

Hughes: Sure. Some hippie kid.

Evans: And they'd go back 10 years. But over those years there was more and more acceptance by the Legislature and by the community.

Hughes: When my oldest daughter was at Swarthmore, people kept coming up to her and saying, "Do you know about Evergreen? Why would you come here?"

Evans: We had *lots* of applicants from the East. (Addressing Legacy Project Coordinator Lori Larson, an Evergreen graduate) I don't know if you would agree with me on this, but I think to go to Evergreen you have to be a little more mature and sort of know what you want to do.

Lori Larson: You really do. You have to take care of your own education, be responsible.

Evans: Exactly. You have to organize it and be resourceful. So a lot of those kids from the East would come out here and loved it at Evergreen.

Hughes: Before we leave the Governor's Mansion that you've done so much to resuscitate, did you have one final nostalgic candlelight dinner or anything there, the whole family?

Evans: No, it was just too hectic to do that. But I did have one night by myself there. I was back just checking to make sure we had gotten everything, personal belongings. And I remember I was standing in the front hall just sort of looking around, trying to plant it in my memory, that I would always remember what it looked like.

Hughes: You spent 12 of the most memorable years of your life—

Evans: To that point.

Hughes: You were 31 years old when you arrived, and left with three pretty well grown up sons.

Evans: It was a wonderful life, and I always say that to people. As difficult as it could be at times, and as busy as it could be at times, and Dan was often times *stretched* thin, and on and on and on, I still thought it was just a great existence for us.

Evans: But we had a hiatus of six months before Evergreen.

Hughes: What did you do for six months?

Evans: Well, we did what we had done shortly after we were married. We took a trip to Europe. Dan said, "Why don't repeat our trip?" So we did with the three boys. And that was *great*. We went all around, skied for several weeks again, and drove around. We went down into Kenya, too. We've been back several times.

Hughes: To Kenya?

Evans: Well, Kenya, Tanzania, and South Africa. It's amazing country. The lighting there is just very different. And you can understand why artists like it so much.

Hughes: What a treat. You and your family really deserved that trip.

Evans: Well, we did. And we have wonderful films that we took and we put those on movies for the kids. It was a good age because they were 10, 13, and 16. So Dan, our oldest son, could drive, and that helped. We picked up a Volvo station wagon after skiing and we drove all over. We rented a house in Surrey, south of London, for six weeks. And my mother came over to stay with us. And we toured around Wales where the Evans came from. And, as I mentioned earlier, we went to Haltwhistle, where the Bells came from in north England.

Hughes: Right up on the Scotland border. Was it a little bit warmer this time?

Evans: No, it was cold. But it was really a wonderful trip. When Mother was with us there were six of us. So Bruce got stuck in the back of the station wagon, at age 10, with the luggage. I think our son Dan had finally had enough of being with the family, understandable you know. So at one point in time he said, "What if I went home a week early? I would like to go to graduation at my high school," where he was a junior and he knew a lot of the seniors. "And then I could get the car and meet you." So we said, "OK." He went home and stayed with friends.

Hughes: Where did he go to high school?

Evans: Charles Wright.

Hughes: Well, what a cool thing to know that you've got a job and time for another trip of a lifetime.

Evans: So, that's what we did. Then we came home and went to Evergreen, which was great. I remember—probably in November or

December—the provost at Evergreen had invited Dan and me to dinner at their home. They were very nice people. And it was fun because we played some games. And I remember going home that night and saying, "You know what? Not once did we discuss politics tonight. Isn't that great?" Because politics always sort of dominated conversation somewhere along the line, no matter who we were with. So that was a complete change for us, and I think it was a very healthy change. We moved into their president's house—they've since sold it—out on Cooper Point. It was just a rambler house, nothing wonderful about it, except that it had space for us all and it had the most glorious view looking out on the very high waterfront over to Mt. Rainier. It was interesting because Evergreen was sort of casual about things. I don't know if that's changed, but at that time it was a pretty casual place and they were great for potlucks. I remember one potluck we were having that included students. A big gathering. That's always a little scary. You don't know what to have out and what all to provide because you've got a large crowd and you've got to have a lot of serving dishes. And one of the students brought a big pot of soup. I enjoyed the people that were there, and the people I worked with. I joined ECCO, which is their community college group, Evergreen College & Community Organization. We would meet and do things, try and promote cooperation and connections with the community. We enjoyed our time there a lot.

Hughes: So the boys are still at home. And Dan Jr. is thinking about college.

Evans: It was a change in schools for the younger boys. You asked me earlier if I get up early. Well, when Dan was a freshman in high school we would send him up to Charles Wright. There was a carpool. Sally Gorton and I, and the Deans. There were four boys—two Deans and then Todd Gorton and Dan Evans Jr. We did the driving. The kids had to be at school at 8. I just remember getting up at 6 o'clock on the days I drove. And I'm not morning person, *at all*. I'm a night person. And I'd get in the car with my son Dan, and then I'd go pick up Todd, and then I'd go pick up these two brothers—the Dean brothers. Nobody was talking. Coming home was worse. I'd get there: "*Hi*, how was school?" "OK." You know with four boys. And then Danny got involved with sports and played football there so he'd get home late. It was just a terrible schedule. And he was still going to Charles Wright when we came to Evergreen. That's when we bought him a car—a little Datsun—so he could drive himself. But the other boys had to come across the city. Bruce went to Jefferson Middle School and Mark went to Capital High School. So that was a big change for them, a whole new group of people.

Hughes: You're still doing a lot of schlepping around as a mom.

Evans: Oh absolutely. But it was fine. It was just fine.

Hughes: When you were at Evergreen did you start getting involved in any new causes?

Evans: I was doing Planned Parenthood in the 1970s. And then I was involved with some things on the campus. And entertaining. I'd still do that sort of thing, but in a different way, without the cook and housekeeper. Well, I had a woman who helped clean, and she was lovely. In fact, we still correspond.

Hughes: Did your mother go with you to the college president's residence?

Evans: Yes.

Hughes: So Mother lived with you until the end of her life?

Evans: No. In those days she was in her 80's. She had congestive heart failure, diabetes and arthritis. Three very common things in older people, but they conflicted with one another. And her arthritis was so painful at times. But with the adult diabetes that she got, it got so bad. She had a sweet tooth and I didn't control her diet as well I should have. It was difficult. Her bedroom was downstairs where two of the boys were. And the stairs were hard for her. But every night after dinner—the boys still can do it—she'd say, "Is there dessert?" And I'd say, "No Mother, there's no dessert." I don't make dessert.

Hughes: You went cold turkey off dessert after the 15 pounds you gained in the first campaign for governor, right?

Evans: I just never did desserts. At any rate, Mother became more frail. And the boys were attentive. It was lovely because they took care of her in many ways. They would take her to the bathroom and shut the door for her when she had to go. It was quite lovely to see this reversal of roles that they had. They adored her, of course. But she was getting more and more frail so somebody had to be there a lot of the time. And she was also getting forgetful. And then when Dan ended up going to the Senate, Mother was an issue. She went over to Sun Valley to stay with my sister Mary for a time. It was very serendipitous in a way. And then we found a wonderful place near my other sister, outside of Portland in a family home where they had two people and had children. It was wonderful because mother loved children. So it was a great place for her. They took good care of her and did her nails, you know, did her hair. So she lived there until 1987 when she died. She was 94.

Hughes: Were Dan's parents still alive during that era?

Evans: Dan's father died in 1979, then two years later his mother, and then my mother.

Hughes: Tell us about the highlights of the Evergreen years.

Evans: Well, there was Willi Unsoeld's memorial service. *(Editor's Note: Unsoeld, one of the founding faculty at the college, died on Mount Rainier in 1979, together with an Evergreen student.)* That was very moving. And the story of Dan rappelling down the clock tower at Evergreen (in the spring of 1973) is pretty interesting.

Hughes: Somehow I missed that one.

Evans: Willi Unsoeld was a real mountain climber, and he just kept saying, "Dan, you've got to do this." And Dan would say, "Willi, I haven't rappelled in a long time." Finally he decided to do it. I think the day it happened was the dedication of the Recreation Center, and the clock tower is part of the Daniel J. Evans Library, which is also the Administration Building.

Hughes: Did you rappel down the clock tower too?

Evans: No! I've never rappelled anything.

Hughes: Quote of the day: "I never rappelled anything."—Nancy Evans

Evans: Those years at Evergreen (1977-83) were a good time for us.

Hughes: But Dan had his hands full. He fought off efforts by Dixy Lee Ray and members of the Legislature to close the school, which they viewed as a haven for hippies. His reputation and moxie probably saved the day. Many believe his tenure was crucial to the school's future.

Evans: That's right. And our lives were changing, too. Our oldest son, Dan, went off to college. And then our next son, Mark, went to college.

Hughes: Where Dan Jr. go?

Evans: To Whitman.

Hughes: Like his mother, his aunts and his uncle.

Evans: And cousins. He had cousins there. A lot of my nephews and nieces went there....All three sons majored in history at their various schools.

Hughes: Well, they'd had a front row seat for history.

Hughes: Had you kept strong ties with your alma mater over the years?

Evans: Yes. Whitman has an unusual, not unique, but unusual governance system. They have the trustees, who are the real fiduciary-responsible board.

The Evans family at The Evergreen State College. Dan rapelled the clock tower in the background. *Evans family album*

Hughes: There's that wonderful word that we all learn when we get on boards. You always need to remember that you have a *fiduciary* responsibility.

Evans: And then there's a board of overseers. And Whitman was styled that way by its first president. He had been a student at Williams College in Massachusetts so he styled it on their system of the board of overseers and trustees. So I was on the board of overseers at that time.

Hughes: And then later became a trustee?

Evans: Yes.

Hughes: Was that often a progression there?

Evans: No, not necessarily. The board of overseers at that time was large. In fact Bob Skotheim, who was the president then, sort of enlarged it. It got as big as 80 sometimes. They had meetings on the campus, and I was on committees so I would come over a little more often. He made it bigger to build goodwill, that sort of thing. But then when we went East I resigned from the board of overseers.

Hughes: When did you get involved with the cancer support group?

Evans: Oh, that was when we came back to Seattle from D.C. in 1989.

Hughes: Did that coincide with your own bout with cancer?

Evans: No. My very dear friend, Barbara Frederick, was the ED (executive director) of an organization here called Cancer Lifeline. And she had built it up. It started with a woman who had breast cancer back in the days when there were very few resources and not a lot of knowledge. She and her husband and friends sat around their kitchen table discussing how to deal with it: Where do you do this, and how do you do that, and where do you buy this, and what have you. And after she died her husband and friends went on with this project. It started out as just a 24/7 free phone line where you had trained people to answer all your questions, except medical questions, or just talk to you if you needed somebody to talk to. It's 3 in the morning and you're feeling confused and vulnerable. Someone was there to say, "I'm here to help you." When Barbara became the executive director it was evolving into other things. So she asked me if I would help. And I said, "Yes, what do you want?" So we decided we would form an advisory committee, like a board, only smaller, which I did.

Hughes: As a cancer survivor, that's really close to my heart.

Evans: And that was in 1990, '91.

Hughes: But we didn't finish up with where we were in 1983. Suddenly and unexpectedly, U.S. Senator Henry M. Jackson dies of a heart attack.

Evans: It was sad to lose Scoop, but the timing was very serendipitous, and that leads to another story. The day before he died we had taken Mark, our middle son, up to SeaTac and put him on the plane for his junior year in college at Williams. Then the next morning we took Bruce, our youngest son, up to SeaTac and put him on the plane. He went to Yale. So we came back home. It was August. Beautiful out.

Hughes: Was there some sort of an exchange going where the children of college presidents got a break on tuition?

Evans: No, no, there was none of that. I can still remember when we were in D.C., and Bruce was at Yale we paid every month for nine months. I can remember writing the last check, and saying, "My God, that's the last check I'm going write to Yale. I'm going to have" whatever it was "$2,500 more a month to…" Well, that $2,500 just dissolved; I don't know where it went.

Hughes: Did you have three in college at the same time?

Evans: No, just always two.

Hughes: Do you know what tuition is at Whitman College now?

Evans: Oh yes, you're going to pay $40,000—$41,000 a year.

Hughes: It's the same as an Ivy League school, and deservedly because it's a comparable school.

Evans: Actually, it was always more. But I think Mark and Bruce, although they never said it, I think they both wanted to go away where nobody knew who they were. Actually, I know that for a fact.

Hughes: They didn't want to go to Evergreen where dad was?

Evans: No, no, that was not an option. I think even Whitman was too close. Just to get away because they'd always been the governor's son, all of them. And it was particularly hard on our oldest son, being a "junior," because he was always identified as the governor's son, and that's really hard on a kid. I know in grade school he would bring home these papers sometimes and I would look at them. And he got an A, and I'd say, "Why did you get an A?" And he said, "Well, that's what they gave me." Well, I know it was because he was Dan Evans' son, and he didn't deserve an A. But Mark and Bruce went East to school, and that was fine. The trouble is that they're still back there.

But anyway, we came home from SeaTac. It was a gorgeous afternoon, and the Evergreen president's house had a deck out in back overlooking the bay and Mt. Rainier. We were having a drink, sitting out there just talking. And I remember I said, "You know, now that the boys are gone...." You hear these stories about families that sort of fall apart sometimes. And I said, "Are we still going to like each other?" And Dan said, "Well, of course." And I said, "I don't know, it just seems strange. What are we going to do?" It was this deep discussion that was going on out there. But we were enjoying the sun. Finally I said, "Well, I've got to go fix dinner." And Dan says, *"Why?"* And I said, "Well, I don't know!" (laughter) So I think I sat back down and we had another drink. We went to bed that night. And at about 11 or midnight, Dan's brother Roger called. He said, "Have you heard the news?" Scoop Jackson had died. Well, we had not heard the news. And the next morning, right after these two boys had gone off to school and we had talked about "What do we do now?" the phone started ringing. The timing of everything was incredible.

Hughes: Would Slade Gorton have been one of the first to call, or would it have been John Spellman?

Evans: Oh no, no, not the governor. I don't have any idea who was the first to call. The press gets on it right away. I just have no clue about who called first. But there was immediate speculation about whether Dan would take the U.S. Senate seat. Each state, you know, has different laws about such things. So they had to figure out what the procedure was and finally concluded that the governor would appoint somebody. Then

The Evans family on the deck at the home of the president
of The Evergreen State College. *Evans family album*

the question was, did it have to be the same party or not? Because John
Spellman was a Republican and Scoop had been a Democrat. Once they
got that figured out, then the speculation really began. But it was something that Dan never thought he wanted to do. It had come up in the past.
Did he want to run for the Senate? Well, we thought Maggie and Scoop
were going to be there forever so why think about it? But Dan just liked
being governor and president of the college. He just didn't think that was
something he wanted to do.

But things happened over the next several days. Slade encouraged him,
and *finally* somebody *(it was Secretary of State Ralph Munro)* suggested
that he should talk to the governor. And Dan said, "Why should I do
that?" And someone said, "Well, because it's just the polite thing to do."
And Dan says, "You're probably right. I should do that." So he called the
governor. He had a breakfast meeting with John Spellman. And he was

walking down the hall, getting ready to leave, and shaking his head. He still didn't know what he was going to say. And *I* didn't know what he was going to say. He just didn't know if this is what he wanted to do. But he met with Spellman and ended up saying to the governor something to the effect that "If you think that I would be a good candidate I would be happy to run." That sort of thing. And then John said he would appoint him to succeed Scoop.

It was a *very* hard time. One of the hardest times in our lives, I think, because he was appointed like that day or the next day, but then had to run for election for two months or something like that while serving in the Senate in Washington D.C. (if he wanted to remain for the last five years of Jackson's Senate term.)

Hughes: Against Mike Lowry. Talk about contrasting styles!

Evans: So, he had to fly back to D.C. We flew Danny out from college at Whitman and brought the boys down from their colleges so they would be there for the swearing in. We went into President Reagan's office and met with him; did all those things. And then I came back home. Now I'm back here in this house, alone, and we have to move out. And Dan had to fly back there every week to learn how to be a senator. Fly home on the weekends, organize and put together a campaign, raise money. And he *never* asked for money. Somebody else had to do that. And he had to campaign out here and then go back and do his work there. So it was particularly hard on Dan. He was doing all the running around. And he got grumpier, and grumpier as the campaign wore on. He really did. And so it was really hard, *really, really* hard. But he won the election.

Hughes: During those six years while you were at Evergreen, did it ever occur to you that there would be any other kind of political jobs that would interest him? Most people were surprised that he actually took the Senate appointment. There's an interesting take on all this that I got from interviewing Booth Gardner. I know now that you're a good friend of Booth's, so I'm sure you've heard this, but Booth told me that near the end of his second term he asked Dan for his advice about whether to run

U.S. Senator Dan Evans with his family at the National Capitol
in the 1980s. *Evans family album*

for the Senate and Dan said, "You're not a legislator, you're a manager. The gridlock will really frustrate you." Because that's what Dan really found out from serving in the Senate. In terms of political temperament, (he and Booth) were really peas in a pod, unlike Slade who just loves—

Evans: *Slade loves it.* He likes the process. Exactly right. I don't think Slade fully understands why Dan never really got into being a Senator.

Hughes: By the way, did you read that remarkable book about the 9/11 Commission that just came out?

Evans: I've read parts of it.

Hughes: Well, did you read the part about Slade and Jamie Gorelick, a deputy attorney general during the Clinton Administration? She served on the 9/11 Commission with Slade.

Evans: Very smart lady.

Hughes: Yes. And John Ashcroft's people tried to say that it was her fault that intelligence information about terrorists wasn't shared (because of a policy memo she had written). All of a sudden she realized what was happening as Ashcroft's testimony unfolded during the 9/11 Commission hearings and she just froze. And Slade put his hand over on hers and said, (whispering) "Let me take care of this." Slade just proceeded to eviscerate Ashcroft because he has such a strong sense of fairness. Everyone stylizes Slade Gorton as being this über partisan person, and here he is defending this liberal Clintonian Democrat—

Evans: Yes. I know he likes and respects her a lot.

Hughes: It was an amazing episode. But I agree with you that Slade so loved the Senate that he probably still can't fully fathom why Dan didn't.

Evans: He loved it.

Hughes: So, was there anything that popped up during those six years at Evergreen when Dan thought, "Ah, maybe I'll run for governor again."

Evans: No. The other part of that story, I guess, that I just remembered is that the week before Scoop died Dan had called the chair of the Evergreen trustees, Thelma Jackson, because he wanted to write this autobiography he's been working on for so long. He had actually started doing some research, and started organizing the governor's years, and going back into his own childhood—those sort of things. So he had gotten that far, but not really doing research like he is now. So he asked for an appointment with her. And he was going to tell her that he would work until the following June, but then he wanted to leave Evergreen. He wanted to write his book and then do something else. He didn't know what—just something else.

Hughes: Boy, fate is fickle, isn't it?

Evans: Yes it is.

Hughes: I knew Henry M. Jackson fairly well, and I got the impression that Henry M. Jackson and Daniel Jackson Evans got along really well.

Evans: Oh I think so. Yes, why not?

Hughes: I mean a lot of times in Washington politics there's not a dime's worth of difference between a conservative Democrat and a liberal to moderate Republican.

Evans: Actually, I don't think Dan and Scoop agreed all that much.

Hughes: Really?

Evans: There are a lot of things that Dan didn't agree with him on, but he didn't dislike him. I thought he agreed more with Maggie than with Scoop, actually. But I'm just speculating.

Hughes: By the way, way back there in 1974 when David Ammons and Mike Layton were talking to you and you were ruminating about what you might do in the future, you remarked that you thought it would be good, sooner or later, for the kids to maybe live for a couple of years in Washington, D.C., because there were "so many opportunities."

Evans: Well, in our discussion before Dan finally said yes to Governor Spellman, I just said, "I'd be happy to do it. I don't care. It's not that I *want* you to do it, because I don't care that much. I just think it would be an interesting time, and an interesting place to live, and maybe a good experience for us"—he and I, as well as the boys, although they were pretty much getting to be on their own. But, yes, I thought it would be a good experience for us, but I didn't care if he didn't do it.

Trova Heffernan (Legacy Project Director): You're married to such an icon of Washington politics—I mean, with the development of the "Dan Evans Republican" wing of the party and everything he did.

Evans: I know. I don't picture him that way, but I know some people do.

Heffernan: That's what I'm wondering. And you must be so proud of him.

Evans: I am.

Heffernan: But about what the most? I mean is it his public life? Is it *who* he is as a father, the person that people don't see?

Evans: Well, I'm proud of him in all ways—all those ways. I can also be very mad at him. You must understand that. I can get so mad at him—and he at me. So we're very normal that way. We have fights, but you know, then you get over it. But I'm constantly learning the depth of knowledge he has about an issue, where I just jump into it. There was something we were discussing just recently, and I just go off, "Da, da, da, da, da, da." And he said, "Yeah, but how do you know that? Just because you read it it's true?" Well, of course later it came out that what I was reading was not true and he was absolutely right. And it makes me *so* mad that he's always right on these things. So I appreciate his unwillingness to jump into forming his ideas just because that's what he thinks at the time. He thinks it through and looks for knowledge, the background, all the facts and details of the issue before he comes to *his* conclusion. And I appreciate that because it's something that doesn't happen often enough. So much of what you read in the paper is this immediate visceral reaction by people, and Dan just never does that. He knows for a fact why he's saying something.

Heffernan: The other question I have is on the mom front. How do you raise three boys and instill confidence in them? It's so important, especially in today's world.

Hughes: Trova has a nearly 4-year-old who is pretty amazing.

Evans: That's great.

Heffernan: But to not feel that they are just Dan Evans' sons.

Hughes: It was hard with our oldest son, and I'm sure he would agree with that, being a junior, and also being the oldest. The other boys came by it a little more easily because they had different names to begin with—not Daniel J. Evans Jr. Dan Jr. had the most struggles with it. Nothing horrendous, but just did. People would point him out, classmates, and friends and what have you. That's hard on a kid. You want to be part of the group.

Heffernan: It just struck me when you were talking about your son that he got a grade on a paper that you felt that he didn't deserve. And as a mother I would want my son to—

Evans: He was in junior high at the time. That's why we sent him to Charles Wright (for more rigorous academic expectations). Along that line, Bruce, who went to Yale, was very young. His birthday is August 21st, so he had just turned 17 when he went to college because he had skipped a grade in grade school. I can still remember he was not driving because he wasn't 16, and he was going to the prom. I think it was the Senior Prom and some senior had asked him to go. And Dan said to him, "Well, how are you getting there? Do you need a ride?" And he said, "No. She's picking me up." (laughing)

Hughes: That's great. This kid's an operator.

Evans: He's always just fine. And most boys wouldn't like that, but he thought it was great to be driven around by a girl. But he went back there to school and he called us one time. There's a time when you go East to school— six weeks, two months, at least these two—and suddenly they realized they're a little homesick. And I can remember Mark called from Massachusetts: "Hi, mom." You know, it was one of those. "Hi, how are things going?" And I said, "How's school?" And he said, "Well, people are really different back here." They both said the same thing. I said, "Well, of course they're different." He said, "And they speak so fast." Well, it's true, Easterners speak fast. And I said, "Remember they think you're different, too. They might think you speak differently." Well, that sort of helped. But then they get over it, and then they're fine, and then they all have great times in college.

So Bruce called one night. It was late and there was noise in the background. I think he was at a party and had had a little beer—my guess, I don't *know* that. But Scoop had just died and everything was unsettled and suddenly maybe we were going to the Senate. But he was having the same kinds of feelings. Finally he said, "Am I going to still have a bedroom?" I almost cried right then and there. I said, "*Of course*, no matter where you are you will have a bedroom, and we will be sure that you're always welcome in our home." They both had this moment of being homesick and being far away from home. And then that disappeared.

Then I got another call from Bruce. Probably November or something like that, and he said, "Well, it's all over." And we said, "What's all over?" And he said, "Well, they know who I am." And I said, "What do you mean?" People would say, "What does your dad do?" "Well, he's an engineer." That's what he always said, "He's an engineer." And then this U.S. Senate appointment came along, and somehow his dad's name was somewhere. One of his friends saw it in the paper, or something, and said, "Your dad is not an engineer." And he said, "I tried all this time to just be Bruce Evans, nobody's son, and here I am again." And by that time he could laugh about it.

Lori Larson: Following up on Trova's question about the "Dan Evans' Republican" idea and Dan being an icon in this state, none of the children really got interested in politics themselves did they?

Evans: They're all very interested in politics, but I don't think any of them want to run for office. Our son Bruce actually works on The Hill (in D.C.). He has a great job. When he graduated from Yale he decided he wanted to take a backpack and go to Europe for a year, which he did. We said, "That's a great idea." He worked in London for a time and the rest of us joined him for Christmas that year. And then he taught skiing to—as he put it—to bratty European rich children—who didn't have to come and ski because they could go and drink in bars. And then he came back as this gorgeous, tall, *very tall*, lean, good-looking young man a year later. I could hardly recognize him because he had lived on the beaches of Greece for a couple of months with a bunch of other guys from Canada and Australia. He hooked up with a lot of Australians and Canadians as it turned out. Then he got a job in Commerce, where he met his future wife.

I ran into Frank Murkowski one day, a senator from Alaska and then later governor. I said to him, "If you're looking for somebody I've got a son who is looking for a job. And he's really a good writer." And he is—he's a *very* good writer. And everybody is always looking for people who write well. Frank said, "Oh, have him come see me." He ended up working for Frank for a while. Then I ran into Mark Hatfield, who was a senator from Oregon but whom we had known as governors. We were at a department store together. He was looking at men's clothes and I said, "I've got a son who's looking for a job." And he said, "Send him over." Bruce went over and ended up working as a staff person on the Senate Appropriations Subcommittee of the Interior, which is Bruce's field. He loves that. So he ended up working for several senators, including Slade for a while, and Mark Hatfield and Ted Stevens, each as they became chair of that subcommittee. He had been on Interior now for several years, and was the lead Republican staff person. And then Pete Domenici asked him to come to Energy, which is the other issue he liked. So he went over to Pete Domenici to be head of that committee staff. Really bright guy, Domenici. They lived across the street from us. So he did that. And he hadn't been there all that long, but he was really liking it because he liked Pete, and he liked the energy issues. His present boss is a senator from Mississippi, Thad Cochran. Thad said, "I'd like you to be head of the Appropriations Committee," the whole committee. So that's what he is now—the lead Republican staff committee person on the Senate Appropriations Committee, which discusses this umpteen-billion dollar budget every year. We all went back especially to see him because he had this gorgeous office in the capitol, right in the Capitol—chandeliers, fireplace, you know, looking down the Mall to the Washington Monument and on and on and on. And then of course the Republicans lost control of the Senate in November, so his office got moved. But he still has a very nice office.

When we were back there a while ago I was talking to him. I said, "Bruce, you ought to run for office. You'd be just so great. You're smart and you're wise and you're honest—all those things." But they live in Virginia and he said, "Well, the trouble is we've got this and that and I haven't really involved myself in local things." You don't have time to do that. His wife is a lobbyist. She works downtown now, but she used to work for some House members. They all talk about it a lot—politics. But no, they're in other areas and probably not interested in running for something.

Hughes: I'd like to go back to 1983 and talk more about that tough decision Dan made. Everything seems to happen in a hurry in your lives. The next thing you know, Dan is sworn in as a U.S. Senator and you're getting people together for that event. Dan's back there. You're house hunting. But he's also immediately gearing up for an election just two months later for the last five years of Jackson's term. Dan found himself in this race with Seattle Congressman Mike Lowry. Had both of you known Mike at all?

Evans: We had known him, but not well. We know him better now.

Hughes: He's a hard guy to dislike isn't he?

Evans: Absolutely. He's a love—he really is. He really loves this country and the state, and he really wants the best for it. And he and Dan a number of years ago started the Washington Wildlife & Recreation Coalition, which has raised millions of dollars to help protect our forests and our wildlife. And they worked at that together very successfully. We're friends with all these people (we've encountered in political life over the years). We all get along very well.

Hughes: Then when Mike and Mary Lowry were in the Governor's Mansion (1993-97) they must have been really cordial and welcoming to you.

Evans: They were.

Hughes: As for the U.S. Senate, the irony, as it turned out, was that it really was a frustrating job for Dan, wasn't it? From being a governor and a college president, as a manager, to being in the Senate, where there was partisan gridlock.

Evans: Well, that was a problem, as was seniority. When he went back there, of course, he was Number 100. It's not like even going in with the class in November, when you could be Number 94 or whatever. But he was 100, but it wasn't the number that bothered him so much. This is why he had never dreamt of becoming a member of the Senate. He really liked to, as he says, "set the agenda." And that's what he had done for years, and I think very well. So it was a huge learning process. He was thrown into it, and it was just a horrendous period of time. He was traveling back and forth across the country every week, and then working seven days a week—doing campaigning and being in the Senate and learning the system. There was a system, and seniority is everything. He immediately took over Scoop's office. And a few of the people were willing to stay on, but most of them went to other jobs and other offices. A few stayed on just to help. They were still cleaning out Scoop's office when we got back there. It was *very* hard for them, and we were trying to be appreciative of their situation. They had just lost their boss, whom they loved, and also their jobs. So it was very hard on everybody. Then Dan had to hire a staff, as well as run a campaign, as well as become a senator and all of that.

Hughes: Did you get involved with that too Nancy—hiring the new staff?

Evans: Oh no, I can't do that. No, that's him. That's when he called on our good friend Bill Jacobs who had been head of L&I (Labor & Industries) in Olympia. When Jim Dolliver became a Supreme Court justice and left the Governor's Office, Dan asked Bill to be his AA, which he did for the last couple of years of Dan's time in office. Bill actually had retired and they had a travel business in Olympia, but he was called back to the Department of Labor in D.C. for a short-term thing, a two-year thing. Bill and his wife Pat are two of our dearest friends. So he was there and due to leave very quickly and go back to Olympia. Pat had stayed in Olympia because this was short-term and she ran the business. Dan asked Bill if he would step in as AA of the Senate Office. I don't remember exactly how this worked but Bill may have said, "Well, for a short time I'd be happy to come and help you get set up, but I'm due to go back to Olympia."

Hughes: Sort of like your mom telling you and Dan, "I'll stay for six months."

Evans: Exactly. That's exactly what it was. Of course, bless his heart, Bill stayed with us the whole time (1983-89). It was great having him there because he was such a good friend. Well, not only a good friend but he

Sporting a hat he was given at a Western-wear shop, Dan Evans campaigns
for the U.S. Senate in 1983 with Nancy at his side. Matt McVay, *Seattle Times*

has so much sensibility about politics and people. He did a great job of
running the office because you hire a lot of young people, primarily. We
kept Sam Spina, who had been one of Scoop's key people. He led the L.A.'s,
legislative assistants, and was sort of their boss, the guy who kept all the
legislation moving. He was great. He'd been there through several senators
and was with us the whole time. All the L.A.s were kids—bright young
people. We still get together with them a lot. In fact, Dan had lunch with
four of them recently. They call themselves "The council"—all women—
and periodically they ask Dan to lunch.

Hughes: That has to be one of the most gratifying things to see all
those really bright young people moving up in their careers.

Evans: All of them have done well. They had a really wonderful working relationship, and part of it was because they all loved Bill. He has a
great sense of humor and he had fun with them. At the same time, he
could be very tough when he needed to be tough and he kept *very* good
control of that office. And they liked Dan as well, of course. And so it was

a fun office to be around. They worked hard and then they played hard. Dan would be in the office and we'd have to go somewhere at 7 o'clock at night, and there they'd all be with the pizzas out and they were all having a good time, still working. Bill was with us for five years and that was a great, great help. Pat stayed in Olympia but she came out a lot.

Hughes: Did you go back to D.C. almost immediately after Dan took office?

Evans: No, I couldn't. I still had a house to run in Olympia, too. I had to transition us out of there. I went back a couple weekends just to house hunt and to try to figure out where we're going to live. Then I had to come home and pack up the house. Evergreen was very nice and let us extend through Christmas, although we didn't spend Christmas there because we were pretty much packed up by then. We actually moved out, I suppose, the first of January. Then after some looking we finally bought a house, which we loved. It was a little 20-foot-wide house that was built in 1878. It had three stories and a garage and a basement. It was quite big by Hill standards. We were on the Hill, two blocks from the Supreme Court

After living in the Governor's Mansion, and even at the Evergreen president's house with a view of Mt. Rainier and all, it was a change. But it was a very interesting place—very up and down, very vertical. The ceiling in our bedroom and in the living room was the old tin—embossed tin squares. And the crown moldings all around were all the original. Fortunately, it had been updated with new wiring and plumbing. We gutted the kitchen, and gutted our bathroom. There was not much closet space anywhere. I looked at houses that had never had closets when they were built.

Hughes: People wonder today why everyone in that era had those big wardrobe cabinets. They were closets.

Evans: Exactly. A lot of those are back there. But in the meantime, we had to find someplace to live temporarily, which was not easy. But we had some wonderful friends. (Washington Congressman) Sid Morrison was one, and early in January we stayed at his condo because he wasn't there an awful lot. It was a big condo, with several bedrooms. So that was just wonderful.

And the boys came and could stay there when Dan was sworn in.

Hughes: Was Joel Pritchard, your old friend, in Congress then?

Evans: Yes, he still was. (*Editor's Note: Pritchard left Congress in 1985.*) And he was also a very good friend of my brother's. Joel was a very close friend of ours.

I finally found a condo that would rent. It's hard to rent a place for just a month or two. And then I had to furnish it. I remember going down to one of these rental places. They had several of them in D.C. I went to a couple of them and figured out which one had the best quality. Everything of ours was in storage because we had no place to move it to. So I picked out a sofa, two end tables, and a coffee table, two lamps, two chairs, a king-size bed with two end tables, and two lamps, and two dressers, and a twin bed for the other bedroom in case a child came to visit. And I had packed four plates, four bowls, a coffee pot—I mean just the basics—and a few glasses and mugs.

Hughes: A lot of people imagine how swell it is to be a United States Senator.

Evans: Many people wrote me letters just out of curiosity (over details like that), asking, "And how much did they give you to move?" Zero! "And do they provide housing for you?" Zero! And, "Do they provide help for you?" Zero, zero! And here I was just struggling to get us settled in. I can remember the first meal I was cooking in this rental place and it occurred to me I didn't have a bowl to make a salad. I had brought a colander along for pasta, and I used it to toss a salad—without the dressing, of course. And I had a little frying pan and a pot.

Hughes: You two were like newlyweds all over again.

Evans: What I discovered was that you can get along so well with so little. It was a good lesson for me. Unfortunately, I didn't pay attention to it because I don't throw things away, and I've acquired too much since then. But we lived that way in this rental situation. One of Bruce's high school buddies came back to visit on his spring break, and of course then I went out and rented a bed because we didn't have one. When I was renting this furniture and asked if they would deliver it, they said, "Payment?" I had a credit card that had Dan's name on it—"Senator Daniel J. Evans." And the clerk said, "Well, he will have to come down and sign this." And I said, "Why?" And she said, "Well, because he is a salary earner." And I said, "But I'm his wife. And it's a 50/50," you know. I did this very calmly. "And isn't there something about community property?" And she said, "No, I'm sorry. He's going to have to…" I said, *"He does not have the time."* And I knew in my mind not only that, but he would not do it. As a matter of principle he would not do it. But I didn't say that to her. Finally I think she said, "You're going to have to take this and he's going to have to write something down." *(Like a note saying she was authorized to use the card.)* So I said, "Then I'm not buying your things because I'm not going to be treated that way. This is 50/50. I said that we would pay the bill, and we will pay the bill." I got quite incensed by the whole process. And eventually it worked and they said OK and I paid the bill. This is 1983, and they didn't know who I was. We were newly arrived, and all of that. Nevertheless, he was in the U.S. Senate, for Pete's sake. You would think that would have helped with something. It wasn't like we were transients moving through, or anything.

But I got the rental furniture delivered, and we lived that way until the rooms in the house were fixed up. Then we moved into this great little house of ours.

Hughes: Eleanor Roosevelt often told the story that when Franklin became assistant secretary of the Navy in 1917 that she had a social obligation as an official's wife to "go calling." And if Mrs. Evans or Mrs. So-and-So wasn't there she'd leave a calling card to be certain that her visit was duly noted.

Evans: And that was how it was done. You know, Washington, D.C., is a very formal city. It's Southern, and it still is to this day. They don't leave their cards any more, I don't think, but there is a great amount of civility there.

Hughes: Was there some residue of all that early protocol when you got there, Nancy?

Evans: Oh yes. There was no more of the calling and leaving the cards, but there were certain formalities.

Hughes: So when you arrived in town in 1983 as Mrs. Senator Dan Evans, there were certain expectations in terms of going to go see some people?

Evans: No, not that sort of thing. But the way parties were given and dinners and things. There was still that. And sometimes the women would retire to the whatever room while the men sat around the table and had the brandy and cigars and what have you. I had some of that in Seattle, actually.

Hughes: And you were first lady and a senator's wife in an era where smoking was still socially acceptable.

Evans: Oh yes, a lot of people smoked. At the Mansion, we were very careful to put ashtrays *everywhere* because we would find residue of put-out cigar butts in planters and places they shouldn't have been.

There's still a lot of smoking going on around this world....I'm a reformed smoker. I haven't smoked since I was married. I quit smoking when we were engaged, actually. But when I go by a young person, which you do a lot in Seattle, they're often standing on the street having a cigarette. They're on a cigarette break because they can't smoke in their buildings any more. And I just want to go up to that person and say, "For personal reasons, I'm telling you, I've had siblings who smoke and you *do not* want to do it because it is a terrible death." But of course I walk on by and I don't say anything.

Hughes: Sometimes they're like little lepers, out there huddled in the cold, feeding their habit aren't they?

Evans: Overcoats on, the wind is blowing, and there they are. I used to have an occasional cigarette after a dinner party. In fact, I used to smoke this little cigar sort of thing. But I couldn't even do that now. My oldest sister, Barbara, died of emphysema, and that's not a nice death.

Hughes: No, it's nasty stuff. I've seen it close-up at the cancer clinic.

Evans: And Bill, my brother, smoked several packs all his life until he was diagnosed with lymphoma. And then, with great, great difficulty, he quit. But it was so hard for him. They have a place in Bainbridge, but it was not convenient for doctors and what have you, so they stayed with us when he was pretty ill. Their bedroom was downstairs. And I remember one time I was walking by and I smelled the smoke. And I called down and said, "Bill, put that cigarette out!" And then I walked on.

Hughes: No little voice came back that said—

Evans: No. And he came up later and said, "How did you know I was smoking?" Sometimes he went into the bathroom and turned on the fan so it wouldn't be smoky. And then I'd say, "You cannot smoke in this house. I will not let you!" It was for his own good, so I was really tough on it. I just kept saying, "I do not want you to smoke. And if you respect me in any way, you will not smoke in this house." There used to be cigarette butts all over the patio.

Hughes: Well, back to politics: In 1987, Dan had had enough. He said he wasn't going to seek another term in the Senate. "I've lived through five years of bickering and protracted paralysis," he said. "Five years is enough. I just can't face another six years of frustrating gridlock."

Evans: Well, he *was* frustrated, but it wasn't just that. He had enjoyed a lot about being a senator. I mean, getting offered the opportunities he wouldn't have otherwise had.

Hughes: For example?

Evans: Well, he was on the Foreign Relations Committee. And every foreign dignitary that came to visit the president always visited with the Foreign Relations Committee. So that was very interesting. And he always has liked that interaction. I thought he was always good at it, too. When we traveled to foreign countries when he was governor, it was always very easy for him to talk to the chief of state, the ambassador, whomever, because he liked that sort of interaction and he was knowledgeable about that country's issues. He always had knowledge of their history and of the country itself, and respect for the leadership. That sort of thing was very interesting to him, and very easy. And so he really liked that. And he also had the opportunity to go on a number of wonderful trips.

Hughes: Did you get to go, too?

Evans: I did many times. So that was interesting, and he really enjoyed that aspect. And he enjoyed some of the other committees that he was on that he was particularly interested in—Energy & Natural Resources, Indian Affairs.

But the legislative process is so slow and so frustrating sometimes. And of course now it's even worse than it was then. But besides the frustration, he also he looked at his life and his age, and he said, "If I don't leave now, I won't be able to seek other opportunities. And that was part of his thinking at that time. So that's an important part of why he didn't go for a second term.

Hughes: Did you make some really good friends among other senators and their spouses?

Evans: Yes, we did.

Hughes: Did you see a lot of Sally and Slade Gorton?

Evans: Well, we did and then he was defeated and they left.

EDITOR'S NOTE: Elected to the Senate in 1980, Gorton was defeated by Democrat Brock Adams in 1986, but ran again in 1988 and won back a seat in the Senate—the seat Dan Evans vacated. Adams did not seek re-election in 1992 in the wake of allegations of sexual improprieties with young women. Adams flatly denied the charges, which were published by *The Seattle Times*.

Hughes: Were you really stunned by those revelations about Brock?

Evans: Well, it was certainly surprising. Brock was a very hands-on person. He was very nice. And Betty, his wife, is a lovely, lovely lady. And it was hard on her. I felt so sorry for her. That was very tough. And she handled it beautifully, I must say.

Hughes: It's really sad in politics when you see a Pat Nixon, or Betty Adams going through a scandal.

Evans: And always having to have a stiff upper lip—having to put that curtain up in front of them, to look happy and be glad to greet people. It is very hard.

Hughes: That's another area where Nancy Evans has been fortunate, haven't you—to be married to a guy with the character of Dan Evans? It has been a really good 50 years of marriage, hasn't it?

Evans: Oh absolutely.

Hughes: Tell us about the most wonderful trip you got to take during those six years in the U.S. Senate?

Evans: We had more than just one. We really had some great trips. One of the most interesting trips we took was just Dan and I and his assistant for the Foreign Relations Committee. It was a young woman, Chris Dawson. We went to the Middle East, including Jordan. The foreign minister there had a lunch at his home for Dan. A very small gathering. We came in and we were greeted by everybody. The wives of cabinet officers were all gorgeous. Diamonds. Lots of jewelry. Chanel. Everything. Then the foreign minister said to Dan, "Well, Senator, we'll go off into this room. We want to talk with you about the issues. And Mrs. Evans and your assistant will go off with the women." Well, Chris, who was a bright, independent, single lady at that time, was furious. She almost turned red right there. I could see that Chris was about ready to say something. So I went over, and I think I whispered, "Just come quietly with me." So she did. We went to this tiny room off the entry and sat there with these Jordanian ladies. They were very nice, but we had nothing in common because all they wanted to talk about was their trips to London and Paris, and shopping. Chris was sitting there seething. And I was sitting there trying to look interested.

But Chris was just *livid*. And rightly so, she was the Senator's foreign affairs assistant and should have been included in the discussion, but was not included simply because she was a woman. I understood how she felt, it was very insulting to her training and professionalism, but I just knew that there was no sense in making a fuss about it at that time. It was going to happen as they wanted it to.

Hughes: Did you also go to Israel or Palestine?

Evans: Yes, we did.

Hughes: Did you form any impressions that have stuck with you as this eternal strife goes on?

Evans: It certainly is eternal, isn't it? We had a wonderful trip there that was hosted by a Jewish friend in Seattle. So he and his wife and daughter and son-in-law and Dan and I went. But Dan had told them up front, "This is a very nice offer, and I would like to do that, but if I do, I want to tell you that I'm not going to just visit Israel. I'm going to visit some other countries because I have to be fair." That was fine, so we did. It's such a wonderful place to visit because of all the history that is still in existence there—to visit the churches and the temples. We happened to be there on Easter, and that was *very* compelling.…There's this one church where three religions converge.

Hughes: The Church of the Holy Sepulchre in Jerusalem.

Evans: And so there were three services. We were there that morning. It was just a mob scene. And to me it was, frankly, so unspiritual. I'm not a real spiritual person, but it was *very* spiritual to the other people who were there. It was old and musty but it was a marvelous atmosphere. And then bells clang, or something, and those worshipers leave and the next group comes in. It was fascinating. That was a marvelous trip because we learned a lot and developed great appreciation for the struggles they have. But it does seem that somehow, sometime, somebody has to figure out that they can't just keep firing back and forth at each other and actually win anything.

Hughes: You immediately empathized with Dan's bright young aide when she was excluded. Being a young woman with progressive views, and coming of age when you did, did you meet emerging female politicians—Jennifer Dunn, for instance—women who really impressed you?

Evans: Jennifer did a good job. She worked hard. Very nice person; died much too young. *(Editor's Note: The former State Republican Party chairwoman and congresswoman from Seattle died at the age of 66 in 2007.)*

Hughes: Have you had a chance to talk with any of the many successful young women in public life today like Chris Gregoire, Patty Murray, Maria Cantwell, Congresswoman Cathy McMorris Rodgers and House Majority Leader Lynn Kessler?

Evans: I've never met Cathy. I've talked to Chris and I've talked to Patty Murray, briefly. But, no, not much.

Hughes: Patty Murray still seems like the school board member she once was—"the mom in tennis shoes…"

Evans: She is. And I think that that's what she prefers.

Hughes: She always returns calls.

Evans: And it gives her a sense of being of the people, so to speak.… There are a lot of bright women in politics today.

Hughes: Did you have any misgivings about not staying back East when Dan left the Senate?

Evans: No, never, no. I was really happy to come home. But I enjoyed much of what we did there. We did a lot of weekend trips. When we were at Harvard after Dan left the Senate, I think we spent one weekend there that whole time. We went up to Maine a couple times. We went off on little trips and we had never done that. We explored so many of the wonderful old buildings and old homes. And when we lived in D.C., my brother was there, so we would do a lot of those things together.

But Dan was gone a lot, so Bill Jacobs and I would do a lot together. He was my saving grace, and we're very good friends. I told him after-

Bill Jacobs, former chief of staff, and dear friend.

wards, "You know, Bill, I always hoped that somebody would see us together and think 'are they a couple?'" because I thought that would be such fun. I think I sort of shocked him. (laughing) But we did a lot together. We'd go to a lot of movies. And whenever Dan could get away, we'd do all sorts of things, including all the museums. That's why I think our family who live in Arlington with their three kids has such great experiences. That's what they do— they go to the Mall and to the museums and a variety of things. And those kids are well imbued with history. They know all the presidents' names. They know this, know that. It's just part of their language.

So we enjoyed all of that. But when Dan decided to come back home (to Washington State) that was just fine with me. Back there, it's a funny life in a way. It's wonderful but it never seemed like a natural life to me. That sounds sort of strange but it's just a superficial sort of thing in many ways. Maybe we just weren't there long enough to fully embed ourselves in the spirit of the thing.

Hughes: Did you make any lasting new friends there?

Evans: A lot of people because I hadn't known anybody to speak of. On our little block there were four senators. The Domenicis were across the street. The night before we drove home we stayed our last night in their home. They're very nice people. And Bob Graham lived three doors down, from Florida. And John Kerry, who ran for president four years ago, from Massachusetts. He wasn't around a lot but he lived there. I would walk everywhere. I would walk to the grocery. I would walk to the cleaners, and I would walk to the book store. It was all within walking distance, all urban. I walked to Dan's office. And we had one car; that was all. It worked because you take the Metro or a cab.

Let me tell you one thing that just occurred to me. I still remember it because it was so unique. They were celebrating the bicentennial of the signing of the constitution. So it was 1987. And they chose the same number of senators as the number of people who signed the Constitution. They planned a celebration and a re-enactment, in Independence Hall in Philadelphia. And Dan was chosen to be one of the senators. So some of the spouses went up with them. You read about the signing of the Constitution and the heavy drapes. It was all true. And there was a little tiny gallery up high above it looking down on the signing room.

Hughes: At Independence Hall?

Evans: Yes. You had to take turns standing up there because there wasn't room enough for all of us. They were reading the speeches and doing a great re-enactment. And then you'd go outside and wait and somebody else would take their turn. And that was fun. Then they had a reception or something and a dinner.

I don't remember if we spent the night or what, but I know that somehow we were coming home by helicopter. We went down to where we were supposed to catch the helicopter. Dan was not there. I think he maybe had to stay behind. But I'm standing in this sort of big area, waiting for the helicopter, together with some spouses and some senators. Strom Thurmond (of South Carolina, at that time the longest serving senator in U.S. history) came over to where I was standing. And he said, "Well Mrs. Evans, how does Dan like being a senator?" Or something like that, because Strom had been governor before being a senator. And he said, "Does he prefer being a governor or does he prefer being a senator?" I said, "Well, he really preferred being a governor because of the ability to set the agenda and organize things a bit more the way you would like to have them." And he patted me on my behind and said, "Yeah, but the Senate is where the *power* is!" And that's the way he said it, "The Senate is where the *power* is," emphasis on the power.

Hughes: "There, there little lady."

Evans: I almost laughed out loud, but I contained myself. That was very memorable for me.

Hughes: That's funny! And did you meet the senior Bushes?

Evans: Oh yes. Barbara came to the Senate wives quite often. The Senate wives would meet once a week. Ostensibly it was still Red Cross oriented but we were actually knitting and making shawls and things for Children's Hospital while we would sit and talk. There was sort of a cadre of a few women who were always there, and I would come often. So you'd come at 10, and then they'd bring lunch in and we'd have lunch. It was very pleasant, and a very nice way to know some of them. And Barbara Bush often came. And she was fun because she is a fun person. She liked to gossip, too, and she would tell us things that were going on—with her kids and what have you, or something about whoever was in town visiting. She was doing a needlepoint rug, and she would bring that and work on it. It was quite large. So yes, we got to know her. And when George Bush was running for president—when he was vice-president—we would see them at a lot of functions. He invited Dan and me over one evening, late afternoon, for a drink. Dan had not declared who he was supporting yet for president, so that's why we were invited. But it was fun. I had been to the Vice President's Residence before for functions and parties, dinners. And I had been there when the Rockefellers were there. That was interesting because the Rockefellers never really lived there. I think Happy was hardly ever in that home. But it was all decorated with very, very contemporary artwork. Rocky's artwork was everywhere. It was just a museum in its way. And then you came when the Bushes were there and it was all the comfortable, lovely chintz. And artwork as well, but it was more of a home. You knew they lived there.

EDITOR'S NOTE: The Vice Presidential Residence is a three-story Victorian-style mansion originally built in 1893 as the home of the superintendent of the *United States Naval Observatory*. It's about a mile northeast of Georgetown University.

So we were sitting there and having a drink and George and Dan were together across from us. Barbara and I were on a little loveseat together. We were chatting away and having a very pleasant conversation. One of their sons was visiting with his wife at the time. And they came down and joined us.

Hughes: It wasn't "W," though? (The future president George W. Bush.)

Evans: No, no, no. We had two martinis, and I'm looking at my watch. I knew we needed to go because they were going to want to eat dinner, and we wanted to eat dinner. So finally I got Dan's eye and we got up and we left. Dan was chuckling on the way home. And I said, "What are you chuckling at?" He said, "Well, I sat there and I was listening to you and Barbara. And you were talking about abortion. And then you were talking about this, and you were talking about that. And George and I weren't discussing things of importance."

Hughes: Your husband was listening to you instead of the vice president.

Evans: And Dan said, "We didn't discuss much. And he never asked for my support."

Hughes: That's funny. Who ran against George H.W. Bush for the GOP nomination in 1988?

Evans: Bob Dole was the primary opponent. He was the Senate minority leader and Dan's colleague.

EDITOR'S NOTE: Besides Robert Dole, Bush prevailed over Jack Kemp, Alexander Haig, Paul Laxalt, Donald Rumsfeld and the perennial Harold Stassen.

Hughes: And Bush went on to beat Dukakis. Poor hapless Mike was running around in a tank with that silly hat on his head.

Evans: Yeah, that helmet. Unfortunately for him. We knew him when he was Massachusetts governor. Very nice person. I liked him. Nice wife.

Hughes: So now it's 1989. You're leaving the Senate, coming home to the real Washington.

Evans: We are. We came home, and then where do we live? Once again we're without a house.

Hughes: The nomads.

Evans: But my brother had this summer home on Bainbridge where we had spent a lot of time when he was living in the East. We asked him if we could rent it. And he was happy to have us rent it. And we said, "You can come and visit…" So that was great. We drove our car across the country and I went to places I'd never been to before.

Hughes: Tell me about that.

Evans: It was a lovely trip. But wait—After Dan left the Senate we went to Harvard for a semester. He was a fellow at the Kennedy School of Government.

Hughes: That must have been fascinating.

Evans: It was fun. It was great. We lived in the business graduate school housing, which was sort of newer housing. We were back to that old bit of two frying pans, two pots...

Hughes: The Tupperware is coming out again. You're like grad-school students.

Evans: A living room with a sofa and two chairs and the coffee table. But it was just great.

Dan would go off to the school to do his thing and I could do mine. They had a dinner every Tuesday night, I believe it was, and the faculty would come. It was not a huge dinner, just around a big long table. They would have different speakers. Oftentimes they would have a program, too, and we would go from the dinner to the program. We met and heard some interesting people. Dan enjoyed that. And I just took classes. I audited classes. I had never spent much time back there; certainly not in the winter time. Now, of course, I have a son who lives there and we've been back there at Christmastime and what have you. But it's *cold* back there. So every morning, my first class was probably at nine. Dan would go off to his classes, and I would put on my boots, my wool coat—that I bought in D.C. because it was cold, and which I still have because I wear it maybe once a year here—my scarf, my gloves and my hat. I'd pick up my books and off I would trudge—a college student all over again. You go across the snowy grass, and over the Charles River. And the wind would always just be blowing there. Then there is another river overpass and the wind would hit me again. But that was my daily walk to my first class. Then you get into the buildings and they're old and steamy. You take off the hat; you take off the scarf; you take off the gloves; you take off the coat, and everything is dumped on the floor. I mean, everybody, all the kids, are doing this. Unbundled, you sit down, open up your notebook and get ready to learn. That was fun! It's wonderful to take classes and not have to get graded. I took about four or five classes.

Hughes: That would be so much fun. What was your most memorable class?

Evans: One was on Beethoven's symphonies, which I *loved*. I still have all the orchestra scores we listened to, analyzed and discussed. It was a big class.

Hughes: Were you the only older student there?

Evans: Oh yeah, pretty much. I also took "Women Authors"—a class on Southern women writers. And I took an art history class. I had another class where they were talking about Machiavelli and early politics. In fact, Dan went to one of those classes with me. The professor was a great lecturer. Then when the semester was over we went back to D.C. Bruce was still living in our house. We packed up for good then, and drove the car south to North Carolina. We crossed the lower tier of the country, through the Bible Belt, which was very interesting. We went down to the Grand Canyon, where I'd never been, and up through Zion Canyon. Our only deadline was that Dan had a speech in Spokane. It was a great trip.

Then we went to Bainbridge. We thought, "Well, this is great. We'll just enjoy the summer here." It was right on the beach with a tennis court. "The kids will come over and it will be great. Then we'll have to start house hunting. And we'll move in, and be there by Christmas." Well, that was our plan. We started to house hunt and houses at that time were having a real surge. We would look at a house and the next week it would be one or two thousand dollars more. People were bidding on houses. It was a terrible time for us because we didn't have big resources. We had no equity in a house to negotiate or anything.

Hughes: A lot of people would think that with the career that Dan and Nancy Evans had had that you'd be pretty well off. But that wasn't the case, was it?

Evans: Well, it was government pay a lot of that time. I'm not complaining, but the fact is we didn't have a lot of money. You know, for 18 years we didn't have a house of our own. Losing the growth in value that those houses had, all our friends had, was significant. We actually wanted to buy a house when Dan became president of Evergreen. And once again because Slim Rasmussen was so down on Evergreen, Dan determined it was not politically wise to not move into the president's house that was provided. It would have been great to have bought a house because the value there then was so relatively low. We could have bought one on the Sound somewhere. But, it didn't happen. So we started house hunting. And it's not convenient to house hunt in Seattle from Bainbridge.

Dan had an office in Seattle, and every morning he would get up at the crack of dawn, getting darker as the winter came on, and trudge to the garage, which was not attached, with his umbrella and his briefcase, grumble, grumble. Drive to the ferry; look for parking because all the places where you could reserve were full. And then you get the ferry and you soon learn that you can't sit wherever you want because that's so-and-so's seat. And he always took the 6:50 or the 7:20. And then he would walk on the other side to his office. It was not a really happy time. It was just hard for him.

I was doing a lot of house hunting. I kept looking and looking. I think it was just because we were a little older. We sort of knew what we wanted, and we just weren't finding it. A lot of the houses we saw we liked, but you knew you had to gut the kitchen and that would add more to the house, and all of that. We had one real estate person—I went through a bunch of them and they would just give up on me, and I don't blame them a bit. But Mary Jane Brinkley was so nice, and she stuck with us. She came to me one day and said, "Well, I've got a house for you to look at. I'm not sure you're going to like the house but it's got the view." We wanted a view.

So she brought us up here in Laurelhurst (on the hillside east of the UW campus). It's two small lots. It was a nice house but it was very small and it didn't really take advantage of the view. It was really more than we could afford, and we knew we were going to tear the house down. There was no practical way to remodel it. But we had our hearts set on a house with that view, designed the way we wanted things. So we bought this property. Then they had this thing with jaws that came in and tore the house down. In one day there was no house. It was just an amazing process to watch.

Hughes: You bought a house, tore it down and went looking for another rental?!

Evans: Well, we were still living on Bainbridge. But finally we rented a house. Then we hired an architect and we started building a house.

Hughes: When did you move in here?

Evans: November of '92.

Hughes: It's an absolutely great house, Nancy.

Evans: Thank you. And this time it was fun to do. When Dan and I were working on the Mansion (renovation) we would have arguments. Two strong people butting heads about silly little things sometimes, but they just seemed important to us—where a door should go. Things like that.

Hughes: And you're married to an engineer.

Evans: Oh yes, there's a lot of that involved. But with this one we didn't have any problems at all, and we knew what we really wanted. We wanted to live on one floor so we could live here a long, long time and they could carry us out feet first—that sort of thing. We made the doors wide so wheelchairs could go through. And the handles are not knobs, they're just levers.

Hughes: You really thought of all the details.

Evans: Yes, we did. And we had an architect we enjoyed working with— someone who listened. So it's been a great house for us. Downstairs is now mostly spare bedrooms and some storage, which is too bad because I fill them up. We used to have one *huge* storage room down there where Dan put up a net, attached it to the wall and then to a post and then to a wall, making an enclosure. I had got him a machine so he could practice his golf swing and actually hit the golf ball. Well, it was just great. He would go down there and swing away. Until one day, the golf ball hit the post and bounced back and hit him in the eye. Fortunately, he was wearing his glasses or who knows what would have happened. He blackened his eye and broke his nose. It was not a good time! And the storage room soon got smaller.

Just before we moved in, one son became engaged. Then a few months later another son became engaged. And both of them were being married in 1993—summer and fall. One son lived out here; one son lived in the East. And then eventually they started having babies.

Hughes: Like people do after they get married.

Evans: And it was fine. We still had enough room (for visits). But then the other son a few years later is engaged and married. So when they would come to visit we had two bedrooms and one bath downstairs. We decided we should build another bedroom. So we took part of this huge storage room and we built a bedroom with a little sitting area and a bathroom. It's sort of a suite, you know, downstairs. So we have three bedrooms and two baths.

I remember looking at drawings. You'd look down the hall toward our bedroom and there was the door to the bathroom. And I said, "Oh, that's not good." That's why you work on paper with pencil with an eraser. And we all agreed. So the architect just took the eraser and we changed it. "Oh, that will do it." I mean it was really sort of fun, the process.

Hughes: Is Dan just a civil engineer?

Evans: Civil and structural.

Hughes: So these are the sort of details he knew about.

Evans: Yes, he really enjoyed that. The house that we rented was not very far from here, and he would drive over every day. And we had a good relationship with the contractor. Probably a lot of the workers wished he'd go away because he would sort of critique and ask a lot of questions. I would be over here almost every day too.

Hughes: How soon after you get back home do you get involved with Whitman College, your alma mater?

Evans: I was asked to become a trustee in 1994.

Hughes: Was Dan a UW Trustee at the same time, so you could spar about who had the better school?

Evans: Well, it's a "regent" at the UW. (Governor Lowry appointed Dan Evans in 1993.)

Hughes: What else do you get involved in right away after building your first-ever permanent home?

Evans: Well, I think I mentioned earlier that I was involved with the Cancer Lifeline—helping organize the Friends of Cancer Lifeline, it was called. And then I went back on the Seattle Symphony board. I'd been on in the 1960s and resigned when we went East. I went back on the board I think in '92 or '91. It was interesting and fun because we had a lot of planning to do. And we got a wonderful new building a few years later, Benaroya Hall. I was very active in that. There were two or three of us on the board who were on the committee that worked with the architects on the design and were involved with the selection of fabrics and chairs and seats and the entire building. We all sat in theater seats, testing them out. It was a busy time. And then there was a lot of work to raising the money. So I was very involved with that and I enjoyed it a lot.

Hughes: Some people think the Benaroyas, generous as they were, donated all the money for that concert hall, but that is not so, is it?

Evans: Oh no, no, no. But they gave us the first big gift that got us started in raising the money. And then they subsequently have given more. But many, many, many, *many* people donated to that building.

Hughes: Well, it's an absolutely incredible venue. It must have been one of the highlights of your career in the arts and philanthropy.

Evans: It's beautiful inside, and it has great acoustics—just a wonderful place for music. I'm still on the Symphony Board. They kept some of us on past our two three-year terms, if we were officers or involved with building. Finally I rotated off. Then I was invited back for two more three-year terms. And then I went off again. And I said, "OK, that's it; it's been great." Then they came back a year later and I said, "No, I really think I've done my thing." Well, I ended up back on the Symphony Board. And now I am chairing the search committee for the new music conductor.

Hughes: That's a big responsibility finding the right person—

Evans: It's a *big* responsibility.

Hughes: The whole chemistry there between a conductor and the orchestra is so crucial.

Nancy at a Whitman College trustees' dinner, 2007. *Whitman College*

Evans: *The whole chemistry.* That's exactly right.

Hughes: Being a musician yourself, you're able to understand the politics of maintaining an orchestra, keeping it happy and productive, and the charisma and the musicianship required to be a conductor. For the record, Nancy is nodding.

Evans: Sometimes it truly is a formidable job, with some orchestra politics involved. And it's unfortunate sometimes. It shouldn't be that way, but it is.

Hughes: Are many of your fellow board members musical as well? Is that sort of a prerequisite for being on the board?

Evans: It's preferable because it just makes it more fun and easier and more enjoyable. But some of them, particularly some of the business people who are representing corporations, do it because they think they would like it. But it really works better if you really do like it because you want to come to the concerts and see what it is you're working for and listen to these amazing musicians. A lot of them come with not a lot of knowledge but then they grow and become very much involved and very knowledgeable about the music just by learning and listening.

Hughes: Do you hit the road looking for a new conductor? Do candidates come to you?

Evans: Well, eventually that may happen, but not now. We bring in guest conductors. The program is already set for next year, for '09-10, and we will have a number of guest conductors. And then we can bring in more in the following year '10-11—guest conductors who we'd like to hear. And they'll send us tapes. But it's really best if the musicians have an opportunity to play under conductors to see how they respond to each other. It's quite involved.

Hughes: What's the most thrilling musical performance you've heard?

Evans: Oh gosh!

Hughes: Just countless?

Evans: Oh yes, absolutely. I heard a pianist at the symphony last Thursday who just blew me away he was so good. It was a Liszt piece and it was wonderful.

Hughes: I love the violin. We've heard Itzhak Perlman in person. And I'm blown away by Yo-Yo Ma, the brilliant cellist.

Evans: We heard Yo-Yo Ma when he first came to the United States when he was a kid. We had good friends, Sherman and Nouchi Huffine, who lived out on Cooper Point in Olympia. She was from the Olympia Brewery family. They loved music, and they had two grand pianos in their living room. They had Sunday soirées, musical programs, and then they served coffee and tea and I suppose cookies or something. And we would go periodically to them. One time it was Yo-Yo Ma, and he was just a kid, a young teenager. But he was wonderful. The next day they were trying to get Yo-Yo Ma back to Seattle. It would have been a Monday because these were on Sunday evening. Dan said, "Well, I'm going to Seattle. I'd be happy to take him." So Sherman drove Yo-Yo up to the Governor's Mansion and left him off. He was very impressed with the Mansion. Then he rode up to Seattle with Dan. We don't really remember this in much detail because at that time we didn't know who he would become. But Yo-Yo Ma remembered it very well because I talked to him later on about that.

Hughes: The technique of those virtuosos is just so incredible.

Evans: And he's wonderful because he's gotten into so many other areas of music, putting together classical cello music or other music with guitars and country music. He's wonderful; he's so creative that way, and he seems to enjoy it so much.

Hughes: How is the Seattle Symphony doing in terms of financial wherewithal? Are you on solid grounding?

Evans: No, it's very difficult right now. *Very* difficult. And we have accumulated deficits. I think we just need to do a better job in the future once we get through this time because it's really tough. Our attendance hasn't dropped *nearly* as much as with orchestras around the country. We actually do quite well on ticket sales, but it has dropped. And that cuts your revenue. People are giving, but not as much. I hate to say it, but every arts organization right now is struggling. It's very, very hard.

Hughes: I keep hearing on NPR and reading that symphonies, great symphonies, are an endangered species.

Evans: A number of the really good ones are. Absolutely. And the other thing is that while we raised this money and built this wonderful new hall, we have never had what some of these older Eastern, Midwest orchestras have—the big endowment. A great deal of their earnings come from the endowment. We have a very small endowment. We were about to start a campaign for the endowment when the economy fell to pieces. So that's been put on hold for now.

Hughes: The Whitman College endowment, though, is still strong, isn't it?

Evans: Yes it is, particularly for a Northwest college. But if you look around the country some of them have endowments that are much, much larger than ours. So we're always trying to grow the endowment. And it's the only way that you can do the things we do in terms of financial aid. Tuition doesn't cover the costs, obviously, of education. And a number of years ago we really knew it was time to do something about faculty salaries because we were a very good school but they were not being rewarded reasonably. So we have continually tried to improve salaries and to bring in new scholars. And when you're hiring new people costs go up, too, because they demand more. And many of them come with spouses who want to teach as well. So it's sometimes quite complicated. Whitman is very solid, but they've lost money, obviously, in their endowment.

Also, we've had a diversity issue because it's Walla Walla, Eastern Washington. In the last number of years, we've worked hard, our presidents, the trustees and everybody—worked really hard at trying to become more diverse as a faculty and student body. And to encourage minorities, particularly African Americans, to come to Whitman. It's expensive, and unfortunately a lot of them need financial aid as well. Sometimes you bus them in or fly them in, trying to get them there just to visit the campus. Then if they like it and want to apply, and even if they're educationally qualified, a lot of them just do not have the wherewithal. But we work really hard and set aside money for that effort.

Hughes: Tell me more about the Friends of the Cancer Lifeline because this topic is really close to my heart. We were very active in the Relay for Life when I was at the newspaper. Is the Friends of Cancer Lifeline an outreach hotline—that if you have just been diagnosed with cancer or you're doing chemo that you can talk to someone?

Evans: Well, when it was started that was what it was—just a 24-hour phone line. Then it went to an 800-line in-state. People fighting cancer needed practical advice. There was just not a lot of data and information available on where to buy a wig—

Hughes: "I'm losing my hair! How can I stop it?"

Evans: Yes. And "What about my children?" and on and on and on. So many questions. So that's how it grew and evolved. It was under the umbrella of Family Services, a United Way agency, and then my friend Barbara Frederick, who was the executive director, thought it was time to break away and grow in different ways. Which, bless her heart, she did. She masterminded the change and we raised enough money to build the building so we could have classes and people could come and do different things. And they have a resource library, and a staff. So we helped with that. They still have the lifeline, the phone line; that's still a very big part of their existence, but they also have classes for lymphedema and other complications. One of the women who has been there ever since I've been around is just wonderful. She deals with young children who are losing their parents, trying to let them know how to express themselves and deal with it. And they have exercise classes. Just a wide variety of things. They also now provide services in several hospitals in the Seattle area.

Hughes: Are you still active with the Cancer Lifeline?

Evans: I'm not now because I was involved for a long time. I just don't have time right now.

Hughes: You were on the KCTS board. I'm really envious of that because I love public television.

Evans: I'm still on the KCTS Board. I'm vice chairman.

Hughes: Well, your new manager Moss Bresnahan, seems—

Evans: Wonderful. He really is doing a great job. He's very nice, very pleasant and he's doing a lot of outreach which we needed. I've been on that board quite a long while, too, and we went through a very bad time.

Hughes: Yes you did.

Evans: There was a time when there were two or three of us who threatened to quit the board if something didn't happen, if things didn't change. We were asked to stay on through some union negotiations which I did reluctantly. And then the president left. Fortuitously, Bill Mohler from Tacoma, the retired head of Bates school and also the public television station down there, called and said, "Can I be of help?" And we said, "Yes, that's just great," because we were just, "whew!" Yesterday we were here and today we're there.

Hughes: You had a terrific budget deficit, didn't you?

Evans: Big deficit, and lots of morale issues. And some of the people worked very, very hard on this. Bill was just great, he came in and he's just an easy person to know him. So the staff was willing to see what he could do and go along with him because he wasn't coming in mad or with demands. He came in and worked with the people and tried to build up the morale. He talked to every employee individually, one-on-one, and he just worked really hard with our staff—and also on the budget. The board worked very hard with him. Every year we would build new challenges for him, and every year he came back and he met his challenges, and succeeded beyond them.

Hughes: He just seemed like such a neat old-shoe kind of guy.

Evans: Bill is wonderful. So he was at the right place at the right time, lucky for us. Then he wanted to go back to golf—his retirement. And he was commuting every day from Tacoma. And so we had a national search. Moss Bresnahan comes from Charleston. He's been with public television for a while. And he's brought a desire to have us reach out. We have such a good sound basis. It's not as bad as other organizations are facing now. Moss didn't know anybody when he got here, and he wants to get to know people, which has been great because they get to know KCTS through meeting him. A number of business people I run into or talk to bring it up: "Gee, I met your new president and he's just great." And he's trying to build alliances between various organizations. "What can we do for you? And what can you do for us?" sort of thing, which has been very nice to see.

Hughes: Newt Minow, the FCC Commissioner in the 1960s, called television a "vast wasteland." I don't know where I'd be without PBS—the Three Tenors, *Sesame Street*, Ken Burns and Julia Child.

Evans: Yeah!

Hughes: Have you got to meet Ken Burns and some of those amazing people involved with PBS?

Evans: Burns was just in town last week.

Hughes: I heard him on NPR.

Evans: We had dinner with him. He was wonderful. I had not met him before. When we learned he was coming to Seattle to promote his new documentary about national parks, we were very pleased because the people who knew him said he's so generous with his time. You set up a horrendous schedule and he'll say, "Sure, I'll do that." And that's just exactly what he had and what he did. He and his co-producer, Dayton Duncan, both came. We had a National Parks Foundation dinner. Dan's nephew—his brother's son—is president of that organization, so we went to that as a fundraiser. Then the next night, KCTS sponsored a presentation at Benaroya Hall. There were 2,000 people there. At the reception beforehand, Ken and I were introduced. We started chatting about funny things—like how do you remember people when you've met them in Seattle and then you see them in New York.

Hughes: Psychiatrists tell us that that's called cognitive dislocation—that you could know Nancy and Dan Evans here in Seattle, but all of a sudden you see them in Los Angeles and you can't remember their names!

Evans: Exactly.

Hughes: *How embarrassing is that?* You're standing there with your wife and your kids and you frantically ask yourself, "Who are these people?"

Evans: It's hard. Well, Ken brought it up, so we all have that happen. This happens to me a lot. People will come up and say, "Hi. Do you remember me?" And people do that to Ken all the time, too. I told him I just say, "No, I'm sorry I don't." But I didn't used to say that. I'm smarter now that I'm older. But I told him that's a terrible thing to do to a person—to say, "Do you remember me?" Now, when I just tell the truth, people invariably say, "You're right" and "I'm sorry." They don't do it to be unkind or mean; they just do it being sort of funny. But I just tell them, "No, I *don't* remember," and "Please don't do that to people. It's not nice." Well, Ken Burns was saying the same thing: "How am I going to remember this person I met in Hoboken?" And I said, "Well, what you do is what Nelson Rockefeller used to do. Even if he knew you, he'd say, 'Hiya fella!' and everybody would think, 'Oh, he knows me!'" So they were ringing the bell and we had to go down to the auditorium to do the show. And I said, "Bye fella." And Ken said, "Bye gal!"

Hughes: When I'm in the car, I've got NPR to keep me company. I love the NPR commercials where somebody pulls into the driveway but doesn't open the garage door. They're waiting for the last of Terry Gross or whatever. I heard an interview with Ken Burns the other morning. He was telling how that in the beginning people were so dubious that he could make a documentary about the Civil War because there was no video back then!

Evans: He did it with still pictures. They moved the camera to focus on parts of a photo to tell a story.

Hughes: Exactly. And someone said to him later, "Where did you get those movies of the Civil War?!" And he laughed, "There are no movies of the Civil War." And the diaries he used to create dialogue are just incredible, too.

Evans: And the different narrations were wonderful. Different voices assume different roles. It's very clever the way they do it. Burns said that some of the photography—the sunrise, sunset, clouds, rain, the moon—for the National Parks documentary "took us 10 years." He was talking about going up to Kilauea in Hawaii. They hiked up at 2 in the morning to get set up and to wait for sunrise.

Hughes: Does Dan do still photography as well as movies?

Evans: No. Not any more. I think I mentioned that I married, among other things, a 16mm camera. Which was great in Europe except it was so heavy to carry around. I remember that we were in Paris in 1960. And we had the camera. It had a wonderful leather case and then all the film. The camera was on the backseat of the car and the case was there. We parked on the street in Paris and we were getting out, and I said, "I don't think we should leave the camera there." And Dan said, "Oh, it's OK." This is the way he always is, even today. "You don't have to lock the door. It's OK." And I said, "I'm sorry." So I took a newspaper and I covered it up. When we came back, the camera case was gone, but the camera was not because I had covered it up with newspaper.

Hughes: Smart woman.

Evans: So thankfully we didn't lose our camera and the film. But at Christmastime when we had all these cousins, nieces and nephews staying with us at the Mansion, and other family members, too, everybody would come down into the drawing room. And the kids would be all excited. There would be our three plus at least 10 others—a big line of them, every year, starting when they were very young. And they can't come in the door until the fire is lit, the cookies and milk are gone, and the camera is ready. "Now, get in line—Line up by height." Dan is yelling through the closed doors, and on and on. And the kids, of course, were just going nuts. And so we have years and years and years of this lineup coming in dutifully and immediately going to the socks, of course, and then the chaos of opening presents. Besides movies, we've got all these slides.

Hughes: There's a gizmo you can get that scans your slides right into Photoshop.

Evans: Yes. We thought about getting one but he just doesn't have the time. Someday I'm hoping he'll have time to really work on that sort of thing because he understands it all. And we have just *tons* of photos and pictures.

Hughes: Dan obviously is enjoying himself and staying active. But don't you kind of wish he was in there in his study, finishing his book?

Evans: That is first and foremost in both our minds.

Hughes: The Parkinson's Foundation. Tell us how that evolved.

Evans: It evolved because my brother Bill's former wife, Tina, developed Parkinson's. Tina was living here in Seattle. And it became more and more difficult. There weren't a lot of doctors who were specializing in that sort of disease. It was just a lot to learn. Bill Bell III, my nephew, had a friend, Craig Howard, whose mother also had Parkinson's. So the two of them dreamed up the idea of forming a foundation mostly to provide help, better education about the disease and ways to alleviate the symptoms—sort of like Cancer Lifeline—and to try to improve the medical scene in Seattle for Parkinson's patients. And of course they came to Dan and me.

Hughes: What year was that, Nancy?

Evans: Oh, '94 maybe. They wanted our support and for advice. We immediately said we would certainly support it, and we became members

of the board. Then they went to the hospitals—to the UW, to Swedish…
different hospitals trying to forge a partnership and build a specialty in
Parkinson's and other movement disorders and diseases. Sometimes there
was no interest; sometimes there was interest and no funds, mostly. They
wanted to see if they could raise funds to help put it all together. Eventually
they hooked up with Evergreen Hospital in Kirkland. It's a good hospital.
They were interested, and they had space for growth. So we really had to
carefully work out the finances—a big undertaking.

Hughes: Was Booth Gardner involved in that as well?

Evans: Not initially. But soon thereafter he was. And the center is
named after Booth. It's the Booth Gardner Parkinson's Center. We brought
in some physicians and therapists who were specializing in the disease and
looking at new ways to treat Parkinson's.

Hughes: It's a tricky disease, lots of different manifestations.

Evans: That's exactly right. And the meds are not the same for everybody. So it's been quite successful, and the hospital is actually making
money. Now the Foundation has newsletters that go to Alaska, Montana…
They've flown to Alaska, flown to Idaho—places where there are no facilities nearby, and had talks. People suffering from Parkinson's come from
all over. They've had seminars twice now down by the airport. People
came from California—all over. They had an all-day session with different
specialists talking about all aspects of the disease. So it's been a wonderful,
very positive thing that these two kids (Bill and Craig)—did.

Hughes: Are you still involved in that?

Evans: Well, not on the board. Neither of us had the time and we
weren't able to do that, but we're still writing checks and we get the newsletter. We keep up with what's going on.

Hughes: Tell me about the department at the UW Dan Evans School
of Public Affairs that was named in your honor.

Evans: Well, that was a huge surprise to me. It's the Nancy Bell Evans
Center on Nonprofits & Philanthropy. They bring in speakers and have
forums on philanthropy and the various issues involved—How to run a

board, not how to raise money so much, but how to achieve transparency in governance and related challenges.

Hughes: When did they spring that surprise on you?

Evans: 2004.

Hughes: That's really a great idea because a lot of people get involved in nonprofits with little knowledge. Yesterday you talked about "fiduciary" responsibilities. It's an important issue.

Evans: That's right. And it's for staff too, the people running agencies like that. It's been very successful and it's a separate fund within the Evans School.

Hughes: Who was behind that besides Dan Evans?

Evans: Dan was not behind it at all. The idea originated with former Dean Marc Lindenberg, who envisioned a center for the study of non-profits and NGO's. At that time he was talking to John Stanton about a variety of things and asked John if he would be interested in funding this effort. John is a Whitman graduate, fellow trustee, former CEO and co-founder of Western Wireless and a former McCaw executive. That's where Dan got to know him. He was on their board of directors. Being a fellow Whitman alum, he very graciously agreed to put forth the original funding for the Nancy Bell Evans Center on Non-Profits & Philanthropy. It was a complete surprise to me and a huge honor to be acknowledged in this way. John Stanton is a very good friend and a model of good community spirit. He has been involved in so many good community enterprises and is a big participant in his own family activities, particularly coaching his sons' baseball teams—a very serious business!

Hughes: Are you still on the Board of Trustees at Whitman?

Evans: I just rotated off. But now I am co-chair of a capital campaign that is just in the formative stages. We've been talking about it for several years. And once again, the economy has slowed everything down. But I am co-chair for Western Washington.

Hughes: Who is the president of Whitman College now?

Evans: George Bridges is his name. I was on that search committee.

We brought George in and he has been a good choice.

Hughes: Well, what are the three Evans boys up to? Tell me about them.

Evans: They're all very happily married. All have three kids.

Hughes: Each has three kids?

Evans: Of both sexes in all families, which is just wonderful.

Hughes: What fun: Nine grandchildren. Tell me more about them.

Evans: How many hours do you have?

Hughes: Plenty.

Evans: We are so fortunate because, of course, we had three sons. And as they were growing up I remember telling them a number of times as they got to be a little older, "Don't even think about getting married until you're 30 years old." I said it rather sincerely, but it was sort of a family joke. But I really wanted them to have fun and be independent young people before they took on that added responsibility. And suddenly as they got to be getting toward their 30s, I realized that Dan and I were getting older too.

Hughes: It's a funny thing about that.

Evans: Yes. I finally said, "OK, forget the wife. I don't care about the wife. I just want the grandchildren!" That was another joke. At any rate, it was interesting because they turned 30 and one by one they became engaged. And within a matter of four or five years we not only had three wonderful daughters-in-law, we started having grandchildren. And bing, bing, bing, they just came along. So, we have three daughters-in-law, three sons, and each family has three children, and they have both sexes represented. So, they planned it beautifully! And the wonderful thing is that our first three grandchildren were girls—Eloise, Emily and Isabelle. Having not had girls, that was a special pleasure for us. So we feel very blessed.

Eloise, our first grandchild, is the daughter of Dan and Celia. Celia was Celia Sheppard and she attended the UW. I've known her mother since the days when I was single, and I double-dated with her father 50 plus years ago. And then Mark and Deb—she has kept her maiden name and goes by Deborah Logan—were living in London and they had Emily.

Then came Isabelle, who was born to Dan and Celia in Seattle. And then we had our first grandsons.

Hughes: The boys are?

Evans: Well, let's do it the other way: Dan and Celia Evans have three children, Eloise is the oldest. She's 14 now and she'll be 15 the day after Christmas. Then Isabelle is 13. And then there's Jackson, who is Daniel Jackson Evans III. He's 11, and he goes by Jackson.

Mark and Deborah live in Ipswich, Massachusetts. Deborah grew up in Massachusetts, went to Dartmouth. And they have three children. Emily is 13, and Benjamin Jackson—another Jackson—is 11. Grace Lilith—her middle name is my mother's name—is 9.

Bruce married Christy Carson from Charlotte, North Carolina. She went to the University of North Carolina. "Go Tar Heels!" I hear that a lot. They have three children. Their oldest is Elizabeth McKay, who is 9. She goes by McKay, which is an old Evans' family name. Then they have Andrew King, and King was a family name on both Christy and the Bells' side. He is 6, soon to be 7. And then they have John, who is 4.

Hughes: You have been incredibly blessed.

Evans: We have been. We are so fortunate. And every one of them is *very, very* different, which is not uncommon, obviously, but it's fun to see within your own family. Nine individuals in sort of a range of ages.

Hughes: Anything else that you'd like to cover as we wrap things up?

Evans: We should talk about Eloise's cancer because it was such a significant time in our lives—the whole family actually.

Hughes: How old was Eloise when she was diagnosed with cancer?

Evans: Oh, I can tell you exactly. We were over at Dan and Celia's house celebrating Dan's birthday, which is October 16th. It was a Friday night. And Eloise, who at that time was two months short of turning four, was just acting very strangely—just melting down way beyond her normal self, because she was a happy, cheerful child. Celia had taken her to their pediatrician, who had logically said it could be an ear infection. So they gave her medicine for that, and that didn't seem to work. So then

The Evans family, including sons, daughters-in-law and grandkids, gather at Sun Valley to celebrate Dan's 80th birthday in 2005. *Evans family album*

she took her to an ENT person who said, "Well, it could be tonsillitis. Try this medicine for a few days. And if that doesn't work, call me back." Well, this was Friday night and she was just melting down. And this was a busy household because Isabelle then was two and a half, and Jackson was six months old. And that night, she had just had a terrible night. I always tell everybody, "Listen to your children," and I give Celia full credit because a day later she picked up Eloise, took her to the Children's Hospital Emergency Room and said, "Something is wrong with this child, and I want to find out what." That was so smart of her. Fortunately she got a doctor who was on-call who agreed with her and ordered an immediate CT scan. They found a mass the size of a tennis ball under her brain.

Hughes: Oh my God!

Evans: And that's what the problem had been. She was diagnosed with rhabdomyosarcoma, a fast-growing tumor of soft tissue, mostly in children. I didn't realize that rapidly growing cancers are very often in the soft tissues. Slower growing cancers are in the hard tissues. So it was not in the brain. It was just under the brain, behind her nose. It was inoperable because it was so inaccessible. So, she was obviously in the hospital immediately, and they started her on chemo shortly thereafter. And here's this tiny little three-year-old.

The other two children came to live with us because we were very close to the hospital and that was the best thing. Jackson was wonderful because he just smiled all the time. He was about seven months old. Isabelle, on the other hand, had a terrible time because she was two-and-a-half and had no clue what was going on. But she knew she was not where she was supposed to be. She was supposed to be home with her mother and her father. And she *adored* Eloise.

Hughes: Yes, missed her sister.

Evans: "Where is Eloise?" she'd ask. And she'd say, "I don't love you Grandma. I don't want to be here, Grandma. I want to be home." And I'd say, *"I know, Isabelle, and I understand."* But this way Dan and Celia could be with Eloise at the hospital and could drop over here. Celia, being a mother, was just torn between the two places. But we were close by and they could come here and sleep or do whatever was necessary. Eloise was in the hospital for a year off and on. She would go there to get her chemo and they would keep her there for a while to make sure her health was not compromised. She'd stay a week or so. Then her blood count would start coming up and they would send her home. She'd just get to feeling better and, wham, back she'd go to the hospital. She had 13 rounds of chemo and was admitted another 13 times or so because of side effects.

Hughes: They'd give her a little respite between doses of chemo?

Evans: Yes. This went on for an entire year. Her brother and sister didn't live with us the entire time, but they were here a great deal, particularly at first. And somebody, some family member, was always in the hospital with her—*always*, night and day. Primarily it was Celia because

Eloise wanted mommy. Our son Dan would stay there, too. The chairs would turn into beds, but they're not the most comfortable thing in the world. And my husband was also occasionally blessed with being asked by Eloise to spend the night with her. It was a rare honor.

Hughes: This is at Children's Hospital?

Evans: Children's. And weren't we lucky to be living *so* close to Children's Hospital?

Hughes: Yes. Just down the block.

Evans: Yes, we were very fortunate. Also, fortunate with the doctors we had and the nurses. The doctor, Doug Hawkins, couldn't have been nicer. He is a specialist in rhabdomyosarcoma—one of the chief rhabdomyo-sarcoma doctors in the nation. We were over there one time and Celia was talking to Doug. She said, "I go online all the time and read about rhabdo. When I have questions, there's this 'Dear Dr. Rhabdo' feature." And Hawkins said, "*I'm* Dr. Rhabdo!" He's one of five or six doctors that take turns answering online questions that patients or parents of patients have, which I thought was wonderful.

Hughes: Is this a disease that primarily afflicts children?

Evans: Yes. Usually up into the teens. It doesn't usually go beyond that. Ten years before that time she would have been dead.

Hughes: And how long ago was it that Eloise was diagnosed?

Evans: It was 1994. Eloise is now 14. That's what Dr. Hawkins did—come up with the proper chemo protocol for children that would help kill the cancer, and not kill the child. We're just lucky that he was here. So, it was very up and down for a long time. And then about half way through the chemo she had six weeks of radiation.

Hughes: Jeeze, that's tough stuff.

Evans: And that was down at the UW Hospital. It was every weekday morning, at 9 o'clock. So Dan and I would go down, or both of us very often, to be there with Celia because she always took Eloise down. Radiation gets to be a routine. Eloise would sit on the table and they would give her a little shot, and she'd say, "Here, Grandpa, take my hand. Here, Grandma, take my hand." And, *boom*, she's out—just like that. The second she's lying down she's out. And then when she wakes up she doesn't remember anything. And 10 minutes later she's fine. It was wonderful to see—the way they did it. Very skilled people. But we always were there with Celia if we could be.

Hughes: Did the tumor shrink away? Is it gone?

Evans: There is a little tissue left behind, but it is checked regularly and there has been no change in its size. They will continue to check, but they think that probably there will be no recurrence of the cancer.

But the big reason I tell this story, first of all, is to emphasize how fortunate we are in this community to have Children's Hospital. And how fortunate we were to be in the neighborhood. The other thing that just stunned me was the support that this family got from friends all over. Dan and I put together an e-mail update network because we kept having so many questions. And, frankly, it's hard to keep telling the story over and over again because it was very emotional. So once every month or so we would send out an e-mail to this long list of people who wanted to know how Eloise was doing. More and more people would ask for it. The other thing was that all Dan and Celia's friends their age put together a dinner thing that went on for months. People would sign up and three days a week, or four days, because every day was too much, they would leave a basket or a box by their front door with dinner for the next two nights.

Hughes: Incredible.

Evans: So they didn't have to worry about cooking for all that time. That was these other parents, all these 30-year-olds helping out any way they could. I just thought that was beautiful that they all did that.

Hughes: You know, here we are, both cancer survivors. But when your kids get sick, to me it's just a million times worse than what you endure yourself.

Evans: And your grandchildren. She was just a tiny little girl—just this tall. Being in Children's Hospital so much, you do get to know other parents. And there were some awful stories. I mean, we knew children who died there. We knew parents who divorced, who did not get through it. We knew one family who lived (a long ways from Seattle). They'd take turns, the mother and the father, coming down. They had teenage kids who had gotten into drugs. I mean, all these associated things that were happening. And the fact that Dan and Celia remained so strong together, and became stronger I think because of all this, really impresses me. A lot of families went the other way, just couldn't sustain the emotional drain that weighed on their marriages.

Eloise is doing beautifully now. In fact, she's a year-round swimmer, racing. Well, all the three kids are racing.

Hughes: I've been to so many swim meets it's a wonder I'm not permanently puckered.

Evans: I love those races!

Hughes: That really is a wonderful story.

Evans: Well, it has a wonderful outcome. But the thing I so often tell young mothers is "Listen to your children." Don't necessarily listen to the doctors because you know your child better than anybody. Follow through on your instincts.

Hughes: And Celia was smart enough to listen and follow her instincts.

Evans: The tumor was so fast growing. If it slid for even a few weeks, who knows what would have happened?

Hughes: Amazing story. And, remind me, Dan Jr. is doing what?

Evans: Dan lives here in Seattle. He has his own business now, consulting with companies.

Bruce lives in Arlington, Virginia. His wife is a lobbyist in Washington, D.C., and he works on the Hill, which I told you about earlier. Mark lives in Ipswich, but he works in Boston for Cambridge Associates. They provide financial investment advice, primarily for foundations, colleges and universities. Deb works for a large retail company located nearby. Ipswich is a beautiful area, but it's complicated getting around there. If they're both gone when we visit we can't get anywhere—unless we go out and hitchhike. There's no public transportation. I wanted to offer to do something for them—"Can I go to the store and get you something?"—I wouldn't know how to get to the store because nothing is the same direction and everything is 20 minutes away in some direction. There are all these old country roads, which at one time were probably cow paths or something. It's very old. A lot of antique shops. And all these little villages. It's lovely. They have seven acres and they board horses. The oldest of their girls, Emily, is 13. She rides and jumps. She's a big rider now, and that's all nearby. So it's great. I think both sets of parents were questioning why they would live there and work in Boston for over an hour commute each way, but once you get there it is lovely. Mark is a gardener. He loves to garden, but he has no time to garden. And they go skiing every weekend in the winter, up in New Hampshire.

Hughes: I wonder if the reason your boys haven't sought elective office is because they had a front row seat to see what it was like for their dad?

Evans: I don't know, because a lot of sons and daughters (of politicians) do go into politics. I don't know. It's just not their choice, I guess.

Hughes: In 1972, you said, "I really hope our boys are busy and active in politics. Not necessarily running for office, but I would be disappointed if they weren't concerned about what our government is doing."

Evans: That's true. But they *are* interested and they do pay attention.

Hughes: You don't have very many regrets, do you? You've had a pretty amazing life.

Evans: I've had a wonderful life. I've been very, very fortunate in *a lot* of ways. A husband and children in primarily good health—not always, but we've gotten through every difficulty that way. Dan's had some cancer. I've had it, and obviously, Eloise. But we've survived those. And we've had wonderful experiences; traveled on our own and sometimes with a delegation of some sort; met amazing people. We're lucky. We're still fairly healthy and active and involved. And I feel fortunate that we can do that.

Hughes: You have always been pretty much who you are, haven't you? Comfortable with who you are. Where do you think you got that sense of confidence and your upbeat outlook toward life?

Evans: Well, you have to go back in your heritage, and my parents were happy. But life was not as easy for them. It was more difficult for them because of my brother's illness and surgeries that he had over those years, and financial reasons during the Depression. But they were very positive. Mother particularly was always very positive about things. "You can do whatever you want to do, you just have to be ready to do it, and say yes." You can go to college if you're willing to work hard, that sort of thing. She was a good influence on our children growing up and they were lucky to have her. And Dan's parents were the same way. Dan's mother was so positive and she applauded everything we did. We'd get a lot of love and support from our family, and that gives you a lot of ability to move on and do other things. That was always the case in both of our families. So we've had good support everywhere—and good friends, lots of good friends.

Hughes: It's a good thing, too, that you didn't marry that guy who asked you to marry him on the park bench the week before Dan asked.

Evans: Or several others elsewhere! Yes, that's right. (laughing) I'm glad Dan was patient and waited for my response because it might never have happened if he hadn't been.

Hughes: Is it fair to say that Dan and Nancy Evans are also really good friends?

Evans: Yes. You have to be. You have to like each other. And that's what attracted me to Dan. I liked him right away. I wasn't sure I loved him, but I liked him. And, as I said, every time I was with him I learned more about him. He just grew on me, he really did. But, yes, you have to be able to laugh at each other and with each other and all of the things that come with life. There are all sorts of corny things people say, but they're very true, I think.

I remember one time I was getting my hair cut at a salon downtown that had been recommended to me by Tina, my sister-in-law. She was actually a former sister-in-law, but she was always a sister to me. And I'd never been to that salon. The stylist was chatting with me and said, "Well, how did you come here?" And I said, "Well, it was recommended to me by my former sister-in-law." And she said, "Well, how long have you been married?" That was probably 10 or 12 years ago. But she was amazed at how long we'd been married. And I was talking about this other friend I had known at

Whitman but who lived in New York and had a place here. And the stylist said, "You still know people you went to college with?" And I said, "Oh, a lot of my very best friends to this day are people I knew in college."

And we started talking about divorce. I said that I hardly knew anybody who was divorced. I mean most of our friends had stayed married, and to this day it's the case. Very few divorces, and they are good marriages, you know. And this young woman—she was probably 30—she said, "You know, I've outgrown all my friends. And they're all getting married and divorced." She

Evans family album

was still single, and she said, "I don't know any of them I want to be around anymore." She was incredulous that we didn't know a lot about divorce, and that Dan and I were together and still friends after 40 years or whatever it was at that time. Which was very surprising to me. It was a lesson to me.

Hughes: Have you changed in some ways over the years that's really profound?

Evans: I'm sure I have. I hope I have. I mean you want to grow and mature.

Hughes: How about Dan Evans? Is he fundamentally different today than 1964 when he was running for governor?

Evans: Oh yes. He's much more sure of himself than he was then. And more at ease with people. Much more at ease. He's a very caring and romantic husband. That's not to say that he's always easy, but he is a loving and thoughtful husband and father. I love him very much.

Hughes: He's a lot more approachable than he was back then. He was always impeccably polite and pleasant but there was sort of a veneer of separation when I first knew him in 1966.

Evans: Really? Well, I think it was the shyness. And he can still have that, actually. Whereas I will go around and say hello to people. I guess it's just what I do. And he doesn't. He'll say hello to people he knows. He's happy to meet and greet people, but he's not going to go out and do it.

Hughes: Well, I think that's what makes you a great team, politically and emotionally. Do you and Dan still get a lot of entreaties to get active politically?

Evans: Dan does. I don't. He gets a lot of requests, all the time. People want him mostly to endorse their candidacies for office. And then a lot of them ask for money. And he's asked to do commercials, radio and TV ads for various candidates. Publicly support—that's the biggie, endorse. And then occasionally do some talks or speeches for them.

Hughes: Well, thank you so much for sharing your life story with us.

Evans: Thank you, John. I've enjoyed it too. ⊠

Nancy and Dan: still best friends after 50 years. *Evans family album*

Q&A WITH NANCY EVANS

You're a pianist, a former music teacher and a trustee of the Seattle Symphony. What's your favorite classical piece?

I love the second movement of Rachmaninoff's Second Piano Concerto. I can get very nostalgic with that music. One Christmas when I was about 13, 33 rpm long-playing records were new. I said, "I don't want anything except Rachmaninoff's Second Piano Concerto!" I still have that record. It just blows me away every time I hear it, and Rachmaninoff is playing the piano!

How about popular music?

I love show tunes. When I was 10, 11, 12, I would imagine myself on Broadway—singing and dancing my way through some show. Well, I could dance but I could never sing very well. But I love all the show tunes—Rodgers & Hammerstein. "South Pacific" is just timeless.

Favorite book?

How can you come up with just one book? Well, I loved "The Kite Runner," by Khaled Hosseini. It's a beautifully written story of a young boy growing up in Afghanistan where they flew kites a lot and had these races in the sky. They're roaming the streets and being boys, but there's racism and war and rites of passage. It's about loyalty, forgiveness, family relationships and redemption.

The story you related to us about your granddaughter Eloise's battle with cancer is harrowing, but it has a happy ending. And you have some advice for parents, don't you?

Yes, I do. Eloise was almost 4 and she just wasn't herself. First, they said it might be an ear infection, then tonsillitis. My daughter-in-law, Celia, knew it had to be something more serious. She took her to the ER at Children's Hospital and said, "Something is wrong with this child, and I want to find out what." They found a mass the size of a tennis ball under her brain. It was so fast-growing; who knows what would have happened had they waited. Eloise is 14 now and doing beautifully, thanks to some great people at Children's and the UW Hospital, so this story has a wonderful outcome. But the thing I so often tell young mothers is this: "Listen to your children. Don't necessarily listen to the doctors, because you know your child better than anybody. Follow through on your instincts."

KEY SOURCES:

HistoryLink.org, the indispensable encyclopedia of Northwest history, features an excellent 2004 essay on Dan and Nancy Evans by Cassandra Tate. **[http://www.historylink.org/index. cfm?DisplayPage=output.cfm&file_id=7167]**

The Washington Governor's Mansion Foundation Web site offers a comprehensive history of the mansion and the foundation, as well as a photo gallery, tour information, newsletters and information on how to make a donation. **[http://www.wagovmansion.org/history. htm]**

The 2009 Whitman College Alumni award **[http://www.whitman.edu/content/alumni/ involved/alumniawards/gordonscribner]**

Miriam L. Bausch of Olympia, a tireless member of the Mansion Foundation, conducted an important interview with Nancy Evans on July 15, 2008, in connection with the mansion's centennial, with transcription by Teresa Bergen.

For a short biography of Nancy Evans and many other first ladies of the State of Washington, plus an historical overview of the mansion, read "First Families" by Mary Lou Hanify. Kendall/Hunt Publishing Co., 1988, ISBN 0840345968

For an entertaining, irreverent history of Washington's capital city and 120 years of state politics, see "Rogues, Buffoons & Statesmen" by Gordon Newell, Superior Publishing Co., Seattle, 1975, ISBN 0-87564-106-7

For more on the colorful career of Speaker John L. O'Brien, who was ousted by the Evans forces in 1963, see Daniel Jack Chasan's "Speaker of the House," University of Washington Press, 1990, ISBN 0-295-96848-6.

For more on the history of the mansion, see "The Governor's Mansion Centennial," by Gerry L. Alexander, chief justice of the Washington Supreme Court, in the winter 2008-09 issue of *Columbia*, the magazine of Northwest history.

"Voices of the Mansion," which includes oral histories on the history of the Governor's Mansion, was published by the Governor's Mansion Foundation, with a grant from the Women's History Consortium, $10, available at the mansion on tour days.

"A Public Mansion, A Private Home," partially funded by the Colonial Dames of Washington, $10, also available at the mansion on tour days.

INDEX